"One of the best books written for the divorcing person...warm, engaging."

—the *Behavior Therapist*

"Deals with the everyday feelings and problems of the divorcing and divorced...hits just the right balance between seriousness and optimism."

—**Florence Kaslow, PhD**, *Journal of Marital and Family Therapy*

"A handbook for the divorcing and divorced that is authentic and which they can employ in the rebuilding of their own lives."

—**Esther Oshiver Fisher, JD**, *Journal of Divorce*

"Warm, simple, and direct...this is a book you will not want to put down."

—*A.R.E. Press*

"I found the book comforting, helpful, and realistic—it is going to hurt, and it will not be easy, but you can do it."

—**Marilyn Anita Dalrymple**, *Affaire de Coeur*

REBUILDING

When Your Relationship Ends

FOURTH EDITION

BRUCE FISHER, EdD
ROBERT ALBERTI, PhD

Impact Publishers, Inc.

Publisher's Note

This publication is designed to provide accurate and authoritative information in regard to the subject matter covered. It is sold with the understanding that the publisher is not engaged in rendering psychological, financial, legal, or other professional services. If expert assistance or counseling is needed, the services of a competent professional should be sought.

Distributed in Canada by Raincoast Books

Copyright © 2016 by Bruce Fisher and Robert Alberti
       Impact Publishers
       An imprint of New Harbinger Publications, Inc.
       5674 Shattuck Avenue
       Oakland, CA 94609
       www.newharbinger.com

Cover design by Amy Shoup

Library of Congress Cataloging-in-Publication Data on file

Printed in the United States of America

22   21   20

10   9   8   7

This book is dedicated to...

... the thousands of people who, while I was attempting to teach them in the rebuilding classes, taught me much of what I've written in this book;

... my children, Rob, Todd, and Sheila, who often, through their love, gave me more reality, feedback, and truth than I was ready to hear;

... my parents, Bill and Vera, because the more I understand life, families, and myself, the more I appreciate the gifts of life and love they gave me; and

... my wife, Nina, who, with her love, often gave me what I needed instead of what I wanted.

Finally, a word of thanks to my coauthor, editor, and publisher, Bob Alberti, who helped it turn out the way I wanted it to.

—Bruce Fisher (1931–1998)

... my parents, Carita and Sam, who showed me—long before I had any formal training in psychology—that divorce, while painful, can be a growth experience for adults and children, and that we all can be healthier and happier at the end of the day; and

... Bruce, who showed us all how to make that happen.

—Bob Alberti

Contents

Acknowledgments

This fourth edition of *Rebuilding* is the first for which I am no longer the "editor and publisher." My excellent team at New Harbinger Publications—copy editor Cindy Nixon, editorial manager Clancy Drake, and acquisitions manager Tesilya Hanauer—have made the transition from "editor" to "edited" much easier and more pleasant than I would have imagined. They showed me just how much we could improve the book after three successful editions and over a million copies. I, along with you readers of this edition, owe them many thanks!

Foreword

Virginia M. Satir, MSW

Divorce is a metaphorical surgery that affects all areas of life of the individual. I have often said that the roots of divorce are in the circumstances and hopes at the time of marriage. Many, many, many people marry with the idea that life is going to be better. Perhaps only a fool would enter into marriage thinking that would not be the case. The depth of disappointment at the time of divorce will depend upon how much more one wants to get out of life or how much more one feels it necessary to add someone to one's life to make life worthwhile.

For many people, divorce is a broken experience, and before they can go on with their lives, they need to be able to pick up the pieces. This period often includes deep emotional feelings of despair, disappointment, revenge, retaliation, hopelessness, and helplessness. People need to develop a whole new orientation to the life that will come. And they need time to mourn what was hoped and to realize that the hope will not manifest itself.

Many books on divorce talk only about the problems. Of course, there are the injury to the ego, diminished feeling of self-worth, constant nagging questions about what went wrong, and many fears about the future. Dr. Fisher has given us a very practical and useful framework within which to examine the grief period, to take a look at where one is, and to determine directions for the future. He offers step-by-step guides to getting oneself in a position to enjoy the life that comes after the divorce. He presents it as a period in which one can learn from the past, get to know oneself better, and also develop new parts of the self that were previously unknown. An apt analogy would be that of the convalescence which occurs after any kind of surgery.

The emotional levels one needs to work through during and following divorce are very much parallel to the stages one goes through at the time of death. At first, there is a denial of the events that have taken place and a consequent feeling of wanting to isolate oneself from the whole situation. Then anger, wherein one blames someone else for one's predicament. The third level is bargaining; a kind of situation in which one wants to look at the ledger to see that things are equal. This is often manifest in the custody of children and property settlements at the time of divorce. Then comes a period of depression, which is where much self-hatred, self-blame, and feelings of failure are present. Finally, after all of this, one comes to acceptance of the situation and acceptance of the self. Out of this comes hope for what can happen.

I believe Bruce Fisher's book makes it possible for people to work through these various levels, stage by stage. It is important to give this rebuilding period the time it needs, to awaken parts of the self that have been paralyzed, repressed, or unknown. Let each self—in this case, the divorced person—come into the next part of life with hope rather than failure!

Menlo Park, California
September 1980

Editor's Note: Virginia Satir (1916–1988) was one of the most well-loved and highly respected contributors to the field of marriage and family therapy. She was recognized as a founder of family systems theory. Her many books, including her best seller *Peoplemaking*, were influential in establishing the framework for family therapy and they constitute a major component of the foundation of the profession as it is currently practiced. Ms. Satir wrote this foreword for the first edition of *Rebuilding*.

Introduction to the Fourth Edition

Robert E. Alberti, PhD

As you begin to read this book, you're probably smarting from the recent end of a love affair. Perhaps you were married for many years. Or you may have been in a committed relationship without the endorsement of church or state. You may have children, or not. You may have initiated the breakup, or you may have received a terse text message. Your ex-partner may have been a wonderful person, or a jerk.

Whatever your own story, right now, it hurts like hell.

We know how overwhelming it seems, but you *can* work your way through the difficult and painful process of recovering from the loss of a love relationship. It's not easy, and it won't happen overnight. But you *can* do it. *Rebuilding: When Your Relationship Ends* will show you how, with a proven nineteen-step process that has helped more than a million readers to recover and rebuild their lives after enduring the pain of a divorce, breakup, or loss of a love partner.

Again and again, we've heard from divorced men and women who have read and worked their way through this process that they are profoundly grateful to their friends who said, "You're going through a divorce? You have to read *Rebuilding!*"

It Will Take You a While

Sure, you can read these pages in a few hours. But the process of divorce recovery is another matter altogether. Use this book well, perhaps for a year or more—whatever it takes. You'll gain a few steps forward, then fall back a step. Most people make faster progress when they take part in a divorce recovery seminar based on the book (the Rebuilding Divorce Recovery Seminars). But whatever else you do, allow yourself the time it will require to work through what Bruce Fisher liked to call "the divorce process." His research showed that it can take two years or more.

Wait. What? Two years? Not what you wanted to hear, huh? Truth is, in the real world, you won't go from married person to divorced person to fulfilled independent person in a few weeks, or even a few months. It will take some time.

It's Like Climbing a Mountain

As you begin your own journey of rebuilding, you'll note right away that's the way we have described the process—like climbing a mountain. (Probably not surprising, since Bruce spent most of his adult life in Boulder, Colorado, at the foot of the Rockies.) It's an apt metaphor; the process can seem slow and difficult. And you'll likely find there are "detours" along the way; like a mountain trail, it won't be a straight path to the top. The nineteen steps are presented here in the order that they most often—though not always—occur in people's lives. You'll probably experience setbacks, switchbacks, and occasional side trips that take you off the path. Don't let that stop you. Each of the steps contains valuable life lessons that are well worth working through. Allow yourself as much time as you need to understand your pain and rebuild your capacity to move on.

You've probably already discovered that there are tons of books out there about how to deal with divorce. Most have to do with legal issues, finances, parenting and custody, finding a new love. *Rebuilding* takes a different approach. It's our goal to help you deal with the almost-inevitable emotional issues you will confront as you put your life back together after this major disruption.

The book starts out with an overview of the process, followed by guidance for the early months, when you'll likely confront significant levels of depression, anger, and loneliness—the darkness before the dawn. As time goes by, we'll help you to let go of the baggage you've been carrying from the past. As you start to recognize your own personal strengths and worth, you can once again risk trusting others and you'll open yourself to new relationships. Eventually, if you keep climbing, you'll discover a life of purpose and freedom. The process probably won't be smooth, but at each point along the way, this understanding trail guide will be at hand when you need support.

If you're reading *Rebuilding* as you take part in a Fisher divorce seminar, you'll find the class will set the schedule for you, and you'll be learning a great deal from discussions with other group members. If you're reading the book on your own, you can set your own pace and tailor your focus to what's happening in your life at the moment. Either way, you're likely to find yourself rereading some material that is important to you as you make your way up the mountain.

How This Book Came to Be

Bruce Fisher was an "Iowa farm boy" (his words) who, after college, became a probation officer working with teen offenders. That experience led him to graduate school to learn more about the emotional forces that impact people's lives. Then a divorce changed the focus of his studies and his career. He began to learn more about how people deal with divorce, and that work led to his development of a scale—a "test" of sorts—to examine the process. His research with that first version of his Fisher Divorce Adjustment Scale uncovered fifteen (later nineteen) key steps that occur with remarkable consistency (though not always in sequence) in the lives of people who are going through the emotional pain that typically accompanies a divorce. You can use an online version of the Fisher Divorce Adjustment Scale at http://www.rebuilding.org/assessment.

As Bruce extended his model to a seminar, guiding others through the divorce recovery process, he began to put his ideas and experience into book form. His early self-published volume, *When Your Relationship Ends,* found its way to me in 1980, in my capacity as editor and publisher at Impact Publishers (and a licensed therapist myself). Bruce and I worked together for a year to create a trade edition of the book, which Impact released in 1981 as the first edition of *Rebuilding When Your Relationship Ends.* Bruce had by then begun training others in how to use the model and conduct the seminar, and his ten-week program was springing up all over the United States and abroad.

The hundreds of facilitators Bruce prepared during his three-decade career provided him with invaluable evidence about how well the process was working for the members of their groups. Those results—the experiences of tens of thousands of seminar participants—provided the evidence base for continuing improvement of the model and the book. By the time of Bruce's untimely death from cancer in 1998, his rebuilding model had expanded from fifteen to nineteen steps, progressed through three editions of the book with nearly a million copies in print and translations in many languages, and spawned hundreds of seminars using his program in community centers, churches, clinics, therapists' offices, and private homes around the world.

And it's not only the personal experience of readers and seminar participants who affirm the value of this process in their lives. Dozens of research studies have been conducted by professors, graduate students, and therapists, most of them published in peer-reviewed professional journals. These studies show that most participants in seminars following the Rebuilding model make significant gains in self-respect, acceptance of the divorce, hope for the future, letting go of the ended relationship, acceptance of anger, and building a new social network. Thus, *Rebuilding* is a well-developed, evidence-based, and proven approach, not just another "pop-psychology" book.

Relationships, They Are A-Changin'

We know that relationships these days are all over the map. Traditional marriage has waned a bit in popularity; fewer young people are marrying, and those who do are waiting longer. Most divorced people marry again, but second marriages are not lasting any longer than the first. Ethnic and religious boundaries are frequently crossed as couples seek happiness that transcends those traditional barriers. Ex-priests are marrying. "Single" is no longer a pejorative in middle age. Trophy husbands are becoming as common as trophy wives, since age difference is not the barrier it once was.

Not much is known about divorce among same-gender couples, since it was only in 2015 that the US Supreme Court brought same-gender marriage into the law of the land. Although still considered sinful by some, these unions are becoming commonplace, and everyone will have to get used to this reality. While *Rebuilding* does not explicitly address same-gender divorce, we know that LGBTQ partnerships do break up (available statistics show the numbers to be similar to those for hetero couples), and we believe the rebuilding process to be essentially the same. When history gives us the benefit of hindsight based on experience with same-gender breakups, we may find notable differences. Until then, we consider this work to be a valuable resource for those of any sexual orientation or gender identity who are experiencing the pain of the end of their relationship. All of us are learning that our similarities are hugely greater than our differences.

Many of the elements of the rebuilding process also address the pain of loss from the death of a partner. While this book does not deal with that personal crisis in depth, we have long recognized that most of the rebuilding blocks do appear in the path widows and widowers must travel. A special section for this group was developed for and by widowed participants in the seminar, and that material has been added to this edition (see appendix D). We offer heartfelt sympathy, and trust that you may find some comfort in these pages as you put your own life back together.

We've tried to make *Rebuilding* as inclusive as we could, but we ask your indulgence if the book doesn't give full recognition to the form your love relationship may have taken. You'll find the process works anyway!

A Few Words About Words

Throughout the book, you'll find frequent references to the group program for divorce recovery that Bruce created. We've tried to label it consistently as "the Fisher divorce seminar," but you'll find it sometimes called "the ten-week class," "the Fisher divorce and personal growth seminar," "the rebuilding class," "the Fisher seminar," and sometimes simply "the class"—different labels, same thing.

Help!

At times as you make your way, you may feel you need extra help. We encourage you to seek out a licensed professional therapist if you find yourself dealing with high levels of anxiety, depression, or anger. Yes, you'll ultimately have to work through the process on your own, but just as with any challenging project, you'll do the best job by using the right tools to help you do the work. Professional support can be one of your most valuable tools if you find yourself stuck.

To get started, however, all you need is available to you right here. I urge you to **read each chapter** (even if it doesn't appear at first to apply to you); **keep a personal journal** of your progress; **(answer the "How Are You Doing?" questions** at the end of the chapters (be honest with yourself!); **avoid jumping into a new relationship** early in your process; **find a Fisher divorce seminar** if you can (see http://www.rebuilding.org), sign up, and take an active part; and, once again, **give yourself all the time you need.**

Prepare yourself for a journey. Pack up your energy, your optimism, your hopes for the future. Discard your excess baggage. Put on a sturdy pair of shoes. Colorado's Rocky Mountains were an important part of Bruce's life. California's Sierra Nevadas have been an important part of mine. And the rebuilding mountain lies ahead for you. Let's get ready to climb together.

CHAPTER 1

The Rebuilding Blocks

You are probably experiencing the painful feelings that come when a love relationship ends. There is a proven nineteen-step process of adjustment to the loss of a love. This chapter provides an overview and introduction to the rebuilding blocks that form that process.

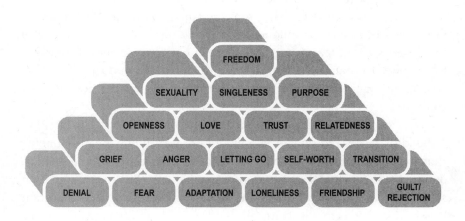

Are you hurting? If you have recently ended a love relationship, you are. Those who appear not to hurt when their love relationships end have either already worked through a lot of hurt or have yet to feel the pain. So go ahead, acknowledge that you're hurt. It's natural, expected, healthy, even *okay* to hurt. Pain is nature's way of telling us that something in us needs to be healed, so let's get on with the healing.

Can we help? We think so. We can share with you some of the learning that takes place in the divorce recovery seminars Bruce Fisher conducted for over twenty-five years. The growth that takes place in people during a ten-week seminar is remarkable. Maybe by sharing with you some of these ideas and some of the feedback we've received from hundreds of thousands of readers of earlier editions of this book, we can help you learn how to get through the hurt also.

There is an adjustment process after a divorce—with a beginning, an end, and specific steps of learning along the way. While you're feeling some of the pain, you're more anxious to learn how to be healed. If you are like most of us, you probably have had some destructive patterns of behavior for years—maybe since your childhood. Change is hard work. While you were in a love relationship, you might have been comfortable enough that you felt no need to change. But now there is that pain. What do you do? Well, you can use the pain as motivation to learn and to grow. It's not easy. But you can.

The steps of the adjustment process are arranged into a pyramid of "rebuilding blocks" to symbolize a mountain. Rebuilding means climbing that mountain, and for most of us, it's a difficult journey. Some people don't have the strength and stamina to make it to the top; they stop off somewhere on the trail. Some of us are seduced into another important love relationship before learning all that we can from the pain. They, too, drop out before reaching the top, and they miss the magnificent view of life that comes from climbing the mountain. Some withdraw into the shelter of a cave, in their own little worlds, and watch the procession go by— another group that never reaches the top. And, sadly, there are a few who choose self-destruction, jumping off the first cliff that looms along the trail.

Let us assure you that the climb is worth it! The rewards at the top make the tough climb worthwhile.

How long does it take to climb the mountain? Studies with the Fisher Divorce Adjustment Scale indicate that, on average, it takes about a year to get up above the tree line (past the really painful, negative stages of the climb), longer to reach the top. Some will make it in less time, others in more. Some research suggests that a few in our climbing party will need as long as three to five years. Don't let that discourage you. Finishing the climb is what counts, not how long it takes. Just remember that you climb at your own rate, and don't get rattled if some pass you along the way. Like life itself, the process of climbing and growing is the source of your greatest benefits!

We've learned a great deal about what you're going through by listening to people in the seminars and by reading hundreds of letters from readers. People sometimes ask, "Were you eavesdropping when my ex and I were talking last week? How did you know what we were saying?" Well, although each of us is an individual with unique experiences, there are similar patterns that all of us go through while ending a love relationship. When we talk about "patterns," you will likely find that it will be more or less what you're experiencing.

These patterns are similar not only for the ending of a love relationship, but for any ending crisis that comes along in your life. Frank, a seminar participant, reports that he followed the same patterns when he left the priesthood of the Catholic Church. Nancy found the same patterns when she was fired from her job, Betty when she was widowed. Maybe one of the most important personal skills we can develop is how to adjust to a crisis. There will probably be more crises in our lives, and learning to shorten the pain time will be a highly valuable learning experience.

In this chapter, we'll briefly describe the trail that we will be taking up the mountain. In the following chapters, we will get on with the emotional learning of actually "climbing" the mountain. We suggest that you start keeping a journal right now, to make the climb more meaningful. After the journey is over, you can reread your journal to gain a better perspective on your changes and growth during the climb. (More about journals at the end of this chapter.)

The rebuilding blocks model graphically shows nineteen specific feelings and attitudes, arranged in the form of a pyramid to symbolize the mountain that must be climbed. The adjustment process can be as difficult a journey as climbing a mountain. At first, the task is overwhelming. Where to start? How do you climb? How about a guide and a map to help us climb this difficult mountain? That's what the rebuilding blocks are—a guide and a map prepared by others who have already traveled the trail. As you climb, you'll discover that tremendous personal growth is possible, despite the emotional trauma you've experienced from the ending of your love relationship.

In the first edition of this book, published in 1981, Bruce described just fifteen rebuilding blocks. His work since then, with thousands of people who've gone through the divorce process, has led to the addition of four new blocks and some changes in the original fifteen. He was grateful to those whose lives touched his, through this book and through the classes. Much has been learned from them, and we'll be sharing their experiences with you in these pages.

Throughout the book, you will find specific ways of dealing with each rebuilding block to prevent it from becoming a stumbling block. (You have probably already stumbled enough!) People often report that they can immediately identify their blocks that need work. Others are unable to identify a problem block because they have effectively buried their feelings and attitudes about it. As a result, at some higher point on the climb, they may discover and explore the rebuilding blocks they overlooked at first. Cathy, a volunteer helper in one of the seminars, suddenly recognized one during an evening class: "I've been stuck on the guilt/rejection block all along without realizing it!" The following week she reported considerable progress, thanks to identifying the problem.

The rest of this chapter presents a "pre-journey briefing" on the climb, addressing the blocks as we'll encounter them on the trail up the mountain. Beginning at the bottom, we find *denial* and *fear*, two painful stumbling blocks that come early in the process of adjustment. They can be overwhelming feelings and may make you reluctant to begin the climb.

DENIAL

Denial: "I Can't Believe This Is Happening to Me"

The good news is, we humans have a wonderful mechanism that allows us to feel only as much pain as we can handle without becoming overwhelmed. Pain that is too great is put into our "denial bag" and held there until we are strong enough to experience and learn from it.

The bad news is, some of us experience so much denial that we are reluctant to attempt recovery—to climb the mountain. There are many reasons for this. Some are unable to access and identify what they are feeling and will have difficulty adjusting to change of any sort. They must learn that "what we can feel, we can heal." Others have such a low self-concept that they don't believe they are capable of climbing the mountain. And some feel so much fear that they are afraid to climb the mountain.

How about you? What feelings are underneath your denial? Nona talked hesitantly about taking the ten-week seminar and was finally able to describe her hesitation: "If I took the divorce seminar, it would mean that my marriage is over, and I don't want to accept that yet."

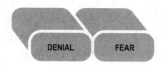

DENIAL   FEAR

Fear: "I Have Lots of It!"

Have you ever been in a winter blizzard? The wind is blowing so hard that it howls. The snow is so thick that you can see only a few feet ahead of you. Unless you have shelter, it feels—and it can be—life threatening. It's a very fearful experience.

The fears you feel when you first separate are like being in a blizzard. Where do you hide? How do you find your way? You choose not to climb this mountain because, even here at the bottom, you feel overwhelmed. How can you find your way up when you believe the trail will become more blinding, threatening, fearful? You want to hide, find a lap to curl up in, and get away from the fearful storm.

Mary called several times to sign up for the seminar, but each opening night came and went without her. As it turned out, she had been hiding in her empty apartment, venturing out only for an occasional trip to the grocery store when she ran out of food. She wanted to hide from the storm, from her fears. She was overwhelmed with fear; coming to opening night of the divorce class was way too scary for her.

How do you handle your fears? What do you do when you discover your fears have paralyzed you? Can you find the courage to face them so you can get ready to climb the mountain? Each fear you overcome will give you strength and courage to continue your journey through life.

Adaptation: "But It Worked When I Was a Kid!"

Each of us has many healthy parts: inquisitiveness, creativity, nurturance, feelings of self-worth, appropriate anger. During our growing-up years, our healthy parts were not always encouraged by family, school, religious community, or other influences, such as movies, books, and magazines. The result was often stress, trauma, lack of love, and other hindrances to health.

People who are not able to meet their needs for nurturance, attention, and love will find ways to adapt—and not all adaptive behaviors are healthy. Examples of adaptive responses include being overresponsible for others, becoming a perfectionist, trying to always be a people pleaser, or developing an "urge to help." Unhealthy adaptive behaviors that are too well developed leave you out of balance, and you may try to restore your balance through a relationship with another person.

For example, if I am overresponsible, I may look for an underresponsible love partner. If the person I find is not underresponsible enough, I will *train* her to be underresponsible! This leads me to "polarize" responsibility: I become more and more overresponsible, the other person becomes more and more underresponsible. This polarization is often fatal to the success of a love relationship and is a special kind of codependency.

Jill stated it clearly: "I have four children—I'm married to the oldest one." She resents having all of the responsibility, such as keeping track of the bank account and paying all of the bills. Instead of blaming Jack for not being able to balance the account, she needs to understand that the relationship is a system, and as long as she is overresponsible, chances are Jack will be underresponsible.

Adaptive behaviors you learned as a child will not always lead to healthy adult relationships. Does that help you understand why you need to climb this mountain?

The next handful of blocks represent the "divorce pits"—*loneliness, loss of friendships, guilt and rejection, grief, anger,* and *letting go.* These blocks involve difficult feelings and pretty tough times. It will take a while to work through them before you start feeling good again.

Loneliness: "I've Never Felt So Alone"

When a love relationship ends, the feeling is probably the greatest loneliness you have ever known. Many daily living habits must be altered now that your partner is gone. As a couple, you may have spent time apart before, but your partner was still in the relationship, even when not physically present. When the relationship is ending, your partner is not there at all. Suddenly, you are totally alone.

The thought *I'm going to be lonely like this forever* is overwhelming. It seems you're never going to know the companionship of a love relationship again. You may have children living with you and friends and relatives close by, but the loneliness is somehow greater than all of the warm feelings from your loved ones. Will this empty feeling ever go away? Can you ever feel okay about being alone?

John had been doing the bar scene pretty often. He took a look at it and decided, "I've been running from and trying to drown my lonely feelings. I think I'll try sitting home by myself, writing in my journal to see what I can learn about myself." He was beginning to change feeling lonely into enjoying aloneness.

Friendship: "Where Has Everybody Gone?"

As you've discovered, the rebuilding blocks that arise early in the process tend to be quite painful. Because of this, there is a great need for friends to help you face and overcome the emotional pain. Unfortunately, many friends are usually lost as you go through the divorce process, a problem that especially affects those who have already physically separated from a love partner. The problem is made worse by withdrawal from social contacts because of emotional pain and fear of rejection. Divorce is threatening to friends, causing them to feel uncomfortable around the dividing partners.

Betty says that her old gang of couples had a party last weekend, but she and her ex were not invited. "I was so hurt and angry. What did they think—that I was going to seduce one of the husbands or something?" Social relationships may need to be rebuilt around friends who will understand your emotional pain without rejecting you. It is worthwhile to work at retaining some old friends—and at finding new friends to support and listen.

It's so easy these days to connect with others online that it's tempting to let your cell phone or tablet or laptop substitute for seeing others face-to-face. The web is a wonderful resource for many things, but we urge you not to let texting or Twitter or Facebook isolate you from in-person contact.

DENIAL FEAR ADAPTATION LONELINESS FRIENDSHIP GUILT/REJECTION

Guilt/Rejection: Dumpers: 1; Dumpees: 0

Have you heard the terms "dumper" and "dumpee" before? No one who has experienced the ending of a love relationship needs definitions for these words. Usually, there is one person who is more responsible for deciding to end the love relationship; that person becomes the dumper. The more reluctant partner is the dumpee. Most dumpers feel guilty for hurting the former loved one. Dumpees find it tough to acknowledge being rejected.

The adjustment process is different for the dumper and the dumpee, since the dumper's behavior is largely governed by feelings of guilt and the dumpee's by rejection. Until our seminar discussion of this topic, Dick had maintained that his relationship ended mutually. He went home thinking about it and finally admitted to himself that he was a dumpee. At first, he became really angry. Then he began to acknowledge his feelings of rejection and recognized that he had to deal with them before he could continue the climb.

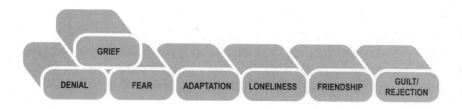

Grief: "There's This Terrible Feeling of Loss"

Grieving is an important part of the recovery process. Whenever we suffer the loss of love, the death of a relationship, the death of a loved one, or the loss of a home, we must grieve that loss. Indeed, the divorce process has been described by some as largely a grief process. Grief combines overwhelming sadness with a feeling of despair. It drains us of energy by leading us to believe we are helpless, powerless to change our lives. Grief is a crucial rebuilding block.

One of the symptoms of grief is loss of body weight, although a few people do gain weight during periods of grief. It wasn't surprising to hear Brenda tell Heather, "I need to lose weight—guess I'll end another love relationship!"

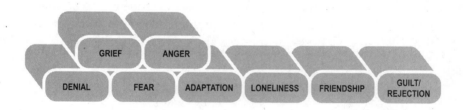

Anger: "Damn the S.O.B.!"

It is difficult to understand the intensity of the anger felt at this time unless one has been through divorce. Here's a true story published in the Des Moines *Register* that tends to draw a different response from divorced and married people: While driving by the park, a female dumpee saw her male dumper lying on a blanket with his new girlfriend. She drove into the park and *ran over* her former spouse and his girlfriend with her car! (Fortunately, the injuries were not serious; it was a small car.) Divorced people respond by exclaiming, "Right on! Did she back over them again?" Married people, not understanding the divorce anger, will gasp, "Ugh! How terrible!"

Most divorced people were not aware that they could be capable of such rage because they had never been this angry before. This special kind of rage is specifically aimed toward the ex–love partner, and—handled properly—it can be really helpful to your recovery, since it helps you gain some needed emotional distance from your ex.

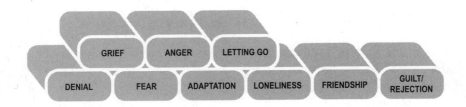

Letting Go: Disentangling Is Hard to Do

It's tough to let go of the strong emotional ties that remain from the dissolved love union. Nevertheless, it is important to stop investing emotionally in the dead relationship.

Stella came to take the seminar about four years after her separation and divorce. She was still wearing her wedding ring! To invest in a dead relationship, an emotional corpse, is to make an investment with no chance of return. You need instead to begin investing in productive personal growth, which will help you in working your way through the divorce process.

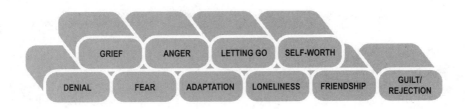

Self-Worth: "Maybe I'm Not So Bad After All!"

Feelings of self-worth and self-esteem greatly influence behavior. Low self-esteem and a search for a stronger identity are major causes of divorce. Divorce, in turn, causes lowered self-esteem and loss of identity. For many people, self-concept is lowest when they end the love relationship. They have invested so much of themselves in the love relationship that when it ends, their feelings of self-worth and self-esteem are devastated.

"I feel so worthless, I can't even get out of bed this morning," Jane wrote in her journal. "I know of no reason for doing anything today. I just want to be little and stay in bed until I can find a reason why I should get up. No one will even miss me, so what's the use of getting up?"

As you improve your feelings of self-worth, you're able to step out of the divorce pits and start feeling better about yourself. With improved self-worth also comes the courage you'll need to face the journey into yourself that is coming up.

Transition: "I'm Waking Up and Putting Away My Leftovers"

You want to understand why your relationship ended. Maybe you need to perform an "autopsy" on your dead relationship. If you can figure out why it ended, you can work on changes that will allow you to create and build different relationships in the future.

At the transition stage of the climb, you'll begin to realize the influences from your family of origin. You'll discover that you very likely married someone like the parent you never made peace with and that whatever growing-up tasks you didn't finish in childhood, you're trying to work out in your adult relationships.

You may decide that you're tired of all the "shoulds" you've always followed and instead want to make your own choices about how you'll live your life. That may begin a process of *rebellion*, breaking out of your "shell."

Any stumbling block that is not resolved can result in the ending of your primary love relationship.

It's time to take out your trash, to dump the leftovers that remain from your past and your previous love relationship and your earlier years. You thought you had left these behind; but when you begin another relationship, you find they're still there. As Ken said during one seminar, "Those damn neuroses follow me everywhere!"

Transition represents a period of transformation as you learn new ways of relating to others. It is the beginning of becoming free to be yourself.

The next four blocks are hard work, but highly satisfying, as you face yourself, learn about who you really are, and rebuild your foundation for healthy relationships. *Openness*, *love*, and *trust* will take you on a journey into yourself. *Relatedness* will ease you back into intimate contact with others.

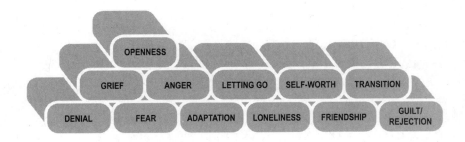

Openness: "I've Been Hiding Behind a Mask"

A mask is a feeling or image that you project, trying to make others believe that is who you are. But it keeps people from knowing who you really are, and it sometimes even keeps you from knowing yourself. Bruce remembered a childhood neighbor who always had a smiling face: "When I became older, I discovered the smiling face covered up a mountain of angry feelings inside the person."

Many of us are afraid to take off our masks because we believe that others won't like the real person underneath. But when we do take off the mask, we often experience more closeness and intimacy with friends and loved ones than we believed was possible.

Jane confided to the class that she was tired of always wearing a Barbie-doll happy face. "I would just like to let people know what I am really feeling instead of always having to appear to be happy and joyful." Her mask was becoming heavy, which indicated she might be ready to take it off.

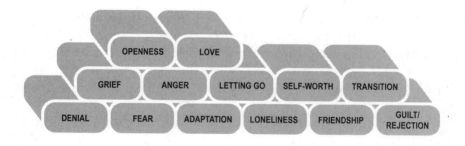

Love: "Could Somebody Really Care for Me?"

The typical divorced person says, "I thought I knew what love was, but I guess I was wrong." Ending a love relationship should encourage one to reexamine what love is. A feeling of being *unlovable* may be present at this stage. Here's how Leonard put it: "Not only do I feel unlovable now, but I'm afraid I never *will* be lovable!" This fear can be overwhelming.

Christians are taught to "Love thy neighbor as thyself." But what happens if you don't love yourself? Many of us place the center of our love in another person rather than in ourselves. When divorce comes, the center of our love is removed, adding to the trauma of loss. An important element in the rebuilding process is learning to love yourself. If you don't love yourself—accepting yourself for who you are, "warts and all"—how can you expect anybody else to love you?

Trust: "My Love Wound Is Beginning to Heal"

Located in the center of the pyramid, the trust rebuilding block symbolizes the fact that the basic level of trust, within yourself, is the center of the whole adjustment process. Divorced people frequently point their fingers and say they cannot trust anyone of the opposite sex. There is an old cliché that's very fitting here: when you point a finger at something, there are three fingers pointing back to you. When divorced people say they don't trust the opposite sex, they are saying more about themselves than about the opposite sex.

The typical divorced person has a painful love wound resulting from the ending of the love relationship, a love wound that prevents him or her from loving another. It takes a good deal of time to be able to risk being hurt and to become emotionally close again. Incidentally, keeping that distance can be hazardous too! Lois says that when she returned home from her first date, there was a mark on the side of her body caused by the door handle on the car—she was attempting to get as far away from the man as possible!

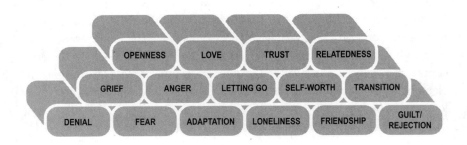

Relatedness: "Growing Relationships Help Me Rebuild"

Often after a love relationship has ended, one finds another relationship— one that appears to have everything the previous union lacked. The thoughts go something like this: *I believe I've found the one and only with whom I will live forever. This new relationship appears to solve all of my problems, so I'll hold on to it very tightly. I believe this new partner is what's making me happy.*

This person needs to realize that what feels so good is that she is becoming who she would like to be. She needs to take back her own power and take responsibility for the good things she is feeling.

The new relationship after a breakup is often called a "rebound" relationship, a label that is partly true. When this relationship ends, it is often more painful than when the primary love relationship ended. One symptom of that pain: about 20 percent of the people who sign up for the divorce seminar don't enroll after their marriages end; they enroll after their rebound relationships end.

You may not be quite ready to think about the next block just yet. But it's time.

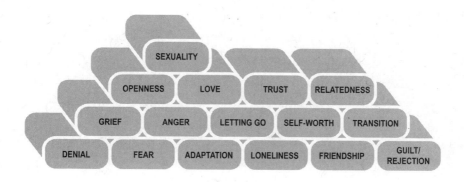

Sexuality: "I'm Interested, but I'm Scared"

What do you think of when the word *sex* is mentioned? Most of us tend to react emotionally and irrationally. Our society overemphasizes and glamorizes sex. Married couples often imagine divorced people as oversexed and free to "romp and play in the meadows of sexuality." In reality, single people often find the hassles of sexuality among the most trying issues in the divorce process.

A sexual partner was available in the love relationship. Even though the partner is gone, sexual needs go on. In fact, at some points in the divorce process, the sex drive is even greater than before. Yet most people are more or less terrified by the thought of dating—feeling like teenagers again—especially when they sense that somebody has changed the rules since they last dated. Many feel old, unattractive, unsure of themselves, and fearful of awkwardness. And for many, moral values overrule their sexual desires. Some have parents who tell them what they should do and their own teenagers who delight in parenting them. ("Be sure to get home early, Mom.") Thus, for many, dating is confusing and uncertain. No wonder sexual hang-ups are so common!

As we near the top of our climb, the remaining blocks offer comfort and a feeling of accomplishment for the work you've done to get this far: *singleness*, *purpose*, and *freedom*. Here at last is a chance to sit down and enjoy the view from the mountaintop!

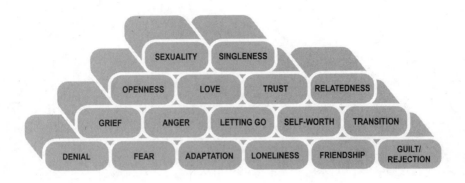

Singleness: "You Mean It's Okay?"

People who went directly from their parental homes into their marital homes without experiencing *singleness* often missed this important growth period entirely. For some, even the college years may have been supervised by "parental" figures and rules.

Regardless of your previous experience, however, a period of singleness—growth as an independent person—will be valuable now. Such an adjustment to the ending of a love relationship will allow you to really let go of the past, to learn to be whole and complete within yourself, and to invest in yourself. Singleness is not only *okay*, it is necessary!

Joan was elated after a seminar session on singleness: "I'm enjoying being single so much that I felt I must be abnormal. You help me feel normal being happy as a single person. Thanks."

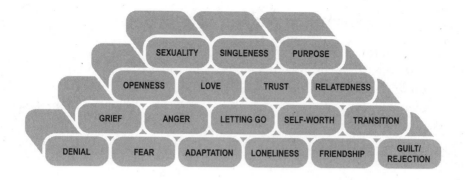

Purpose: "I Have Goals for the Future Now"

Do you have a sense of how long you are going to live? Bruce was very surprised during his divorce when he realized that, at age forty, he might be only halfway through his life. If you have many years yet to live, what are your goals? What do you plan to do with yourself after you have adjusted to the ending of your love relationship?

It is helpful to make a "lifeline" to take a look at the patterns in your life and at the potential things you might accomplish during the rest of your life. Planning helps bring the future into the present.

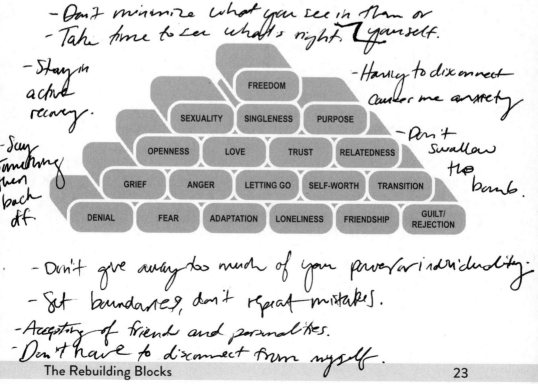

- Don't minimize what you see in them or
- Take time to see what's right for yourself.

- Stay in active recovery.

- Having to disconnect causes me anxiety

- Say something then back off.

- Don't swallow the bomb.

- Don't give away too much of your power/or individuality.
- Set boundaries, don't repeat mistakes.
- Accepting of friend and personalities.
- Don't have to disconnect from myself.

Freedom: From Chrysalis to Butterfly

At last, the top of the mountain!

The final stage has two dimensions. The first is freedom of choice. When you have worked through all of the rebuilding blocks that have been stumbling blocks in the past, you're free and ready to enter into another relationship. You can make it more productive and meaningful than your past love relationships. You are free to choose happiness as a single person or in another love relationship.

There is another dimension of freedom: the freedom to *be yourself*.

Many of us carry around a burden of unmet needs, needs that may control us and not allow us freedom to be the persons we want to be. As we unload this burden and learn to meet needs that were formerly not met, we become free to be ourselves. This may be the most important freedom.

Looking Backward

We have now looked at the process of adjustment as it relates to ending a love relationship. While climbing the mountain, one occasionally slips back to a rebuilding block that may have been dealt with before. The blocks are listed here from one to nineteen, but you won't necessarily encounter and deal with them in that order. In fact, you're likely to be working on all of them together. And a big setback, such as court litigation or the ending of another love relationship, may result in a backward slide some distance down the mountain.

Reconnecting with Your Faith

Some people ask how religion relates to the rebuilding blocks. Many people working through divorce find it difficult to continue their affiliation with the religious community they were part of while married, for several reasons. Some faith groups still look upon divorce as a sin or, at best, a "falling from grace." Many people feel guilty within themselves, even if their faith doesn't condemn them. (It is worth noting that in 2016 Pope Francis offered a ray of hope to divorced Roman Catholics: without changing church law, he noted that divorced people are not automatically excommunicated, and should be met with an attitude of welcome in their parishes.)

Many churches, temples, mosques, and synagogues are very family-oriented, and single parents and children of divorced people may be made to feel as if they don't belong. Many people become distant from their faith community since they are unable to find comfort and understanding as they go through the divorce process. This distance leaves them with more loneliness and rejection.

There are, happily, many congregations that are actively concerned for the needs of people in the divorce process. If yours does not have such a program, we urge you to express your needs. Let the leaders know if you feel rejected and lonely. Organize a singles group, talk to an adult class, or ask how you can help to educate others about the needs of people who are ending their love relationships.

The way each of us lives reflects our faith, and our faith is a very strong influence on our well-being. Bruce liked to put it this way: "God wants us to develop and grow to our fullest potential." And that's what the rebuilding blocks are all about—growing to our fullest potential. Learning to adjust to a crisis is a spiritual process. The quality of our relationships with the people around us and the amount of love, concern, and caring we're able to show others are good indications of our relationship with God.

Children Must Rebuild Too

"What about the children?" Many people ask about how the rebuilding blocks relate to children. The process of adjustment for kids is very similar to that for adults. The rebuilding blocks apply to the children (as they may to other relatives, such as grandparents, aunts, uncles, and close friends). Many parents get so involved in trying to help their kids work through the adjustment process that they neglect to meet their own needs.

If you're a parent who is embarking on the rebuilding journey, we recommend that you learn to take care of yourself and work through the adjustment process. You will find that your children will tend to adjust more easily as a result. The nicest thing you can do for your kids is get your own act together. Kids tend to get hung up on the same rebuilding blocks as their parents, so by making progress for yourself, you will be helping your children, too.

In our discussion of each rebuilding block in the chapters to come, we will take up the implications of that stage for the kids. And appendix A concentrates specifically on the process as it relates to children should you wish to develop a more structured approach to helping your children adjust to the divorce.

Homework: Learning by Doing

Millions of people read self-help books looking for answers to life and relationship problems. They learn the vocabulary and gain awareness, but they don't necessarily learn from the experience at a deep emotional level. Emotional learning includes those experiences that register in your feelings, such as: mothers are usually comforting; certain kinds of behavior will bring punishment; ending a love relationship is painful. What we learn emotionally affects our behavior a great deal, and much of the learning we have to do to adjust to a crisis is emotional relearning.

Some things you believed all of your life may not be true and will have to be relearned. But intellectual learning—thoughts, facts, and ideas—is of value only when you also learn the emotional lessons that let it all make sense in your life. Because emotional learning is so important, we have included in this book exercises to help you relearn emotionally. Many chapters have specific exercises for you to do before continuing your climb up the mountain.

Here's your first set of homework exercises to get you started:

1. **Keep a journal** or a diary in which you write down your feelings. Use your tablet, a laptop, or a small notebook—whatever fits your personal style. You might journal daily, weekly, or whenever it fits your schedule. Start a lot of the sentences in the journal with "I feel"—that should help you concentrate more on feelings. Keeping a journal will not only be an emotional learning experience that will enhance your personal growth, but it will also provide a yardstick to measure your personal growth. People often come back months later to read what they wrote and are amazed at the changes they have been able to make. Every report we've heard from those who have kept a journal has described it as a worthwhile experience. We suggest you start writing the journal as soon as you finish reading this chapter. You may want to write in your journal after reading each chapter, or perhaps once a week, or on some other regular schedule. But "regular" or not, do make this a part of your rebuilding process.

2. **Find a person you trust** and can ask for help, and learn to ask. Call someone you would like to get to know better and start building a friendship. Use any reason you need to get started. Tell the person about this homework assignment if you like. You're learning to build a support system of friends. Make that connection when you're still feeling somewhat secure, so that when you are down in the pits (it's tough to reach out when you're down there!), you will know you have at least one friend who can throw you an emotional lifeline.

3. **Build a support group for yourself.** Because a support system is so important, this is a key part of your first homework assignment. We suggest you find one or more friends, preferably of both genders, and discuss with them those rebuilding blocks with which you're having difficulty. This sharing may be easier for you with people who have gone or are going through the divorce process themselves because many married people may have difficulty relating to your present feelings and attitudes. Most important, however, is your trust in these people.

If you choose to form a discussion group of supportive friends, you may find this book a helpful guide. We do caution you to be aware that not all "support groups" are supportive. Choose carefully the others with whom you work through this process. They should be as committed as you are to a positive growth experience and willing to maintain confidentiality of personal information.

4. **Answer the checklist questions.** At the end of each chapter, you'll find a series of statements, most of them adapted from the Fisher Divorce Adjustment Scale, which we have included as checklists for you (the complete version of the scale is available at http://www.rebuilding.org/assessment). Take the time to answer them, and let your responses help you decide how ready you are to proceed to the next rebuilding block.

How Are You Doing?

Here is the first checklist to respond to before you proceed to the next chapter. Assess your response to each question as "satisfactory," "needs improvement," or "unsatisfactory."

☒ *I have identified the rebuilding blocks that I need to work on.*

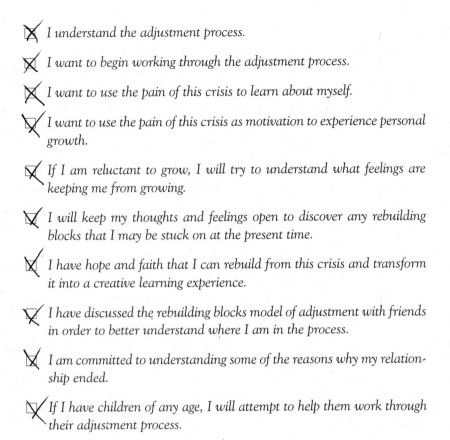

☒ I understand the adjustment process.

☒ I want to begin working through the adjustment process.

☒ I want to use the pain of this crisis to learn about myself.

☒ I want to use the pain of this crisis as motivation to experience personal growth.

☒ If I am reluctant to grow, I will try to understand what feelings are keeping me from growing.

☒ I will keep my thoughts and feelings open to discover any rebuilding blocks that I may be stuck on at the present time.

☒ I have hope and faith that I can rebuild from this crisis and transform it into a creative learning experience.

☒ I have discussed the rebuilding blocks model of adjustment with friends in order to better understand where I am in the process.

☒ I am committed to understanding some of the reasons why my relationship ended.

☒ If I have children of any age, I will attempt to help them work through their adjustment process.

How to Use this Book

On your own. Most readers of *Rebuilding* are recently divorced individuals who are reading this book on their own. If that description fits you, we suggest you start at the beginning and take it one chapter at a time. Do each chapter's homework before going on to the next chapter. The chapters are arranged in the approximate order most people experience the rebuilding blocks, although you may find that your life doesn't follow the sequence exactly!

On the other hand, we have found that many readers want to devour the whole book first, then go back and work their way through the stages, doing all of the homework then. Whichever approach you choose, we suggest you use a highlighter as you read the book in order to better understand the information. Some readers have found it helpful to use a different-colored highlighter each time they read the book, because each time you read it, you will find new and different concepts that you missed before. You hear only what you are ready to hear, depending upon where you are in your personal growth process.

There are many different reactions from individuals who read this book. Some readers are overwhelmed with some of the information. You may, for example, realize you left your relationship too soon and need to go back and work on some of the unfinished business with your love partner. One seminar participant, George, reported that after he had read the first chapter, he experienced so much anger that he threw the book against the wall as hard as he could!

In a group. Even better than reading the book on your own is to form a small group to discuss a chapter per week together. It takes a minimum of leadership to do this, and you will be pleased to discover how much support you get and how much more you learn from the book by discussing it with others.

In fact, experience and research have shown that the most personal growth and transformation comes in a group setting, including but not limited to that offered by the ten-week Fisher divorce recovery seminar (see http://www.rebuilding.org for information on the Fisher seminar). Most people are amazed at the transformation that takes place throughout the course of a group recovery program, where participants are guided through taking control of their lives and learning to make "loving choices" in the way they live. When you're putting your life back together after the ending of a love relationship, you may find this approach even more helpful than individual therapy, so check out what's available in your local area.

A note of caution. It is rewarding to see that many religious and community organizations have developed programs for divorce recovery. In some such programs, however, guiding texts like this one are accompanied by an "expert" lecture each week on a related topic. With this method, you must adjust not only to your crisis, but also to a new viewpoint each week. Instead of giving you an opportunity for active discussion and learning from your peers—a "laboratory" in how to take control of your life—the lecture approach keeps you listening passively. We therefore endorse a participation-centered program over a lecture-based approach, so that group members can bond and connect with one another in a meaningful way.

Don't get us wrong here. There is nothing wrong with gaining lots of information about divorce. There are many excellent books—you'll find a list of some of our favorite resources at the end of this book—and we encourage you to read them and broaden your knowledge of the complexities of the process. But information alone will just put a Band-Aid on your pain; it doesn't allow you to really heal and transform your life.

We don't claim to have all the answers, but we do know that the program described in this book works. It has been successful for hundreds of thousands of individuals going through the divorce process, and it can help you deal effectively with your crisis and take control of your life. We believe you'll find in these pages strong practical support for your desire to learn, to grow, to heal, to become more nearly the person you would like to be. We wish you every success in climbing the mountain!

CHAPTER 2

Denial

"I Can't Believe This Is Happening to Me!"

Ending a love relationship may be the greatest emotional pain you will ever experience. The pain is so great, in fact, you may react with denial or disbelief. This only prevents you from facing the important question: **Why did my love relationship have to end?** There are rarely simple answers, so it will take some time and effort. Until you can accept the ending, you will have difficulty adjusting and rebuilding.

Owl is crying forlornly in the dark,
I heard him calling to his mate last night.
I waited with him to hear the familiar answering cry,
And my heart fell with his
as the silence fell, louder than a cry.
He is still calling tonight,
Only to be answered by longer silences.
I have never seen the owl.
I have only heard him calling
And waiting...

—Nancy

Look at the big crowd gathered at the trailhead waiting to climb the mountain! There are so many kinds of people waiting—all sizes and colors, all ages, both men and women, some wealthy, some poor. Some people think that only losers get divorced, but many of these look like winners. Some are eager to start the climb and are doing calisthenics. Some look in shock—as though they have just witnessed a death. There are some who look up the mountain and act overwhelmed, as though they expect never to be able to climb to the top. Many are waiting around, expecting their former love partners to pick them up so they won't have to make the climb.

Many act confused and disoriented. John is shaking his head and mumbling, "I thought we had a good marriage. I had been the captain of the football team in high school, she was a cheerleader. Everyone predicted we would be perfect together. Then last week she dropped the bombshell on me. She said she was unhappy, that she didn't love me, and she wanted a divorce. She left with our two children to stay with her parents. I was dumbfounded. I thought it would never happen to me."

Mary is impatient to start the climb. She is telling a passerby, "I was so unhappy in our marriage. I wanted a divorce but was afraid to initiate any actions. Then he was killed in a train wreck, and everyone thought I was weird because I felt so little grief. But his death left me free to climb this mountain. When do we start?"

We hear Rita saying, "He has left me and is living with another woman, but I know in my heart that he will always be my husband. God made this marriage and God will have to end it. I refuse to climb this mountain and will stay married until I die. Maybe when we get to heaven, we will be together again."

David is warming his feet by stomping on the ground and appears to be cold and in shock. "I had a good marriage. We never fought. But last night, she told me she had fallen in love with my best friend and she was packing her bags to leave. I went in the bathroom and was sick. This morning, I called my lawyer and asked him to start divorce proceedings."

Maria is a gray-haired grandmother. "I lived with him and gave him my whole life. I planned to share the harvest of our years in old age with him. But he left without giving any reasons. My harvest is destroyed, and I am too old to plant another crop."

We could fill this whole book with stories similar to these—similar yet unique stories of people who are reacting in many different ways to the ending of their love relationship.

It is hard for anyone to be comforting when you are hurting so much. The most help we can offer at this point is to listen to your reality of the crisis. You may feel as though you have failed, as though you have been hit in the stomach and had your emotional wind knocked out, as though you have just experienced death even though you are still living. The initial shock is easier for those of you who made the decision to leave and who were more prepared for this crisis, but the ending is still painful no matter what the circumstances.

Why Did It Have to End?

The big question you may be asking is "Why?" You feel a strong need to understand what went wrong, to perform an "autopsy" on the dead relationship. You want to know why, yet denying the pain often prevents you from accepting the results of this emotional autopsy. To understand why it ended helps you overcome the denial, so in this chapter and the next, we'll discuss some of the reasons love relationships die.

It's fun to start a talk with teenagers by asking them, "How many of you plan to get married?" Usually, about half of them raise their hands. Then the next question: "How many of you plan to get divorced?" There are never any raised hands after this question.

No one plans to get a divorce. And most of us deny it at first even if it does happen. We want to bury our heads in the sand like ostriches to avoid the storm. But, like the ostrich, we have problems in our love relationships that are more obvious to others than they are to us.

There are three entities in a love relationship—two individuals and the relationship between them. It is analogous to a bridge: the two people are the foundations at each end of the bridge; the relationship is the span that connects the two foundations. When change occurs in one or both of the foundations at the ends of the bridge, it strains the bridge itself. Some changes are too great for the bridge to handle, and it falls into the river. In people, such changes may result from personal growth, education, religious experiences, attitude shifts, illness, anxiety, anger, relocation, or maybe a reaction to stress or trauma. (One way to prevent such stress on a relationship is to never grow or change—not a very healthy way to live, is it?)

You may recognize that you or your love partner recently went through a period of change and personal growth, and that upset the system of your love relationship, tumbling your bridge into the river.

If you need to doubt and question yourself and your abilities, you may feel that you should have been able to adjust to this stress resulting from change. If you had been, you would be unusual. Two of the most important abilities we need to learn in our lives are how to build and maintain the bridge between two people in a love relationship and how to parent our children. And where do we receive education and training for these two important roles? From our parents mostly. And TV. And other adults. Not always helpful or well-informed sources. In a talk to a group of about a hundred women, Bruce asked them how many would like to have a marriage like that of their parents. Only one raised her hand! Did the rest receive good training from their families on how to have a happy love relationship? Did you receive good training and education on how to adjust to a strain in your love relationship?

Perhaps relationship counseling would have helped you to adjust? Perhaps. We are terrific marriage counselors when both parties want to work on the relationship, but lousy marriage counselors when only one wants to work!

What was the reality in your love relationship? Were both you and your partner wanting to work and improve the system, or did only one of you want to work on the relationship? If only one is willing, then it is not very likely that the relationship will improve. A team of horses will not pull a very big load when one of the horses is lying down.

You may be punishing yourself with feelings of failure in your love relationship by playing the "if only" game: "If only I had listened more.... If only I hadn't become so angry....If only I had made love to her every time she wanted to....If only I hadn't been such a bitch."

We hope by now you have satisfied your need to punish yourself. We suggest you let it go. Your hindsight is much better now. You have learned a great deal about life and about yourself since the troubles began in your love relationship. Your awareness and your insights are much improved. How about using the new awareness and insight as a basis for further *growth* rather than self-punishment? Do something for the rest of your life, not the past. Try saying, "I did the best I could with what I knew and what I had to work with," and leave it at that. Now you're going to work on today, and tomorrow, and the next day, and the next....

Maybe your relationship failed because there was a third party involved. It is easier to be angry at that third party than it is to be angry at your former love partner or yourself. There is a catch-22 in being angry at your former love partner: "You're damned if you do and damned if you don't." How can you be angry at the person you loved? It is easier to be angry at the person who came in and "took your spouse away from you."

There are many reasons why one partner leaves a relationship to become involved with another. You may feel that the other person had something to offer that you didn't have. That may be true in some cases. But every love relationship has some cracks in its foundation, and in many cases—and for many reasons—these cracks may result in a breakup. Patterns of development and interaction start long before love relationships end. If there were such serious cracks in your relationship, it may be difficult for you to see and understand them at this time.

Here's an example. Many people have not freed themselves from their parents' influence when they marry. They don't have identities of their own, separate from being children of their parents. Such a person may later decide to dump a love partner. But when you examine what is really going on, you see that he or she is actually dumping the parents' control and influence. To rebel against the spouse may be, in reality, to rebel against the parents.

So the crack in your relationship may have begun even *before* you married. And if there was a crack in your relationship, it is easy for a third party to become involved by filling that crack. It often is easier—or seems easier—for a person outside of the relationship to fill the deficiency than it is for a person who is part of the relationship. A good marriage counselor may be able to help you explore and understand some of the cracks and deficiencies in your past love relationship.

There is another important phenomenon that frequently contributes to the demise of a marriage. Many couples make the mistake of investing all of their time and energy into a project external to the love relationship. Examples might be building a new house or business or going to school. This external project may keep the couple so occupied that they have little energy or time to invest in their love relationship. In fact, the project may become a method of avoiding each other. When the house is finished, the couple finds they have nothing in common anymore, and the new house becomes a monument to their divorce.

Why Did It Begin in the First Place?

Many people ask, "Why did so-and-so get a divorce?" Sometimes a more relevant question is, "Why did that couple marry?" (Bob recalls a college paper he wrote that began, "The basic cause of divorce is marriage." Not profound, perhaps, but not far off when we look at the facts surrounding most divorces.)

Many people marry for the wrong reasons, among them (1) to overcome loneliness; (2) to escape an unhappy parental home; (3) because they think that everybody is expected to marry; (4) because only "losers" who can't find someone to marry stay single; (5) out of a need to parent, or be parented by, another person; (6) because they got pregnant; and (7) because "we fell in love." And on goes the list.

We'll talk more about love in another chapter, but for now, let it suffice to say that there are many levels of love and not all are mature enough to provide a sound basis for getting married. It's common to develop an idealized image of another person and to fall in love with that *image* instead of the real person. When the honeymoon is over (a long time passes before reality hits), disillusionment follows; that person is not living up to the idealized image. Perhaps "falling in love" is an attempt to fill some emptiness, rather than a sound basis on which to build a marriage.

Those who get married for these wrong reasons (including "falling in love") might be described as "half people" who are trying to become whole and trying to find happiness by getting married. Even the usual wedding vows talk about "two people becoming one." During a talk with a group of ministers, one asked if Bruce thought the marriage vows were contributing to divorce. When he replied "yes," the discussion grew lively, and a few of the ministers began to consider changing the vows in the marriage ceremony.

Similarly, Bob has often objected to the common marriage ritual in which two candles (representing the two partners) are used to light a single candle (representing the relationship)—okay so far—but then *the two are extinguished*! What happens to those individual partners when their "candle" goes out?

When you are ready to face life alone and have found happiness as a single person, then you are ready to face life together with another person. Two whole people who have climbed the mountain of personal growth and self-awareness will tend to have a much more dynamic relationship than two half people joining together in an attempt to become whole.

Most of the wrong reasons people get married can be summarized by stating that the unhappy person expects that getting married will bring happiness. Do you remember movies about marriage in the *old days*? (Television has seen to it that no one is too young to have seen them!) The movies were all about the *courtship* of the couple. When they married, the movie ended. The subtle message was that you became married and without effort lived "happily ever after." Such a fairy tale!

Bruce's son Todd writes his ideas and thoughts on paper, and often they are profound. As a young man, he described a good reason for getting married: "At some time in the future during my growth toward becoming a full person, there will come a day when my cup runneth over so profusely that the need will arise for another person to soak up the excess."

When It's Over...It's Over

Recognizing the ending of an unhappy and unproductive relationship may help you look at your divorce as a decision reflecting good mental health. Take a look at your former relationship, your former partner, and yourself. Set aside for a moment all of society's reasons why you were "meant for each other." This is the time for painful honesty. Ask yourself:

Were you and your partner friends?

Did you confide in each other?

What interests did you share? Hobbies? Attitudes toward life? Politics? Religion? Children?

Were your goals for yourself, for each other, and for the relationship similar/compatible?

Did you agree on methods for solving problems between you (not necessarily the solutions, but the methods)?

When you got angry with each other, did you deal with it directly, hide it, or try to hurt each other?

Did you share friendships?

Did you go out together socially?

Did you share responsibilities for earning money and household chores in a mutually agreed upon way?

Did you make at least major decisions jointly?

Did you allow each other time alone?

Did you trust each other?

Was the relationship important enough for each of you to make some personal sacrifices for it when necessary?

We hope these questions were not too painful for you. Your honest answers will probably help you recognize that your relationship really was at an end in many ways, even before the formal separation or divorce. It is tough to acknowledge some of those shortcomings. It is even tougher to accept that you were part of the problem (easy enough to blame your partner, society, or someone or something else). Acceptance, however, is the all-important positive side to the *denial* rebuilding block.

Take some time with this. And remember: you do not have to take on a load of guilt in order to accept that your relationship is over! Stay out of the "if only" game. The reasons, the contributing factors, are as complex as those structures that support a bridge. It takes a great deal of analysis of *known* forces and stresses and loads and strength of materials to build a successful bridge. How infinitely more complex is a successful love relationship! And how little most of us really *know* about the interpersonal forces and stresses and loads and strength of our own materials!

You'll learn much more as our journey up the mountain continues. For now, take a deep breath and say it: "My love relationship has ended."

Now let yourself cry for a while.

From Denial to Acceptance

Now that you are up to your tears in the reasons why relationships end and you have taken a hard look at the cracks in your own former love relationship, you may be feeling "sadder but wiser." And maybe a bit down on yourself. You are not alone.

In fact, one subtest of the Fisher Divorce Adjustment Scale was designed to measure acceptance of the ending of a love relationship, and data from this scale over the years has revealed that feelings of *acceptance* and self-worth are significantly related. More specifically, the better your sense of self-worth, the easier it is for you to accept the ending of your love relationship.

If you have difficulty starting the journey up this mountain because you refuse to accept the ending of your love relationship, you may need to work on improving your self-concept. When you are in the shock of a recent ending, telling you to improve your self-concept is like blowing in the wind—it does not change much. Still, you will find it true. Especially after we deal with self-concept more in chapter 11, you will experience the difference for yourself as you discover more of your own value.

As you come closer to standing alone, to accepting that your relationship has really ended, the emotional pain will get pretty intense. And the pain you are feeling is real. Divorce and death of a spouse are probably the two most painful experiences you will feel in your life. Millions of other people have felt the same things you are feeling as your relationship ends. It hurts. And even knowing you're not alone helps only a little. But we need to use our pain to learn. To flow with the pain rather than denying it. To use it as motivation to grow and turn the crisis into an opportunity instead of an experience that leaves us with wounds that never heal. We can use the pain as an excuse to remain bitter, angry, unhappy; or we can use the pain to grow. Which do you choose to do?

Those of you who believe that you will be getting back together with your former love partner probably feel there is no reason to climb this mountain of adjustment. What's the best plan of action for those of you who want to get back together? Do you have to climb the mountain? If your relationship has become fractured to the point of physical separation and you are talking about divorce, you may need time apart to change the old patterns of interaction. You may need to close off the bridge to traffic while you shore up the foundations. Experience individual personal growth before you start working on the bridge. It's pretty easy just to move in together again, but it's difficult to make the old relationship more meaningful and productive unless both people go through changes. You may need to climb the mountain before you go back to your former love partner!

Suffer the Children

There are three areas relating to denial that cause problems for kids.

The first is that children of divorce will continue to maintain some sort of a fantasy of their parents getting back together again. They have difficulty accepting the reality that their parents' relationship is over. It may be surprising for you to learn how strong this fantasy is in your children. You continually need to present them with the reality that the relationship is over so they don't continue to invest in this fantasy.

Your kids may use all kinds of manipulative behavior to try to get the two of you back together again, to have you spend time together, or to get you talking to each other. Kids have a large emotional investment in not accepting the ending of their parents' relationship and in hoping that their parents will get back together again. Respond gently but firmly and persistently with your own decision—that the marriage is over.

The important second aspect relating to kids in this denial stage is their belief that they did something to cause your breakup. The last time that they disobeyed—when they didn't go to bed or clean up at mealtime or do their household chores—they think this led to your fight and then to your divorce. Try hard to help your kids see that it's not their fault and that divorce is a grown-up problem.

Third, children fear that now that they have "lost" one parent, could they then lose the other? They tend to be very clingy and dependent upon their parents at this point, and they need a lot of reassurance that neither will leave them. Parents do divorce each other, but they do not divorce their children. You need to reassure your children that even though Mom and Dad are divorced from each other, *you will never divorce them.*

Thoughts about Friends and Lovers

I want to become somewhat parental and talk to you about how vulnerable you are to becoming involved in another love relationship as a way of making your pain go away. My belief is that you need *friends* rather than *lovers* right now.

Have you read Homer's *Odyssey?* This Greek myth tells of sailors on a journey filled with various obstacles. One of these obstacles is an island where beautiful female sirens attempt to seduce the sailors into stopping. (The sailors have been forewarned that stopping will lead to their destruction.) They prevent the sirens from tempting them by tying themselves to the ship's mast and blindfolding themselves.

Like Homer's sailors, you will need to tie yourself to the mast of self-discipline and avoid becoming too deeply involved in another love relationship until you have healed some of the emotional pain. Almost always, a relationship that is started when you are in deep pain will add to your misery in the long run. But friendships are helpful; and if you can build friendships rather than love relationships, it will be more productive for the present.

Imagine a circus tightrope act. The platform at one end represents the security you had in the love relationship. The platform at the other end represents the security you need to find within yourself. You need to walk across the tightrope in your adjustment process to find that inner security.

You can fall off one side by withdrawing into your home and not making any friends.

You can fall off the other side by becoming deeply involved in another long-term, committed love relationship—if you're investing more in the relationship than you are in your own personal growth. You wake up one morning and discover you're trying to please the other person and trying to make the relationship work, but you're not trying to become the person you wish to be.

But having friends is the balance pole that will help you keep walking across the tightrope. Friends give you honest feedback that is not biased by a need to have your love. Friends are more objective than lovers, and you need objectivity at this point in your life. Set yourself a goal: learn to be happy as a single person before you become coupled again!

—Bruce

How Are You Doing?

You may be making this journey even though you don't want to, even though you are still married in your heart. The emotional pain is so great that you know you have to climb. It will benefit you to learn as much from this journey as possible, so decide to make it a positive experience rather than one you undergo begrudgingly.

In the next chapter, we'll continue our exploration of why love relationships end. Before you go on, however, take time to complete this chapter's checklist, to help you decide if you are ready to move on to the next portion of the trail. Use it to check out your progress. No one is grading you, so be very honest with yourself.

☒ *I am able to accept that my love relationship is ending.*

☒ *I am comfortable telling my friends and relatives that my love relationship is ending.*

☒ *I have begun to understand some of the reasons why my love relationship did not work out, and this has helped me overcome feelings of denial.*

☒ *I believe that even though divorce is painful, it can be a positive and creative experience.*

☒ *I am ready to invest emotionally in my own personal growth in order to become the person I would like to be.*

☒ *I want to learn to become happy as a single person before committing myself to another love relationship.*

☒ *I will continue to invest in my own personal growth even if my former love partner and I plan to get back together.*

CHAPTER 3

Fear

"I Have Lots of It!"

Fear can be paralyzing until you're able to recognize it as a part of you that is your friend. Fear then becomes a motivator and a way to learn more about yourself. Fears are a major part of the feelings you experience when you are in the pits of divorce.

Fear was my biggest obstacle. I was afraid of all the changes I had no control over, and at the same time, I was afraid nothing would ever change. My whole life was being influenced by my fears! I was afraid of being alone, and at the same time isolating myself, afraid of never really being loved again and yet pushing love away when it got too close.... I was completely stuck, paralyzed by my own fear.... It wasn't until I admitted my fears, listed them and talked about them openly, that they lost their power over me.

—Jere

I spent thirty-three years as a homemaker, raising a large family. I had the security and comfort of upper-middle-class living. When I became a single parent, with responsibility for our youngest child and faced with the task of becoming self-supporting (with few if any marketable skills), I was literally paralyzed with fear.

—Joanne

The trail looks a bit intimidating, doesn't it? Some would-be climbers are showing their fears with comments like these: "Don't take that trail; you'll fall off the side of the mountain!" "The trail is too steep. I'm afraid I can't climb it." "I don't know what kind of wild creatures will jump out at me while I'm climbing." "I don't think I want to do this." "I'm afraid of what I'll learn about myself if I make this climb."

Ending a love relationship results in fears of all kinds. Some are fears you didn't know you would ever feel. Some are old fears you've had most of your life but had been successfully denying.

It's easy to allow fears to immobilize you. You feel too afraid to make the climb and become almost paralyzed by your fears. A little fear can be motivating. But too many fears makes it difficult to function and to get on with your life. There are a couple of key things we've learned about fears that can be helpful in learning to deal with them.

The first is that fears not yet identified can be the most powerful. When you identify them, take a look at them, and face them, you'll find they aren't as scary and powerful as you thought. One simple thing you can do that really helps is to make a list of your fears. Identify the things you're afraid of so you can get in touch with just what you're feeling.

Another useful insight is that *feared situations that you don't face are the very ones that are likely to occur.* If I'm afraid of being rejected, I find many ways of avoiding rejection. I may become a people pleaser, or become over-responsible, or avoid expressing anger. While these behaviors might appear to insulate me from rejection, they can actually increase my chances of being rejected. People sense I am not being real, honest, and authentic and may reject me for that.

Until we face our fears, what we are afraid of will most likely happen to us. So, as you become aware of your fears, it's best not to deny them, but to face them openly. That alone may be enough to chase some of them away!

What Are You Afraid Of?

Let's take a look at some of the common fears we've heard people express in the past. This discussion of fears that often come up in the divorce process will help you access and identify your own. As you read what follows, how many of these fears are you experiencing too?

One of the greatest fears is fear of *the unknown future:* "I don't know what the trail up this mountain is like. I don't know what I'll learn about myself or about others. I can't visualize how I'll be able to make it as a single person."

These fears about the unknown are based in our formative years. Like the ghosts you thought you saw when you woke up in the middle of the night as a child, the fear is real, but the objects aren't really there; they're figments of your imagination. You need to learn that you can face the ghosts of the unknown future, living one day at a time. You can learn to trust the process and know that you'll eventually be able to face every new experience that occurs as you end your love relationship.

Another common fear is that of *becoming a divorced person:* "What will people think? They'll discover what a failure I am. If I can't work out the problems in my love relationship, what is there left for me? It's as if I spilled food on my clothes while eating, and now everyone is shouting, 'Look at that person who is so stupid and foolish that she spilled food all over herself!' I feel embarrassed, awkward, found out, ashamed, and afraid people won't like me anymore."

It is also fearful to *have others discover our family secrets.* Often we haven't thought about it, but many of our family secrets are not secret anymore: "When we were together, I could have a fight with my spouse, but no one knew about it. We felt ashamed of having problems in our marriage, but at least the whole world didn't know about it then. When you separate, it's hard to keep the kids' teachers from knowing. Friends soon discover there is another phone number to reach my ex. The post office found out right away that her mail was to be forwarded to another address. The utility company had to be notified that the bill wouldn't be paid until some of the financial decisions had been made. It seems everyone in the whole world knows about the dirty linen that only the two of us knew about before."

Then there are fearful practical, financial, and legal matters: "I feel fearful because I don't know *how to make the decisions I have to make.* What lawyer do I contact? What therapist will I go see? How do I decide which bills to pay when I won't have enough money to pay them all? My partner handled the checkbook—how do I learn to manage the accounts? I don't have any idea of how to have my car serviced. I'm sure the repair shop will take advantage of me because I never had to take the car in before. Just learning all I need to know so I can make good decisions is a full-time job. I'm too overwhelmed emotionally to care much about my car."

"I am fearful about *money*. How can I make it financially when there are now two houses to maintain? I'm afraid I'll be fired because all I do is cry at work. I can't concentrate and do an adequate job. Why would anyone want to have me work for them when I'm so inefficient? I don't know where I'll find enough money to pay the bills and feed my children."

And speaking of children: "I'm afraid of *being a single parent*. I'm barely functioning on my own, and I just don't have the patience, courage, and strength to meet the needs of my kids by myself. I no longer have a partner to take over when I'm overwhelmed. I have to be there for my kids twenty-four hours a day, seven days a week. I want to crawl into bed and hide my head under the covers. I wish there were someone whose lap I could crawl up in, someone who would hold me, instead of me having to pretend I'm strong enough to hold my kids on my own lap."

"I'm afraid of *losing my kids*. My ex is talking about filing for sole custody. I've always been the primary parent for my kids, and they say they want to be with me. But my ex has more money and is able to buy the things the kids want. I'm sure my kids will be swayed by the promise of so many material things that I can't provide; surely they'll want to live with him. If we have a custody hearing, what will my kids say? Will they talk about how distraught Mom is and that she's too busy and upset to spend any time with them?"

"I'm afraid about *whom to talk to*. I need someone to listen to me, but will anyone understand? Most of my friends are married and have not been through a divorce. Will they gossip about what I share with them? Will they still be my friends now that I'm divorced? I must be the only person in the whole world feeling these feelings. No one else can possibly understand me when I can't even understand myself."

"I'm afraid of *going to court*. I've never been in court before. I thought only criminals or those who have broken the law go to court. I have heard the 'war stories' of what's happened to others in court when they were going through a divorce, and I'm afraid some of the same things will happen to me. I know my ex-partner will find the best barracuda attorney around, and I'll lose everything. I don't want to be mean and nasty, but I am afraid I'll have to be in order to protect myself. Why does the court have so much power over what happens to me, my family, my children? What have I done to deserve this kind of treatment?"

And other common fears, of course, are simply about feelings: "I'm afraid of *anger*. I'm afraid of my own anger and of my partner becoming angry. As a child, I used to feel terror when my parents were angry and fighting. I learned to avoid being around anger. My ex and I never fought or showed anger in any way. I find myself feeling angry sometimes, and it really frightens me. What if I become angry? It would take away any chance of getting back together again. I feel angry a lot of the time, but it's not safe or right for me to get angry."

"I'm afraid of *being out of control*. The anger feelings are so great inside of me. What if I were like my parents when they got angry and lost control? I hear stories of people being violent when they are divorcing. Might I do something violent if I get out of control?"

"I'm afraid of *being alone and living alone*. If I'm alone now, who will take care of me when I am old? I have seen couples take care of each other and avoid going to a nursing home or retirement center. But with no one to take care of me, I'll spend my old age alone. And what if I get ill? I might just die in my empty apartment and no one will know. There's no one to take care of me when I'm ill, and no one to find me if I become so sick that I can't function or call for help."

"I fear *discovering that I am unlovable*. If my ex-partner, who knows me better than anyone, doesn't want to live with me, I must be unlovable. How can I live the rest of my life alone and feeling unlovable? I was always afraid of being abandoned, and now I feel I have been abandoned. I've been discarded like a toy that isn't wanted anymore."

"I feel afraid I am *becoming mentally ill*. I feel crazy enough to be admitted to a mental hospital. I feel crazy enough that the idea of being taken care of completely in a psych ward, with even my meals provided, is almost appealing. Never before in my life could I imagine being crazy enough to think a psych ward would sound desirable. But it does in a way. I want to be little and have someone take care of me, even if I have to go to a psych ward to have it happen."

"I'm afraid of *being hurt even more than I have been hurt*. I never knew I could hurt so much. The person I loved—and I thought loved me—has hurt me more than anyone else has ever hurt me in my life. I want to hide so I won't be hurt anymore. I hurt so much, I find myself feeling numb, as though I have calluses on my feelings. I'm afraid I will crack and not be able to survive being hurt again."

"I am afraid of *change*. What changes are going to happen to me? Will I have to move from my home? Will I have to find a new job? Will I have to make new friends? Will I have to make changes in myself and my personality in order to survive? These unknowns are pretty frightening; I don't know what changes I will have to make as a result of this crisis."

"The thought of *dating and being with another person* is so fearful that I don't allow myself to even think about it."

Allowing Fear to Become a Friend

A few people deal with their fears by doing risky and dangerous things. They want to face their fears and find that taking risks allows them to feel their fears. As part of the divorce process, they will climb cliffs, drive their cars dangerously, or put themselves in other perilous situations that cause them to feel fearful. Rarely are such extreme behaviors productive. Instead of trying to push the limits of fear, it's more valuable to let fear become a friend.

Therapists often ask those who are feeling a great deal of fear to think of the worst thing that could happen. Are you going to die from this crisis? Are you going to become ill? Are you going to be sent off to prison? Usually, the worst thing is that you're going to live with a lot of hurt for a while. The most likely outcome is that the crisis will lead to being transformed and experiencing life in a deeper, more profound way.

Fear is a normal part of each of us, and we can make it a friend. It keeps us from taking unnecessary risks, putting ourselves in situations that are dangerous to us, exposing ourselves and becoming vulnerable. Without fear, we might not live very long, because we would expose ourselves to life-threatening situations. We need fear to help protect us. You suffer a physical burn from a fire and learn to respect and fear the fire; you know it can hurt you. The same thing is true with an emotional burn. When you're hurt, you learn to protect yourself from becoming too intimate until you have healed the emotional burn.

Fear also can be a motivator. It can motivate us to develop coping skills in order to survive. It can motivate us to develop better defenses. It can motivate us to become stronger emotionally and physically. We can use fear as a motivator to work through the adjustment process. For example, you could say to yourself: "I don't want to be in this much pain. I want to work through the process and overcome my fears."

The best way to overcome fears is to allow yourself to feel them. You've heard the old adage: "The only way out is through." You need to discover your fears, to be committed to overcoming them, and to use them as an avenue to understanding yourself better. The things you're afraid of lead you to knowing yourself better.

You may, for instance, have fears about parenting and dealing with your children. Working through this crisis can result in you becoming a far better parent than you were before. Facing and dealing with your fears allows you to have more time and energy to devote to personal growth, career development, building better relationship skills, becoming a better parent.

Dealing with Fear

When you are feeling fear, it can help a lot to pay attention to your body so you can determine where you are experiencing the fear. Most people experience fear in the solar plexus—that area just above your belly button. But you can feel it elsewhere, such as an accelerated heartbeat or tension down the backs of your legs. Identifying where in your body you are experiencing fear helps you to accept and start to deal with the fearful feelings.

Here's an exercise that can help. Find a comfortable place to sit or lie down and do some deep breathing. Breathe in as much air as you can. Fill your lower lungs with air by doing belly breaths—inhaling deeply into your abdomen and exhaling slowly. Get the oxygen flowing in your blood, especially to your head.

Now relax. Allow all the muscles in your body, from your toes to your forehead, to release tension and become deeply relaxed. Keep breathing deeply as you relax more and more fully. Close your eyes for a few minutes and imagine yourself in a very calm, relaxing place (on the beach, in a mountain meadow).

Then begin to visualize your fear. Think: *Is this fear life-threatening? Where did I learn this fear? Is it a present concern or a remnant from my past? For example, when my ex is expressing anger toward me, does it remind me of how fearful I felt when my father became angry when I was a child? Does my fear remind me of a time when I was emotionally or physically hurt in the past? What would be an appropriate action for me to take when I am feeling this fear? Is the fear I am feeling going to overwhelm me, or can I use it as a method of better understanding myself?*

Keep breathing deeply as you consider these questions. Come "back to the room" slowly and open your eyes when you're ready. Use this deep relaxation exercise often, as a way to discover more about your fears and to deal with them more effectively. Processing fear in this way will help you allow fear to become your friend and help you take more control of your life. The more choices you can make, the less fear will control you.

Of course, one session of deep relaxation won't cure your fears. You'll need to keep at it, practice relaxing regularly, face those fears as best you can and "work through" them. If they're overwhelming you or keeping you from getting on with your life, seek professional help. Ask your minister, rabbi, imam, physician, or trusted friends for a referral to a licensed psychologist or family therapist.

You can experience a great deal of personal growth and transformation because of the crisis of ending your love relationship. Facing and overcoming your fears can help you turn the crisis into a creative experience.

Your Children Are Even More Scared Than You

> After I told my eight-year-old daughter I was leaving, I went to pack my clothes. When I came back to kiss her good-bye, she was hiding under the bed. She was so scared, she doesn't remember this and denies to this day that she was hiding.
>
> —Bruce

Imagine the fears children feel when their parents divorce! Their whole world is threatened: "Do my parents still love me? Where will I live? Will I go with Mommy or with Daddy? What will my friends think? Will I even have any friends? What's going to happen to me?"

Children often fear that they'll be left alone: "Mommy is leaving me; will Daddy leave too?" "I didn't have anything to say about my daddy moving out. I wonder when my mommy will move out and leave me all alone."

As introduced in the last chapter, the message we need to give our kids is that *parents may divorce each other, but they will never divorce their children.* The marriage may end, but parenting is forever. Reassurance on this point, in words and actions, is extremely important at this time.

Fears are extremely powerful. Children, like adults, can learn to identify their fears, talk about them, and handle them more comfortably. All of us need to recognize that it's okay to be afraid; everybody is sometimes.

Incidentally, the relaxation and deep breathing methods described in this chapter are very valuable for kids too. If they learn them early, they can apply them in all kinds of life situations that bring up anxiety and fear (like exams, or public speaking).

How Are You Doing?

Here is a checklist to help you determine if you have completed this part of the journey. It will be hard to really climb the mountain of adjustment until you have become courageous enough to deal with your fears.

- ☒ *I have identified and made a list of my fears.*

- ☒ *I have found a friend or a helping person with whom I can share my list of fears.*

- ☒ *I am learning that fear can be one of my friends.*

- ☒ *I am changing fear from a paralyzing into a motivating feeling.*

- ☒ *I am learning more about myself by facing my fears directly.*

- ☒ *I am practicing deep relaxation regularly as a way to help deal with my fears and with everyday stress.*

CHAPTER 4

Adaptation

"But It Worked When I Was a Kid!"

Growing up, we all learned a variety of ways to adapt when our needs for love and attention were unfulfilled. Some of those strategies may have helped us get by as children, but they are excess baggage for grown-ups. An over- or underresponsible style, for example, is not effective in adult relationships. The process of rebuilding offers many opportunities to change your unhealthy parts into authentic, relationship-enhancing behaviors.

In my first marriage, I was the parent taking care of him. In my next love relationship, I would like to have a parent to take care of me and nurture the little girl inside of me. And then in my third love relationship, maybe I can become balanced and have a healthy relationship.

—Janice

Y ou're still trying to figure out why your love relationship ended, aren't you?

Before we continue our climb up the mountain of rebuilding blocks, let's take some time to explore that question. Almost everyone going through the divorce process wants to find out more about why their love relationships ended; this chapter will help you answer that question.

Nothing is 100 percent when you are ending a love relationship. When you were considering divorce, your feelings were probably about 80 percent favorable to the divorce and 20 percent against it. When you are in crisis, it is confusing—but quite normal—to hear these competing voices inside of you.

Each of us has many parts. When you drive by the ice-cream store, one voice says, "Let's stop and get an ice-cream cone." Another voice says, somewhat critically, "Do you remember your New Year's resolution to lose twenty pounds? You won't do it by eating ice cream all the time!" Best of all is a mediating voice that says, "It's okay to have a small ice-cream cone once a week as a reward for being such a good person."

Listen to your self-talk and you will better understand your different subpersonalities. As you listen to the different voices inside yourself, try to identify the parts that are represented. If you're like a lot of people going through a divorce, there may have been an "internal war" among the parts that eventually became an "external war" with your love partner and resulted in the ending of the relationship.

Getting in touch with the diverse parts of yourself can be of great benefit to your healing process and will also improve the self-understanding you'll need for building more solid relationships in the future.

Healthy Relationships

Why do so many people, when they have a choice between a healthy relationship and an unhealthy one, often choose the unhealthy one? What does health look like, anyway? How does it feel? How can we create healthy relationships with ourselves and with others?

Let's begin to deal with those questions by looking first at what might be called "healthy personality parts."

Each of us has a *feeling part*, which some refer to as the "inner child." It's important to be able to access and identify feelings. There is evidence of a correlation between how much one can *feel* and how much one can *heal.* The person who isn't able to access and talk about feelings will take much longer adjusting to a crisis.

We also have a *creative part* that thinks of new ways of doing things or thinking about things. The creative part is a wonderful gift that allows us to be not only artistic, but original, unique, individual, and self-actualized. Being creative feels good and leads us to be more human and less robot-like.

The *magical part* reads garden-seed catalogues and believes that the seeds we plant will produce flowers and plants that look like the catalogue pictures. This part enjoys going to see *Aladdin* movies and believes we, too, could fly with a magic carpet. The magical part allows us to balance out our serious and rational sides so we can have fun and not always have to be eating bran, broccoli, and other things that are good for us.

We have a *nurturing part*, but often we become unbalanced with our nurturing. We nurture others quite easily but neglect to nurture ourselves. We bought the idea that it is better to give than to receive, and then we often pay the price of giving ourselves away. The healthy alternative is to give to both others and ourselves.

We have a *spiritual part* that allows us to connect through faith to whatever our supreme being looks like. This is often more of a childlike part, because faith may not be rational and intellectual. The spiritual child part allows us to surrender to a power greater than we are, but at the same time, to use our free will to make loving choices in our lives.

Can you name other parts of you that are healthy? Take some time and think about it. Write down a list of other healthy parts.

Did You Grow Up Healthy?

There are some important questions for you to think about. How much did your family and your childhood home encourage your healthy parts? Were you, particularly if you are a male, encouraged to cry? If you're female, were you encouraged to be appropriately angry—and to show it? Were you encouraged to be inquisitive and creative? Were you encouraged to be independent and think for yourself, or were you told to "do as I say because I'm your parent"?

How about other influences in your childhood, such as school? Were you encouraged to be unique, or did being different cause you problems? Were you encouraged to express anger? To cry? To talk about feelings?

What grades did you receive for being nurturing, being spiritual, believing in magical fairy tales?

What about your religious training? Did your religious community encourage creative doubts in your beliefs? Did you find encouragement to be angry, or was anger looked at as sinful and not religious? Was nurturing of yourself encouraged? Or were you taught it is better to give (and give and give) than to receive?

Feedback from seminar participants indicates that some of us received more encouragement to acknowledge our healthy parts than others. Some of us grew up in families that allowed us to be creative, to believe in magic, to both give and receive nurturance. Others had schools that, along with teaching the three Rs, still allowed us to be individual and unique. Some families and schools and churches taught us how to be more loving, but too many emphasized fear and control to make us behave as we were "supposed to."

For a variety of reasons, many of us failed to learn how to acknowledge and encourage our healthy parts. As adults, we forget to pay attention to our feelings, to be creative, to take time for ourselves, to invest in our spiritual well-being. We internalized the rejection of these healthy parts in order to get along, to belong, to get good grades, to make money, to be what others wanted us to be. Now we feel more or less unloved, not nurtured, not okay. We may have low self-esteem and look for ways of feeling better from our relationships instead of looking inside ourselves. No wonder we're uncomfortable when we find healthy relationships with others. We're uncomfortable with any healthy parts we may have within us.

Healthy and Unhealthy Adaptation Strategies

We humans are amazingly adaptive creatures. Our highly developed intelligence gives us the ability to express our individuality, as well as to respond to an infinite variety of circumstances presented by our natural and social environments.

If life treated us well in our early years, our adaptive capabilities helped us to be creative, exploratory, self-expressive, loving, and responsible.

Those of us whose emotional and psychological needs were slighted in our formative years found it necessary to discover ways to adapt to those nonnourishing situations. We developed alternative—and often unhealthy —"adaptive behavior" parts that allowed us to survive in such conditions.

The more stressful and traumatic a childhood was, the greater the need for such adaptive behavior parts. Let's take a look at some of these unhealthy adaptation strategies.

Caren developed an *urge to help* part of her personality. If others in the family were unhappy, quarreling, angry, or using drugs to excess, she felt better when she "helped" them. Her pain and discomfort were lessened when she focused on their pain and discomfort. Now in her adult relationships, whenever she sees someone needing help, she wants to pitch in: picking up hitchhikers along the road; talking to anyone in the grocery store who appears to be feeling sad or irritable; finding stray cats and bringing them home. She may choose to marry someone in need, because she's looking for someone to help balance out her own "urge to help" part.

Gerald learned an adaptive *overresponsible* behavior. An oldest child, he changed his siblings' diapers, babysat the younger ones, helped with preparing meals. These activities gained him recognition, attention, and love. He grew up continuing to take care of the rest of the family—just what he had resented doing as a child. And he found someone underresponsible to marry (and when she wasn't underresponsible enough, he "trained" her to be more underresponsible!).

Lots of us grew up with adults who were very critical. Joe was given the job of taking care of the yard at an early age. He learned that if he mowed every blade of grass off evenly with no long stems sticking up, if he trimmed around each tree and along the sidewalk, mowed the grass diagonally so it looked like a golf green or major league baseball diamond, he might receive less criticism. He gave up early on looking for any "attaboys," praise, or encouragement. He found the only way he could receive compliments was to go to the neighbors: his father often bragged about his son to others but never praised him directly.

When Joe grew up, it was very difficult to go shopping with him because he had a great deal of difficulty making up his mind what to buy. He was afraid of making the wrong decision because he had internalized a part of his father that might be called an *inner critic* part. Many of us have a big adaptive "inner critic" part that keeps reminding us that we should strive to be perfect and that we are definitely not behaving as perfectly as we "should." Each decision, even what to buy when we go shopping, should be the best possible decision. Like Joe, we strive to be perfect so the inner critic will not shout so loudly inside.

What does this type of adaptive perfectionist look for in a partner? Maybe a people pleaser who will continually appease the inner critic, which easily becomes an "outer critic" in adult relationships. The only thing more difficult than living with another perfectionist is living with one's own internal perfectionist part. Some perfectionists marry an opposite—like the Pigpen character from the Peanuts comic strip—so that the perfectionist can continually find something to criticize in the other person's messy behavior.

Charles grew up with a lot of chaos in his childhood home: family members always coming home drunk, acting off-the-wall, behaving irrationally, or just being angry and emotional all of the time. Charles made a choice to always be rational, logical, and sensible, and to avoid feelings of any kind. He learned to adapt to the chaos by being completely *intellectual and unfeeling*, because when he got into his feelings, he felt hurt, criticized, and not okay. He learned to stuff feelings of any kind, particularly angry feelings. Becoming angry was okay for the "big people," but not for him.

What kind of mate would a buried-feelings person like Charles look for in a relationship? Well, since he had become unbalanced with his all-intellect, no-feelings approach, he needed a very emotional, expressive partner to balance him out. (It seems easier for males to become nonfeeling people, but it can happen to either gender. Often the female is the more feeling person because growing up female in our society usually means learning to be aware of and to trust feelings.)

When emotional individuals marry nonfeeling opposites, the emotional partners keep trying to draw feelings of any kind out of their reluctant mates. And the harder they try, the more the other person becomes focused on thinking rather than feeling. And the more one is thinking, the more emotional the other becomes. Such relationships may become polarized, with one person carrying virtually all of the thinking parts and the other carrying all of the feelings for the relationship.

Most folks think they married because they "fell in love." There's an argument to be made that "falling" in love is actually an unstable condition—maybe even an emotional illness! Oftentimes it has to do with *the way the partners are unbalanced*, rather than having anything to do with love. Some of us marry our disowned or disused personality parts and call it "falling in love."

Why Relationships End

What do adaptation strategies have to do with the ending of relationships?

Think about personality as a car with one of a person's unhealthy parts in the driver's seat. (We're talking human driver here, not a self-driving machine!) Other people in that person's life are going to have to put up with the way that part is driving, particularly if that part is a rigid adaptive behavior. And the more unmet needs there are that led to the unhealthy adaptive behavior, the more rigid and controlling the adaptive behavior is likely to be. If the driver is overresponsible, for example, everyone will have to deal with a lot of controlling behavior and will learn to be underresponsible (if they elect to stay in the relationship). On the other hand, if the personality in the driver's seat is a people pleaser, everyone will have to tell the driver how and where to drive—people pleasers don't like to make any decisions on their own.

Everything can work okay for a while with an unhealthy adaptive personality part in control. Sooner or later, however, one partner is likely to grow tired of the imbalance.

Nancy was an overresponsible person (an "OR" for short) who tired of always being in control. She developed a lot of resentment toward underresponsible (UR) Jack, her partner, because he was a walking example of a part of her that she didn't want to own or admit. Nancy saw Jack having more fun, being less responsible, and not carrying his share of the load. She became angry and resentful because Jack couldn't even handle the checkbook; checks were bouncing all over town because of insufficient funds. Sometimes Jack never got the checks written or the bills paid until the phone calls started coming. Nancy decided to end the relationship.

Like Nancy, ORs quite frequently become tired of their role and leave their marriages. As for Jack and other URs, the crisis can serve as an opportunity to wake up and become more responsible. If not, they will look for another mommy or daddy figure to marry so they can carry on the same pattern in the next relationship.

Had Jack decided to take more responsibility during the course of their marriage, however, he might have resented Nancy for not "allowing" him to grow up; he himself may have decided to end the relationship. URs often become rebellious, frustrated, irritable, and angry, wanting to get away from the smothering behavior of ORs.

As for Nancy, if she doesn't take the opportunity to look at herself and her adaptation strategy, she will probably seek out and find another stray cat to take care of so her OR trait can keep driving the personality car.

When people are asked to identify when they first noticed an event that upset the system in their love relationship, many mention things like a baby being born, the at-home partner starting to work outside of the home, the breadwinner being transferred to a new job, a parent or grandparent becoming ill or dying, or barely surviving a catastrophe such as a major flood. If asked how they were able to adjust to this change in the relationship, they usually say the relationship was too rigid to adjust. The major life change was the beginning of the end of their relationship.

Did you have an event that upset your system and that eventually resulted in your relationship ending?

The Bridge Across Responsibility

To return to an analogy used earlier, here is a metaphor to help you think about this OR/UR relationship. Imagine the love partners (Jack and Nancy or you and your partner) as the ends of a bridge. The two of them are supporting the relationship bridge: it is the connection between them. The overresponsible person (Nancy) is the bridge sweeper who keeps the whole bridge clean—all the way across to Jack's end of the bridge. The underresponsible person (Jack) is sitting on his end of the bridge with a fishing pole. Nancy resents Jack fishing all of the time instead of keeping his end of the bridge swept. Fisherman Jack resents Nancy never taking time to enjoy fishing herself, not to mention her scaring away the fish with her persistent sweeping.

We're discussing this particular over-/underresponsible adaptive behavior more than some of the others because it was the most common unhealthy adaptation strategy with the two thousand people Bruce taught personally in the divorce class. The over/under responsible pattern seems to be a major cause of divorce. It might be called a parent-child relationship, a caretaker-taker relationship, or an alcoholic-enabler relationship. It is a specific form of codependency, in which each person is dependent upon the other to keep the system in balance (or, rather, *imbalance*).

What kinds of adaptive behaviors have you developed? Are they driving your personality car? Would you like to be better able to choose which of your parts you want to be driving? How will you go about changing and taking charge of your life?

Feelings Underneath Adaptive Behavior

Overresponsible people usually give to others what they would like someone else to give to them. They have unmet needs—most often from an unsatisfying childhood—that lead them to develop this unhealthy adaptive behavior so they'll feel better and more comfortable. The same is true of other adaptation strategies. The way to take charge of your life is to learn how to meet the needs that were not met in your formative years. This starts with understanding some of the feelings underneath adaptive behavior.

Julie developed an unhealthy adaptive behavior pattern because "I don't want to feel *rejected* and *abandoned*. If I take care of him, he won't dare leave me. He'll feel obligated to not reject me." She takes care of others so she will feel less rejected.

Wayne takes care of Susan because, he told the class, "I would feel *guilty* if I didn't. If I do things for myself, my inner critic starts telling me how selfish I am. How I never do enough for others. How I need to be more loving. By giving to Susan, I feel less guilt."

Fear of criticism is one of the most common feelings behind adaptation strategies. Bill explained it this way: "I learned to feel somewhat anxious inside because of the large amount of criticism I heard from one or more of the significant adults in my childhood. I need to make my world as perfect as possible because I feel *fearful* when my external world is not perfect. I've developed my adaptive behavior so I will feel less fear."

Here is Edward's story: "The only time I feel worthwhile is when I am doing something for others. I don't have much *self-esteem*, but I feel better when I am doing my adaptive behavior. I didn't feel loved as a child, and I learned to be seen and not heard. So I am a people pleaser because I feel worthless if I am not pleasing you."

"I feel *angry*," Alec admitted, "and I don't know how to express it or even allow myself to feel it. So I become very critical of you as a way of adapting. I saw my father as being angry but never showing it openly. But he was very critical of others. I become critical and controlling as a way of disguising my disowned anger."

Jennifer grew up with an all-too-common experience: "As a female, I saw my mother being the caretaker of the family, so my unhealthy adaptive behavior was learned from her *modeling*—take care of others."

Michael also learned from parental modeling: "As a male, I saw my father being the breadwinner of the family, so the adaptation strategy I learned is to make enough money to be as good a breadwinner as my father was. It is more important to me to work long hours than it is to spend time with my family."

Making Peace with Your Inner Critic

Most of us have a well-nourished and thriving "inner critic" part, which often drives our "personality car." The inner critic is good at finding ways of controlling us, just as critical people in childhood found ways of controlling us.

When the members of one divorce seminar were asked to think of a name for their inner critics, most of them gave the name of one of their parents. Most of us developed our inner critics from the criticism we heard from one or both of our parents.

"I've often thought of the inner critic as me, or as *who I am*," Beverly told the group. We pointed out to her that it is important to identify it as just one of the many parts of her personality and to put up some internal boundaries between the essence of who she is and the part of her that is critical. When we understand that the inner critic is just one of our many parts, we begin to diminish the power it has over us. *Your inner critic is smaller than you are, and you can be bigger than it is.* Many of us tend to respond to our inner critics in much the same way we did to our parents. If we believed our parents' criticism, which often resulted in lower feelings of self-esteem, we similarly believe our inner critics and allow the criticism to continually lower our esteem. Those of us who rebelled against our parents may well rebel against our inner critics.

We must remember that we are controlled if we always *obey* one of our parts. But we are also controlled if we are forced to always *rebel against* one of our parts. If we tuned out our parents and didn't listen, we probably will tune out the inner critic as well.

How do you react to the voice of your inner critic? Do you react the same way as you did to your parents? Do you want to react differently? How will you do that?

Instead of trying to disown or disuse your inner critic by ignoring it or by believing it, start listening to what it is saying. Think of it this way: If you keep ignoring the person sitting next to you, she will probably try harder and harder to get your attention. She might even start shouting at you or inflict some physical pain or discomfort.

The inner critic is even more powerful than that frustrated person at your elbow, and it's harder to keep ignoring it when it lives inside your head! Consciously make a decision to start listening to that part. You might even write down what you hear it saying. It probably has been sending *you-messages*: "You are really dumb." "Can't you ever do it right?" Acknowledge the voice, and it will eventually start softening the words it uses. When it is feeling heard, feeling important, and feeling understood, it will start sending *I-messages* instead: "I didn't like the way I handled that situation." Notice how much more constructive that statement is and how much more valuable it is to you when you accept it as your own.

When your critic has finished speaking each time, you may respond with a simple "Thank you."

What is really happening is that you are making peace with your "inner parent." The messages of your inner critic are usually very much like the admonitions of your parent(s) when you were a child. As you listen to and begin to own your inner critic, it'll become a new and healthy "good parent."

Homework to Help You Take Charge of Your Life

Among the major goals of this book are to help you understand what went wrong with your past relationship and to help you learn how your unhealthy adaptive behavior keeps you unbalanced.

If your adaptive behavior in the past relationship was being *overresponsible*, you were probably a good giver and a poor taker. You were responsible for others, but you were not responsible for yourself. You need to become balanced in your giving and receiving so you can do each one equally well.

Here's a homework assignment designed to help you start becoming more balanced. First, ask someone to do something for you. (We can just hear some of you saying, "I can't do that." Not ready to let go of your unhealthy adaptive behavior, huh?) There is a second part of the homework: say no when someone makes a request of you. Do you see the value of this homework exercise? It can help you to balance out your giving and receiving. The important thing for you to be aware of is how you feel when you do this homework: rejected, guilty, fearful, angry, worthless? Or were you simply unable to perform the assigned behavior?

If your adaptive behavior in your past relationship was being *underresponsible*, you will need to put your money where your mouth is and carry out specific changes in responsible behavior.

Dave shared an example of his homework in this regard. In the past, his former wife was overly responsible. After they divorced, he would ask her what their teenage daughters would like for their birthdays. As an OR, she, of course, was able to state exactly what they would like. The situation seemed to be working for everyone: Dave was able to continue his underresponsible behavior by following his ex-wife's recommendations; she was happy to continue her overresponsible behavior; and their daughters were happy to get what they wanted for their birthdays. But for his homework, Dave shared with the class: "I decided on my own what my daughters would like for birthday presents, and I got it for them without asking anyone what I should buy. It wasn't anything they'd asked for, but they seemed thrilled anyway!"

If your adaptive behavior in your past relationship was being a *perfectionist*, your homework is to not make your bed when you get up this week. ("Oh, I can't do that. I will be thinking about the messy bed all day and not get anything done at work. The room looks really messy when the bed isn't made. What if the plumbing should break down and someone would come and see the messy bedroom?" Still not ready to change, huh?)

Remember to ask yourself what you are feeling so you can become aware of what's underneath your adaptive behavior.

If your adaptive behavior in your past relationship was being a *people pleaser*, your homework is to do something that will likely displease someone. It might be saying no to a requested favor, or it might be not doing something that you resent doing but have been doing nonetheless for fear of displeasing someone. The problem here is that if we suggest a specific homework assignment, you might do it just to please us. So it may be valuable for you to create your own homework, to think of a way to counter your people-pleasing tendency. Just be aware of the feelings underneath as you do so.

If your adaptive behavior in your past relationship was taking on the role of the *thinking, nonfeeling* person, your homework is to write ten "*I feel*" *messages* each day for the next week. An "I feel" message is simply a statement of your feelings—not what you think, what you *feel*—at any moment, like "I feel angry," "I feel confused," *not* "I feel that you're being unfair" (that's an opinion, a thought). Be aware of how it feels to talk about your feelings. (More about I-messages in chapter 9.)

If your adaptive behavior in your past relationship was being *unorganized* as a way of hiding under the mess, then your homework is to create a daily to-do list. Be aware of your feelings underneath.

If your adaptive behavior in your past relationship was being *rebellious*, your homework is to make a list of ten "*I am*" statements. "I am" statements are self-descriptions about something meaningful, not just factual: "I am a person who hates rules" fits this assignment; "I am a resident of Ohio" does not. This exercise is designed to help you gain an identity of your own instead of allowing someone else to be in charge of your life, which is what's happening when you feel you *must* rebel.

And finally, if your adaptive behavior in your past relationship was *whatever you decided,* then you will have to decide what your homework will be also!

Learning to Nurture Yourself

This is homework for everyone, regardless of whatever unhealthy adaptive behaviors you may have: do something nice for yourself, something that will make you feel good. Stop for a treat before you pick up the kids. Take a long bubble bath. Read a book that you have been wanting to get to for a long time. Develop a new hobby. Get a full-body massage. Have someone take care of and nurture you for a whole evening. Write twenty things you like about yourself on slips of paper and post them where you can read them until you believe them.

Children and Adaptation

This part of the trail is especially important for children. As we have seen in this chapter, it is the formative years—and usually in response to parents—when unhealthy adaptive behaviors develop: when we're not getting our needs met; when we feel frightened; when we need more attention and love.

Not surprisingly, the need to develop adaptive behavior is even greater in children when their parents are separating and divorcing. Ever notice how the oldest daughter becomes a pseudomom when she is with her dad? Or how the boy becomes the "man of the house" when he is with his mom? How often children become overresponsible when their parents in the divorce pits are behaving underresponsibly!

We adults often encourage our children to develop unhealthy adaptive behaviors by our own need to be little. We have difficulty working through our own process and want somebody "big" around because we don't feel we can do it ourselves. It's understandable, but it's not a good idea. We need to be careful not to use our children to meet our own needs.

Let's encourage our children to become independent as they grow and develop—to be themselves instead of being caretakers for their parents. Let's help them build their creative and inquisitive parts. Let's help them make peace with the inner critic and learn how to use it as a friendly guide to a responsible and independent life.

How Are You Doing?

The crowd on the trail is growing restless. Most want to get on with the journey. Before you go, check out the following questions to see if you're ready to move ahead:

☒ *I have become aware of my adaptive behavior part(s).*

☒ *I am committed to becoming more flexible and balanced through self-nurturing.*

☒ *I have identified and completed the homework designed to help me take charge of my unhealthy adaptive behavior.*

☒ *I have become aware of the feeling(s) underneath my adaptive behavior.*

☒ *I have made a list of healthy parts that I would like to encourage within myself.*

☒ *I have a better understanding of why my love relationship ended.*

CHAPTER 5

Loneliness
"I've Never Felt So Alone"

It is natural to feel extreme loneliness when your love relationship ends. But healing can come from the pain, if you listen to it. You can learn how to grow through loneliness to the stage of aloneness—where you are comfortable being by yourself.

Loneliness is a disease
That grows slowly and
Undetected. Its symptoms
Are terrifying.
Loneliness is a dark,
Unseeing veil that covers
You with sadness, and a
Desperate race to conquer the
Complete spiritual and
Emotional emptiness...
In an unmerciful world.

I am experiencing this
Disease, and wish I could
Find a cure—
But even a ray of sunlight
Is a blessed thing.
For loneliness demands; it takes
Everything from you and
In return gives you nothing
But solitude; as if you
Were the only person.

—Elaine

As we observe others climbing this mountain of rebuilding blocks, we see a lot of lonely people. There are those who have withdrawn into their "caves," just peering out once in a while, looking very sad and dejected. And there are the lonely people who insist on being with somebody else, so they're always holding hands or following somebody around. And then there are the busy ones—always busy doing this and that so they never have to face their loneliness. Some express their loneliness like a vacuum—"sucking up" everyone around in order to fill the void. For others, it's like an iceberg—trying to gain warmth by staying as close as possible to whomever they can.

Loneliness is pain. But it is a pain that tells us we have something important to learn.

The formerly married do not have a corner on the loneliness market. Untold numbers suffer from the affliction. For many, it began in childhood and persisted through the marriage and into the divorce. (Another cause of divorce, for those of you who are keeping track.) This may be a crucial part of the climb for you if loneliness has been a stumbling block for years.

The loneliness that comes when that special person is gone is often more intense than any you have ever felt. Suddenly, you have no one with whom to share meals, your bed, or the special moments in your children's growth. Used to having the sounds, smells, and touch of that other person in the home, you now know nothing but silence. There is a strange emptiness in the house—even a house full of children—as though a gong were struck and produced no sound. You can find no one in the whole world to see, hear, or feel as you do. Friends who do try to reach out seem distant, even as you most need them to be close and real.

A voice within you may warn, "Withdraw, withdraw, and you won't be hurt again!" You want seclusion, like a wounded dog that retires to parts unknown until its wound is healed. At the same time, you crave emotional warmth, to be a child, to have someone care for you.

Some who have been lonely in marriage are actually relieved to end the relationship. But there is now a different kind of loneliness. They were never really emotionally close to the loved one; life with that person may have been painful, anger-filled, frustrating, distant—and lonely. (Another cause of divorce—are you keeping track?) So ending the relationship comes as a relief...but a new loneliness is there nonetheless.

Stages of Loneliness

Many of the rebuilding blocks have a three-stage pattern. For loneliness, the first stage is *withdrawal*—you may withdraw or at least fantasize about it.

Some people hide at home and brood so that others will not suspect their loneliness. Another approach is to play the "poor-little-me game," hoping that someone will come along and feel sorry for them. The goal is to keep others from seeing how much one hurts, while at the same time letting the former partner know.

The quiet is a constant reminder during this stage that your partner is gone—really gone. The silence can be crushing. An inability to concentrate makes reading difficult. Watching TV or surfing the web seems boring. Nothing feels exciting. There is a nagging, restless desire to do something—but what?

Withdrawal may be appropriate for some during this period because—let's face it—the lonely are not very good company. Their need for emotional warmth is insatiable. The need often stifles friends, engulfs them, and denies them space to be themselves, to be friends. There is an old nursery story about millions and billions and trillions of cats that began to eat one another up until there were no cats left. Close friends can "eat each other up" during this first stage of withdrawal until there is nothing left of either!

Life is often like a pendulum, swinging from one extreme to the other. Seeking ways to escape extreme loneliness, many people leave behind their withdrawal to enter the second stage of loneliness: *becoming "busyholics,"* with an activity planned for each night of the week and two on Saturdays and Sundays. They work long hours and find all kinds of excuses to keep working rather than coming home to emptiness. (They also may have been workaholics while married, perhaps to keep from coming home to a lonely marriage. Add that one to your list of why relationships end.) They go out with people they really do not enjoy just to avoid being alone. A party for singles may last all night—no one wants to go home to be alone!

These people are running from themselves—as though a frightening ghost lurks inside them, the ghost of loneliness. For those who have been truly lonely, the ghost may even seem real. They never take time to stop and look at what they are doing or where they are going because they are so busy running. Instead of climbing up the mountain, they are running around it in circles. (Sound familiar?)

This "busy-ness" stage of loneliness varies in length and intensity from person to person. Some may only want to be busy, while others actually keep themselves so busy that they have to walk on tiptoes to keep their posteriors from dragging. Eventually, all get tired and begin to realize that there must be more to life than running from the ghost of loneliness. That's when the slowdown period begins into the aloneness stage.

And Then You're Alone

Aloneness—what one friend calls the "all-oneness" stage—is finally achieved at the point of being *comfortable* by yourself. You may choose to be at home alone by the fire with a book rather than going out to be with people you really do not like. Development of your inner resources leads to interests, activities, thoughts, and attitudes that make it comfortable to be alone with yourself.

How do you get there from here? Start by facing the ghost of loneliness and realizing that it *is* a ghost. You have run from it, feared it, avoided it. But when you turn to that ghost of loneliness and say, "Boo!" often the ghost loses its power and control. You have accepted loneliness as part of being human, and you thereby become more comfortable being alone.

Accept also that loneliness has healing qualities. A period of time alone with yourself allows introspection, reflection, growth, and development of the inner self. Hollowness and emptiness are replaced by inner fullness and strength. You have made a giant step toward independence when you become comfortable by yourself, no longer dependent on the company of others.

We encourage you to go slowly in seeking new relationships at this point on the trail. You really need to learn to be alone with yourself. What's more, choosing to be with another person to escape loneliness is a very unhealthy reason to begin another love relationship. There is tremendous therapeutic value in being by yourself, even lonely for a time, before you start another love relationship.

Time really is the best healer. A period of loneliness—and self-discovery—is part of the remedy you need. This is an important growth stage in your life. Later, when the time is right, you can *choose* to enter into your next relationship because you want to, not because you *need* the next relationship to overcome loneliness.

A mentally healthy person maintains a balance between being with others and being alone. You need to find the proper balance for you.

All the Lonely Children

Children suffer loneliness too after their parents divorce. They have the same kind of empty feelings inside them that their parents have. They have the same need to be with others to fill up that loneliness, but they also fear being close to others.

How they feel around their peers can vary greatly. In one community we heard about, divorce was so prevalent that when one boy told his school friends that his parents were getting a divorce, another kid said, "Your parents are finally getting with it, aren't they?" In another community, though, divorce can still be so uncommon that your son or daughter could be the only child of divorce in the grade.

Children's daily living habits are altered by divorce just like those of their parents. At home, there is only one parent at a time now to spend time with, to play with, to put them to bed. And the kids feel the loneliness of the house, too—whether it's a new house altogether or the same one after one parent moves out. In one parental home, there may not be familiar books or toys to play with. Often one parent's new home is not set up for children or may be located in a new neighborhood, away from friends.

Kids need to work through this loneliness—just as parents do—in order to develop their own healthy feelings of aloneness. Kids need to learn that they have the resources within themselves to spend time alone without having to have another person around.

Many kids may have been lonely before the divorce because the interaction within the family did not help them to feel that they belonged. Divorce tends to increase this feeling of not belonging or not being okay. However, perhaps the crisis itself can be used to help deal directly with the problem.

This is a special time for parents to help their children feel that they belong, that they are loved, and that they are an important part of a new (restructured) family. They need help in learning to live with a single parent, two parents living apart, new stepparent(s) and maybe even stepsiblings. (Again, we caution you not to develop serious new relationships too soon!)

As with all of the rebuilding blocks, when you're dealing with your own loneliness, it is very difficult to have enough emotional time and energy left to devote to the kids' needs. Like putting your own oxygen mask on first in an airplane emergency, it may be necessary for you to work through your own rebuilding blocks first; then you'll be better able to help your children.

How Are You Doing?

Do some work *now* on your own capacity for being alone. If you can honestly answer "yes" to most of the items listed below, you have developed a healthy *aloneness* and you are ready to move on up the mountain. If more than three or four of these areas need work, spend some time going over this chapter so you can become more comfortable being by yourself.

- ☒ I am taking time for myself rather than keeping too busy.

- ☒ I am not working such long hours that I have no time for myself.

- ☒ I am not hiding from loneliness by being with people I don't enjoy.

- ☒ I have begun to fill my time with activities important to me.

- ☒ I have stopped hiding and withdrawing into my home or apartment.

- ☒ I have stopped trying to find another love relationship just to avoid being lonely.

- ☒ I am content doing activities by myself.

- ☒ I have stopped running from loneliness.

- ☒ I am not letting feelings of loneliness control my behavior.

- ☒ I am comfortable being alone and having aloneness time.

CHAPTER 6

Friendship

"Where Has Everybody Gone?"

The support you receive from lifeline friends is very important and can shorten the time it takes you to adjust to the crisis. Friends are more valuable to you than lovers right now. You can develop friends of both sexes without becoming romantically and sexually involved. Divorce is threatening to many married people, so your married friends may slip away from you.

Maria and I had lots of friends and family around all the time. Most weekends, we'd have a barbecue or go over to her sister's place or take a picnic with two or three other couples. Since we split up, none of those people ever call me or drop by. How come married people don't seem to want us around when we're single?

—José

As we climb the mountain, notice the different ways people handle the problems of friendship. While going through the pain of separation, some people insist on walking alone. They tend to withdraw, and they feel uncomfortable being with anybody else. You will notice others who are continually clinging to each other, as though they cannot be alone for a single minute. Always walking arm in arm, they even plan ahead so that they have no part of the journey to walk by themselves. Note also how few people continue to have any communication with friends from the days of their love relationship.

It appears that we have to find new friends as we journey up the path. In this stage of our climb, finding friends seems to be a very difficult problem.

Ain't It Great to Be Single?

Did you ever, when you were married, look at your divorced friends with envy and wish you could be part of all of those interesting activities they were into? That you could go to the exciting events that your spouse was reluctant to go to? Well, now you are free! What do you think about the "glamorous" single life now? For most of us, especially when we first separate, the single life is not glamorous—in fact, it is downright lonely and scary.

It is lonely, in part, because we tend to lose the friends we had when we were married. There are four main reasons for this.

First, consider that, when you are ending a love relationship, you suddenly become a possible love partner for one of the people in a marriage. Thus, whereas you were formerly invited to parties and events as a couple because you were safe, now you are a single person and a threat. Suddenly, people look at you as eligible, and invitations to married friends' events diminish accordingly.

When Bruce was first divorced, he was working side by side with a married woman. One day, three months after his separation, he walked by her desk and she said, "You're sure a lot more sexy now that you are separated and getting a divorce!" He responded, "I don't really believe I've changed very much, but you're looking at me differently now. It makes me feel like an object rather than a person." Though flattered by her interest, he was uncomfortable being cast as a potential threat to her marriage.

The second reason we tend to lose friends is that divorce can be very polarizing. Friends tend to support one partner or the other, rarely both. Thus, we tend to lose the friends who have sided with our former spouse.

The third reason is probably the most important: the fear that "If it can happen to you, it can happen to me." Your divorce is very threatening to many marriages around you, so married friends slip away. Although you may feel rejected, it is actually their problem, a reflection on them rather than on you. It is likely true that the shakier your friends' marriages, the quicker they will fall away from you. So instead of feeling rejected, understand that your divorce has caused them to feel insecure about their own marriages. They withdraw from the friendship because they fear divorce may be contagious.

There is a fourth aspect of friendship that is important to understand while you are going through divorce. Although cultural norms around marriage are changing somewhat, married people are still considered to be part of the mainstream, accepted, couples-oriented society that is the cornerstone of our way of life. Divorced people, however, become part of the singles culture—a part of our society that is less acceptable to many. This singles culture may not be evident until you become a single person yourself. To be pushed out of the mainstream couples culture into the singles culture is a difficult adjustment.

There are different standards, mores, and values in the singles culture. People live a little bit "looser," a little bit freer, as if in a large fraternity or sorority. At a singles gathering, the words "I'm divorced" become a valuable conversation opener, rather than a turnoff. If, as is often the case, the other person is also divorced, you suddenly have something in common and you can start talking to each other. Because the standards and mores are different, formerly coupled people are not quite sure how to behave in the singles culture, and their first reaction can be somewhat of an emotional shock. You think, *Somebody's changed the rules, and I don't know the new rules!*

Building Friendships

As you begin to work at rebuilding your friendships, you will find a three-stage process. In the first stage, you are so hurt, lonely, and depressed that you *avoid friends* unless it is very safe to be with them. The second stage begins when you can at last take the risk of *reaching out* to people, even when the fear of rejection looms large. The third stage is *becoming comfortable* with people, finding out that you are okay, and beginning to enjoy people without fear of being rejected.

Recently divorced people frequently ask: "How do I make friends after a divorce? Where can I find someone to date?" The problem is that many formerly married people are out looking desperately for another love relationship, instead of just enjoying the people around them. Your goal for now should be to get to know people; some of these new acquaintances *may* become special friends or even lovers. But be patient and go slowly. Start by expanding your "pool" of acquaintances. You can meet new people wherever you go—the grocery store; church; classes in computers, tennis, ceramics, cooking, language, or personal growth; community groups; volunteer activities; the library; work; or just out walking the dog. (And, yes, we know that online communities and interest groups offer venues for meeting new people, but we encourage you to connect in person when you can.)

As you do begin to explore ways to make new friends, you'll find that when you are genuinely interested in the people with whom you come in contact, you send out "vibrations" that make people want to respond. But if you come across as lonely, desperate, and needy, people will not want to be around you.

The vibrations we're talking about include your body movements, the way you walk, the tone of your voice, your eye contact, your style of dress, and all the subtle ways you show how you are feeling. Experienced people in the singles culture can often tell if you are single by your nonverbal signals. Note that even if you do not intend to do so, you are sending out some sort of signals. Are you inviting others to get to know you?

When you are ready to make friends and feel comfortable doing so, there are some specific steps you might want to take. For example, you can enroll in a Fisher divorce seminar to work on the rebuilding blocks with others. You can check with clergy people, your counselor or therapist, or local colleges or community centers to see if there's a seminar near you, or some other type of support group you'd be interested in joining.

If you don't find a group nearby, you may want to start your own with five to ten people who are interested in working through this book together. Meet in one another's homes. Have a time for work and a time for play; spend some time in group discussion and some time just socializing. Share your common concerns and feelings. It may be advantageous for the group to consist of people who do not know one another, so you will not fall into old patterns of gossip. This kind of group can provide some of the most memorable and enjoyable evenings in your divorce process. There are literally hundreds of divorce recovery groups around the country (and in other countries as well) that meet weekly and use this book as a discussion guide (go to http://www.rebuilding.org to see if there's one near you).

When trying to establish new friendships after a breakup, we now also have available to us the virtual variety. Let us offer a word of caution, however, in this age of instant electronic friendships. You will find hundreds—even thousands—of opportunities to connect with people online: chat rooms, interest groups, divorce and singles sites, and much, much more. The web is basically infinite. Online friendships can be seductive, but they may keep you from making connections close to home—and that's where you really need them right now.

So go online for information, for sharing ideas, for broadening your horizons. Join online hobby or activity groups. Take part in chats on topics of interest to you. But don't let an electronic screen be your primary source of friends. Face your fears and seek out friendships in the world around you. In the long run, they're likely to be much more satisfying and much more likely to last.

We've all read and seen movies and TV shows about e-mail romances, and no doubt there are many that have actually worked out beyond the virtual world. But research shows that the chances are slim that a successful face-to-face relationship will result from an online connection, and the energy (and fantasy) you invest there is likely to detract from your real-world growth.

As for online dating, it's become mainstream, of course. In fact, with a reputed total of more than 1,500 dating websites, it is now the most common way couples meet. However, the chances of connecting with someone you'd rather avoid are at least as great online as in a bar or at a singles party. The major sites do some background checking, but there are no assurances, much less guarantees, about the caliber of people you'd meet. So check out the online dating sites if that appeals to you, but take care. *Consumers Digest* examined online dating in 2013 and reported that "all of our experts recommend that consumers who use an online dating service proceed with caution. Awareness is the best defense."

And speaking of dating…

It's Not Time for Romance Yet!

There is one concept we feel so strongly about that we want to give it special emphasis:

We suggest you not get involved in another long-term, committed love relationship until you have emotionally worked through the ending of the past love relationship.

Getting involved too soon results in carrying emotional garbage from the past relationship into the next one. You would likely marry someone just like the one you left or someone just the opposite. Either way, the chances of the same problems occurring in the next relationship are great.

A healthy process of divorce is well described as "learning to be a single person." Many people never learned to be independent individuals before they were married. They went directly from their parental home to the marital home. If you have not learned to be a single person, it is easy for you to *hide* in another relationship. Because your emotional needs are great when you are ending the love relationship, the comfort of another love relationship is appealing. Nevertheless, there is truth in the paradox that when you are ready to face life alone, then you are ready for marriage.

But you do need friends and relationships with potential love partners based upon friendship. If you can build open, trusting, honest relationships with good communication and opportunities for both people to experience personal growth, then you will probably work through the divorce process more rapidly.

Sometimes it is hard to tell whether a current relationship is limiting personal growth. The best criterion might be to ask, "Am I learning to be a single person?" If you feel you are losing your identity because of your love relationship, then you probably need to back off from it. (This is easier said than done in many instances. But we stress again how important it is to get *yourself together first!*)

We'll have more to say about growing relationships in chapter 16.

Can't We Just Be Friends?

Here is an exciting concept that you may learn for the first time: it is possible to develop a close, nonsexual, nonromantic friendship *with a member of the opposite sex!* This may be the way it happens for you: You tentatively make friends, but you are very cautious because of your fears of closeness and intimacy. The friendship becomes important, and you suddenly realize that you want very badly to maintain this friendship because it feels so good. You have a feeling down inside somewhere that if the quality of the friendship changes to a romantic, sexual one, it will become less meaningful, not so special anymore. Then you realize that you want to keep this friendship very much and will go to great lengths to invest emotionally so that it will continue to grow. Such a friendship brings a free and exhilarating feeling. It also destroys the myth about members of the opposite sex not being able to be just friends.

There's an old wives' tale about this kind of friendship destroying marriages, which you will now recognize as pretty phony logic. There are just as many kinds of friends as there are vegetables; and trying to make a tomato into a zucchini is difficult, if not impossible! You have learned something that will enrich your next marriage if you choose. To have friends of both sexes is one indication of a healthy relationship.

While you are working to develop new friendships, you may also be hearing a barrage of negative comments about marriage in the singles culture. There are people who rant and rave and shout from the hilltops that they will never get married again. They compile long lists of all the painful and negative aspects of marriage. And if there is someone who decides to remarry, they even send cards of *sympathy* to the couple! You need to realize that these people are as threatened by marriage as some people are threatened by divorce. Perhaps a bad marriage led to feelings that they could never have a happy marriage, so they project their unhappy biases about marriage onto others.

There *are* a lot of unhappy married people. But much of that is due to individual personalities. Some folks would be unhappy wherever they are; the marital situation may have little to do with it. A marriage, after all, can be no happier than the two individuals in it.

Building a support system of lifeline friends will shorten the time it takes you to adjust to a crisis. We all need friends who can throw us a lifeline when we feel we are "drowning." A friend whom we can talk with is a real "lifesaver" during a crisis. If you have not developed such a support system, then you need to start doing so—it may save your life.

Children Need Friends Too

Children have a problem with friendships also, often feeling isolated and "different." In some communities, they may think they are the only children of divorce in the whole school. They may not know anybody else whose parents are divorced, partly because children often don't *talk* about their parents getting divorced—it is a painful experience for them, after all. Of course, a youngster may go to school and say, "Guess what? My parents are getting divorced." And these days, other kids are likely to respond, "Welcome to the club!"

Just as their parents tend to become friends with only formerly married and single people, children may begin to seek out friendships with kids from divorced or single-parent families. Some children may withdraw, just as parents withdraw, and shut out all friendships whatsoever. Children who are going through the pain of their parents' divorce really need friends to talk to, but they may find it difficult to reach out or to discuss personal things. Schools are concerned about this, and many are providing some sort of counseling service to help kids who shut themselves off, whether because of their parents' divorce or for other reasons. It is a valuable service for children experiencing emotional trauma. (What's more, it may go a long way toward helping to prevent some of the tragic acting-out behaviors that have devastated many communities in recent years.)

Parents can help their children find somebody to talk to. Maybe it is the time for other relatives to get involved. (Caution: relatives—or friends or neighbors—who are highly emotional and who may have unresolved concerns themselves are *not* good people for the children to talk to. They are likely to be more concerned with meeting their own needs.) Also, while it is often helpful for children to talk to adults, this is the time that they need to talk to other children of divorce if possible.

We need to be aware and supportive of the needs of our kids as they are going through this process. We can encourage them to become involved with others through after-school activities and community programs. Having friends to talk with will shorten children's adjustment time, just as it does for the adults involved.

How Are You Doing?

Now might be a good time to sit down off the trail, rest for a moment, and take a look at the people around you. Have you taken the time to get to know any of them, to see them as actual individuals rather than as potential love partners or people to avoid? Do any look interesting enough to have as a friend? You'll find it easier to make the rest of the climb up this mountain if you have a friend to hold your hand, to give you a hug, and to catch you when you slip. Why not take time right now to invest emotionally in some friendships? If you worry about rejection, remember that that person may want a friend just as much as you do!

Use the checklist below to assess your progress with friendships before you go on to the next chapter. And remember that friendship does not just *happen*—like anything worthwhile, it takes continuous effort.

- *I am relating with friends in many new ways since my crisis.*
- *I have at least one lifeline friend of the same sex.*
- *I have at least one lifeline friend of the opposite sex.*
- *I am satisfied with my present social relationships.*
- *I have close friends who know and understand me.*
- *People seem to enjoy being with me.*
- *I have both single and married friends.*
- *I have discussed ideas from this book with an important friend.*
- *I communicate frequently about important concerns with a close friend.*

CHAPTER 7

Guilt/Rejection

Dumpers: 1; Dumpees: 0

Dumpers end the love relationship, while dumpees have it ended for them. The adjustment process differs since dumpers feel more guilt and dumpees feel more rejection. Dumpers start their adjustment while still in the love relationship, but dumpees start adjusting later. For the "mutuals," people who jointly decide to end the relationship, the adjustment process is somewhat easier.

I laughed so hard...
It was the funniest joke I ever heard:
"He doesn't love you."
And it was even funnier
When you told it yourself:
"I don't love you."
And I laughed so hard
That the whole house shook,
And came crashing down upon me.

—Megan

As we begin this segment of our climb through the rebuilding blocks, let us explain where we are headed in the pages ahead. The four key concepts of this chapter are so closely intertwined that it may get confusing at times. We will be viewing the two main characters in the divorce drama as "dumper" and "dumpee." And we will take a look at two of the very strong feelings that accompany the trauma of divorce: *guilt* and *rejection*.

We notice different groups of people on this portion of the trail. There are those who are in shock, lying on the ground trying to get their emotional wind back. Some are walking around looking guilty and trying not to look at those on the ground. Then there are others who are walking around holding hands with their former lovers. (What are *they* doing here, anyway?) Everyone looks sad.

On the ground are the dumpees, who were walking the pathway of life and enjoying their love relationships when their partners announced they were leaving. Sometimes the dumpees had some warning; sometimes they had none. They are having a great deal of difficulty accepting the ending of their relationships.

Those looking guilty are the dumpers. They had been thinking about leaving their relationships for some time, maybe a year or two, trying to get their courage up because they knew it would hurt the dumpees a great deal. They avoid looking at the dumpees because that makes them feel more guilty. They are usually better climbers because they had been thinking about the climb, preparing for it, while still in their love relationships.

The ones holding hands—the "mutuals"—have decided jointly to end the relationship. Notice how few of them there are! Many people ask them why they are ending the relationship if they are such good friends. They may be very unhappy *together* and want to end the relationship for the benefit of both. They are good climbers because they do not keep tripping each other as often as the dumpers and dumpees do. Mutuals do not enjoy the game going on between dumpers and dumpees, the game of "don't let my ex climb faster than me."

To get us started up this portion of the trail, here is an oversimplified summary of the chapter:

Dumpers are the partners who leave the relationship, and they often feel considerable guilt; dumpees are the partners who want to hang on to the relationship, and they often experience strong feelings of rejection.

Of course it is not really as simple as that. We will get into much more detail in the pages ahead, but that gives you an advance look at the topography of the area we are about to enter.

Rejection Really Hurts

Nearly everyone has been a dumpee in some relationship, and no one enjoys rejection. After being rejected, you might become very introspective, continually examining yourself to see what fault causes people to reject you. Such a self-examination can help you see yourself more clearly—perhaps you will want to change the way you relate to other people. In any case, to accept the fact that feeling rejected is an expected part of the ending of a relationship—particularly a love relationship—is helpful in itself.

One step toward overcoming those feelings of rejection is to learn that the breakup of the love relationship is perhaps not your fault. As we've explored during earlier stages of the climb, everyone brings much of the past into a love relationship, and the past often determines the course of events in the relationship. Because the love relationship ended does not necessarily mean that *you* are inadequate or inferior or that there is something wrong with you. Relationships do end. Maybe that ending is not an indication of inadequacy at all.

The goal is to say, "If we have a problem, it's not because there is something terribly wrong with me. If we can't work it out, then he (she) has as much to lose as I have—maybe more." Feeling that good about yourself is a difficult goal to reach emotionally. Don't be discouraged if it takes quite a period of time to admit that the responsibility is mutual, not yours or your ex-partner's alone.

You are a worthwhile person, capable of loving and being loved. You have something special to offer to others, and that is your own unique individual self. You really ought to believe that. You could even get to feeling so good about yourself that you might believe that anyone who dumps such a neat person must have a problem!

A Little Guilt Goes a Long Way

Let us look now at guilt. It may sound strange, but the ideal may well be to have the "right amount of guilt" in your personality. If you feel no guilt at all, nothing other than being caught deters you from doing harmful things to yourself or to others. A sense of guilt is helpful in making decisions about the way you choose to live. Unfortunately, many people experience so much guilt that they become very inhibited and controlled, unable to do the productive things that can bring happiness. The happy balance is "just enough" guilt to help maintain a sense of direction without severely restricting your options.

Ending a love relationship tends to make one deal realistically with guilt feelings. The dumper, especially, feels a large amount of guilt and says, "I'm feeling very bad about hurting somebody I love, or used to love, and I wish I could meet my needs without feeling so guilty." Guilt—or the tendency to feel it—appears to be deeply ingrained in the human personality and is difficult to overcome. The best solution appears to be rational thinking about the breakup: listen to your head right now, not your heart (and its feelings of guilt). To end a love relationship may be *appropriate* if it has been destructive for *both* people. Under those conditions, instead of sitting around feeling guilty, those involved may be able to say, "This is probably the best decision for both of us."

One way to resolve guilt is to be punished. Bruce recalled, as a middle school teacher, marching a misbehaving seventh-grade boy into the hall and giving him such a lecture that the boy began crying. Bruce felt somewhat mean and hurtful until, after school that day, the boy came to the classroom and acted as though Bruce were his long-lost friend. By punishing him, Bruce helped him overcome his guilt, and he appreciated that. Someone had cared enough to set limits for him, to pay attention when he misbehaved, and to balance the scale of justice by exacting a penalty for his behavior.

When we're feeling guilty, we often seek ways of punishing ourselves to relieve the guilt. If you see that you are trying to punish yourself by setting yourself up to experience pain in relationships, maybe you should look for feelings of guilt that may be motivating your behavior.

Guilt is usually a result of not living up to some standard of behavior. If the standard is one you have freely chosen for yourself, and if it is a *possible* one, it is probably healthy to feel some guilt about falling short. But if the standard is someone else's, or society's, or the church's, and not one you have adopted for your own, your guilt feelings are not productive. Give yourself a break! It is tough enough to live up to your own standards; you can't expect to please everyone.

"But," you'll say ruefully, "staying married *is* one of my standards. I feel guilty because I didn't make the marriage work, so I failed one of my own standards." We hear you, and we understand that feeling. What we hope for you is that you can come to accept your own humanness. Nobody is perfect. Maybe you could take another look at that feeling of guilt and consider a more useful response to the situation.

Try this one on for size: "My love partner and I aren't able to make our love relationship meet our needs and provide us happiness. It appears that, somehow or another, we didn't learn enough about loving and communicating with another person."

Remember in school, taking a test you hadn't prepared for? You probably did poorly on the test and felt pretty bad. But you didn't fail the whole course! As an adult, you feel bad because your love relationship didn't work. Maybe you can learn from this experience so you can do better the next time. You might even help your ex learn something positive. Maybe, if you can accept your guilt as appropriate for this situation, you can change yourself into a better person who can build a productive, meaningful relationship in the future.

All Guilt Is Not the Same

Let's compare two types of guilt: *appropriate guilt* and the large reservoir of *free-floating guilt* that seems to reside within each of us. Appropriate guilt is the feeling that comes when you do something wrong or do something to hurt somebody and then feel bad about it. You've broken one of your own standards or values. When a love relationship ends, it's very appropriate to feel bad about hurting somebody else or hurting yourself. Appropriate guilt is a current process that you can work through.

Some people, however, carry long-standing guilt, usually from childhood—a large reservoir of unexpressed guilt feelings. When an event comes along and taps this reservoir, the result is such a strong sense of guilt that the person feels anxious, afraid, and fearful.

The guilt may feel overwhelming because it does not seem to be attached to anything or related to anything. It just feels huge and enormous.

If you have this sort of free-floating guilt within you, you may need help from therapy to work through and minimize the guilt and get it under control. Again, maybe the crisis of divorce will motivate you to work on something you have needed to do for a long time.

Acceptance is an important aspect of dealing with rejection and guilt. In the Fisher divorce seminars, the emotional atmosphere values acceptance of one's own feelings and strong mutual support among the members. Being with people who help you feel accepted and supported can heal feelings of rejection and guilt rapidly. If you can find warm, supportive, accepting friends and/or a supportive group, you will be able to heal these feelings.

Rejection and guilt are closely tied to feelings of self-worth and self-love, which we will discuss farther up the trail. You will find that as you improve your feelings of self-worth and self-love, you will be less devastated by life's inevitable rejections.

Which Are You?

In the Fisher seminars, approximately half of the people state that they were dumpees, a third state they were dumpers, and the rest believe it was a mutual decision to end their relationship. We don't know if this is true of the general population of divorced people. Theoretically, of course, we would expect an equal number of dumpers and dumpees in society. However, in some situations, one person feels like a dumpee, and the other (usually a dumper who doesn't want to feel guilty) feels it was a mutual decision.

The divorce process is different in many ways for dumpers and dumpees. Research with the Fisher Divorce Adjustment Scale indicates that dumpees experience more emotional pain at the point of separation, especially in the areas of letting go and anger. However, if dumpers' pain could be measured while they were still in the love relationship, they would very likely show more emotional pain than the dumpees. The dumpers began to let go before they left the relationship, so they have been able to back off from being lovers to being friends with the dumpees. The dumpee, however, is usually still deeply in love with the dumper when the relationship ends. (Mutuals tend to score like dumpers, but they experience less grief.)

Occasionally, there are people who have a strong negative reaction to the words "dumper" and "dumpee." They fail to see any humor in the words. They usually have not been able to accept their divorces, and they definitely have not been able to accept the idea of being a dumper or a dumpee. Despite such strong reactions, it helps to use the terms because we each need to accept the reality of either dumping or being dumped in nearly every dissolution. You can climb the mountain of rebuilding more rapidly if you accept your role.

You may not know if you are a dumper or a dumpee. First of all, you may not have thought about it. Second, the roles may switch back and forth. George and Margaret, for example, were childhood sweethearts who married soon after graduating from high school. During the courtship and marriage, George was continually going out with other women, leaving home for short periods of time, and acting like a dumper wanting out of the relationship. Finally, Margaret reached her "martyr's tolerance limit" and filed for divorce. Immediately, George's behavior and vocabulary became those of a dumpee. Margaret and George had switched roles.

It may occur to you to ask if the person who files for divorce is the dumper. Not always; filing is not the deciding factor. And you may ask if there are more male or female dumpers. We don't know about the general population, but in the divorce classes, there is exactly the same percentage of male and female dumpers.

The Language of Dumping

Language is an important clue as to whether you are a dumper or a dumpee.

It is often possible to identify someone as a dumper or a dumpee just by the questions he or she asks. Questioners are surprised to be identified as one or the other ("Are you a mind reader?") until we point out that there are dumper and dumpee vocabularies.

Dumper vocabulary goes like this: "I need some time and space to get my head on straight. I need to be out of this relationship in order to get this time and space. I care for you, but I don't love you enough to live with you. Don't ask me why I don't love you—I just know that I need out. I feel bad for hurting you, but there is nothing I can do about that because staying with you would also hurt you. Can we be friends?"

Dumpee vocabulary goes like this: "Please don't leave me! Why don't you love me? Tell me what is wrong with me and I will change. There must be something wrong with me, and I don't know what it is. Please tell me what I did wrong. I thought we had a good love relationship, and I don't see why you want to leave. Please give me some more time before you leave. I want to be friends, but I love you. Please don't leave me."

The dumper may reply, "I have been trying for a long time to tell you that I was unhappy in the relationship and that we needed to change. You just wouldn't listen. I have tried everything. I don't have any more time. You keep hanging on to me, and I just want to be friends."

Dumpees at this point are likely to be hurt and to cry. They become introspective and try to understand what went wrong: "Why am I unlovable?" and "Why did our relationship have to end?" Often there is denial of feelings while the dumpee gains time to recover from the shock. The emotional pain is great for the dumpee.

The vocabulary seems universal; almost all dumpers and dumpees use the same words. The problem of timing is evident. The dumper claims to have been trying for "months and years" to do something about the problem, thinking about leaving during much of that time. The dumpee has not heard this dissatisfaction, perhaps because he or she had been "in denial" long before the dumper actually left. But when the dumper makes the announcement, the dumpee really starts denying and refusing to believe there is anything wrong. "We have such a good relationship!"

Notice the difference in priorities. The dumper wants to work on personal growth: "I have to get my head on straight." The dumpee wants to work on the relationship: "I need more time and feedback about what I need to change." Listen carefully to the words the dumpee is saying to reflect the hurt. Can you hear the anger beneath the words? But the dumpee does not express this anger because the divorce is still in its honeymoon period.

During this period, the dumper is feeling much guilt, acting super nice, willing to give the dumpee anything. The dumpee is feeling rejected, anxious for the dumper to come back, and afraid to express anger for fear it will drive the dumper even farther away. The dumpee is acting nice also. Eventually, anger replaces the feelings of guilt in the dumper and the feelings of rejection in the dumpee. Then the "divorce honeymoon" ends.

This phase often begins around three months after the separation, but the timing may vary a great deal. "Good court settlements" are often negotiated while dumpers feel so guilty that they will give up everything and while dumpees will settle for anything in hopes of getting the dumper back. Dumpers: "I want out so badly that I don't care about property or money." Dumpees: "I won't ask for anything because all I want is for her (him) to come back."

There is a strategy to change the honeymoon period, in case you are interested. Both parties feel better and can speed up the adjustment process when the dumpee can express anger quickly. Dumpers feel less guilty when dumpees express anger, because the anger helps them deal with their guilt. And dumpees feel less depression by expressing anger quicker, because some depression is the result of unexpressed anger. But it is not always possible to shortcut the process, because the dumper may have a need to feel guilty for a while, and the dumpee may have a need to feel rejected and depressed for a while. Working through feelings takes time.

There is an exercise that will help you understand this dumper-dumpee concept better. Find a friend to role-play with you—one of you as dumper, the other as dumpee. Begin in the middle of a room, then have the dumper walk out of the room using dumper vocabulary. The dumpee should follow after, trying to keep the dumper from leaving the room by using dumpee vocabulary and behavior. Change roles so you can experience being both a dumper and a dumpee.

The symbolism of the exercise is good. The dumper is looking toward the door and trying to get out. The dumpee is looking at the back of the dumper and trying to figure out a way to prevent the leaving. (There have been dumpees who follow the partner out of the room, out to the car, and then hang on the car as the dumper drives off.)

How does it feel to be a dumper in the exercise? Did you feel guilty? Did you feel the other person was hanging on to you to keep you from leaving? Did you feel reluctant to look back at the other person? Did you try to keep looking at the door? Did you feel like walking faster or maybe even running?

How does it feel to be a dumpee in the exercise? Did you want the other person to look at you? Did you feel the desire to physically grab the other person? Did you want to cry and plead with the other person not to leave? Did you feel rejection and loneliness as the other person left the room? Did you feel anger?

Good News, Bad News

At the risk of confusing this discussion more, we want to introduce a further breakdown in the dumper-dumpee categories. The terminology is strong and somewhat judgmental, but it is helpful in better understanding the dumper-dumpee concept. Namely, there are "good dumpers" and "bad dumpers," along with "good dumpees" and "bad dumpees."

The good dumper is a person who has tried to work on the love relationship in order to make it last. A good dumper was willing to make changes, invest emotionally in trying to change, and go for marriage counseling if appropriate. But the dumper finally realized that the relationship was destructive to both people and that it was better to end an unhealthy relationship than to continue to destroy each other. This person has the courage and strength to end the relationship, and it often takes a great deal of courage and strength.

Bad dumpers are very similar to runaway kids. They believe the grass is greener on the other side of the fence and all that is needed for happiness is to get out of the relationship. There is often another love relationship waiting in the wings. The bad dumper avoids dealing with feelings and looking inside at attitudes that might need to be changed. Bad dumpers often leave quickly without even a "good-bye" conversation or an explanation of their intent to end the partnership.

Good dumpees are open, honest, willing to work on the relationship, and willing to go for counseling if appropriate. They seldom have had an affair and have likely worked hard on communicating. They are not "innocent victims" in the sense that they, too, have done things to hurt the relationship. They are basically at the wrong time and place when the internal explosion and the need to be out of the relationship occurs within the dumper.

Bad dumpees are people who want out of the relationship but do not have the courage and strength to be a dumper. They make it miserable for the other person, who then is forced into being the dumper.

There are few who fit perfectly into one of these four categories. Most of us are a combination of both good and bad dumpers or dumpees.

"Maybe I'll Come Back After All"

Another important phenomenon in the dumper-dumpee dynamic is the "pain cycle." The dumper is not hurting as much when the relationship ends, but the dumpee's pain is great and motivates rapid growth and adjustment. When the dumpee is reaching a good emotional adjustment, the dumper frequently comes back and begins talking about reconciliation. This really blows the dumpee away. Gordon exclaimed, "I devoted all my emotional energy to learning to accept the ending of the relationship, and I'd given up completely the hope that Juanita would come back. And then she called me!"

There are many different ways to interpret this phenomenon: perhaps the dumper, in contrast to the sense of euphoria experienced when she or he first left, has found it so scary out there in the single world that the security of the old love relationship looks good. "There ain't nothing out there but turkeys, and the old lover looks better all the time." Another interpretation is illustrated by dumpee anger: "She made me the dumpee. Now she wants to make me the dumper, to share the guilt!" Perhaps the best explanation comes from observing that the dumper comes back around the time the dumpee is "making it" successfully. Maybe when Juanita no longer felt the guilt and responsibility of having Gordon cling with dependency, she felt free to come back into a more equal relationship.

The typical dumpee reaction is not to take the dumper back. Dumpees find that they can make it on their own, that being single has advantages, and that it feels good to experience the personal growth they have been going through. If you get a dumpee to talk long enough, you will learn what was wrong with the relationship. It is only during the first period of denial that the dumpee maintains there was nothing wrong with the relationship. "Now I can see what was happening all those years! Besides, I don't see that much change and personal growth in Juanita, so why should I want the old relationship back?" At this point, the dumper usually gets dumped!

Down in the Dumps

It is no wonder that dumpers and dumpees have trouble working together! The timing is different for each, with the dumper often starting the adjustment process while still in the relationship. The feelings are different, with the dumper tending to feel more guilt and the dumpee tending to feel more rejection (although you may experience both, whether you were the dumper or the dumpee). The attitudes are different for the two people because the dumper feels pressure to leave the relationship (wanting "personal growth" of some sort) and the dumpee fears the relationship ending. The dumper has already let go much more than the dumpee, causing problems in communicating and interacting. These different attitudes and behaviors add to the trauma of adjusting to the ending of a love relationship.

One last note on the terms "dumper" and "dumpee." Despite differences in timing and attitudes, the two people are not that much different. Most times, both have contributed fairly equally to the relationship not working. Even differences in their attitudes are not major. Once a dumpee begins talking about the love relationship, he or she will say almost the same things that the dumper was saying about their problems, only using dumpee vocabulary of course. *Timing* remains the essential element that separates the dumper from the dumpee.

This discussion of dumpers and dumpees may be a bit confusing at first (you'll want to read it over again), but it will help you to see that feelings of guilt and rejection are part of the process. Intellectual understanding is often the first step of awareness that leads to emotional understanding. Feelings of guilt and rejection are normal and typical during the ending of a love relationship—in fact, you may have been experiencing these feelings before. But the ending of a love relationship tends to magnify and emphasize feelings, so you can be more aware of them and thus learn to deal with them more adequately.

Don't Dump on Your Children

The dumper-dumpee concept has interesting implications for the children of divorce. Often the children are very angry at the parent who decided to leave, and they have a great deal of difficulty maintaining a relationship with that person. They blame the breakup on the dumper, so they take out their pain and frustration on that person. They probably fail to see that there is not that much difference between the dumper and the dumpee, since both of them contributed to the ending of the relationship, only in different ways.

Almost always, the children of divorce can be looked upon as dumpees. They had very little to do with the decision, thus they may feel the same frustration and anger that dumpees do. Kids, however, are not like dumpees in the sense that they often recognize that the marriage is ending—sometimes before their parents do!

Kids have a definite problem with rejection and guilt. Youngsters may have problems with guilt when they feel they are responsible for their parents' marriage not working out. They may need help in seeing that it is not their fault, that divorce is a grown-up problem.

Kids frequently feel a tremendous amount of rejection because it seems one parent is leaving and rejecting them. The rejection a child feels is often long-lasting and can even persist into adulthood. Adults who have never fully accepted their parents' divorce find that their own love relationships can be adversely affected.

Children must be assured that they are not guilty, they are not responsible for their parents' divorce, and they are not being rejected. If the parents can maintain a quality relationship with the children after their separation and divorce, the children will be able to deal with these feelings.

How Are You Doing?

Let's rest from our climb for a while. You may want to think about the differences between dumpers and dumpees, try to understand the feelings and attitudes on both sides of the issue. Maybe you have changed your mind about whether you are a dumper or a dumpee after reading this chapter. In any case, take time now to consider the different perspectives partners get of *what happened* during a dissolution.

We hope this chapter has helped you gain a better view of the end of your own relationship. After completing the checklist below and treating yourself to some time to think about these ideas, you'll be ready to move on up the mountain!

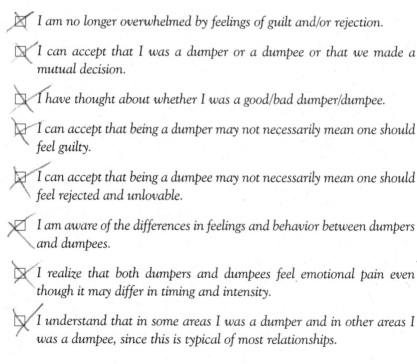

☒ *I am no longer overwhelmed by feelings of guilt and/or rejection.*

☒ *I can accept that I was a dumper or a dumpee or that we made a mutual decision.*

☒ *I have thought about whether I was a good/bad dumper/dumpee.*

☒ *I can accept that being a dumper may not necessarily mean one should feel guilty.*

☒ *I can accept that being a dumpee may not necessarily mean one should feel rejected and unlovable.*

☒ *I am aware of the differences in feelings and behavior between dumpers and dumpees.*

☒ *I realize that both dumpers and dumpees feel emotional pain even though it may differ in timing and intensity.*

☒ *I understand that in some areas I was a dumper and in other areas I was a dumpee, since this is typical of most relationships.*

☑ I understand that the concept of dumper-dumpee is most meaningful at the point of separation; as I grow, it becomes less and less important.

☑ I have looked at my life patterns to see if rejection or guilt feelings have controlled much of my behavior.

☑ I am working to overcome the influence of rejection and guilt in my life.

CHAPTER 8

Grief

"There's This Terrible Feeling of Loss"

Grief is an important part of your divorce process. You need to work through the emotions of grief in order to let go of the dead love relationship. An intellectual grasp of the stages of grief can help you become emotionally aware of grief. Then you can do the grieving that you may have been afraid of before.

Weekends are...
All the lonely hours poured into remembering,
All the lonely thoughts poured into trying to forget,
The harder we try to forget, the easier it is to remember.
The past can't die and the future can't live,
But the present exists.
If silence is deafening, then what is quiet?
Quiet is weekends and weekends are hell.
Wake up and face reality—why?
Weekends enforce reality, weekdays subdue it.
Saturday—it's a world of two plus two,
Where one has no meaning and no value.
Sunday—the body rests,
But where's the "off button" for the mind?

—"Honey"

We are now entering one of the most difficult and emotionally draining parts of the climb. All along the path sit people who are crying mournfully. Some will stop crying for a while, then suddenly start in again. Others are trying to comfort them but seem uncomfortable and not quite sure what to do. What is happening?

These people are experiencing grief. Whenever there is a loss of someone or something important in our lives, we suffer grief. Perhaps you had not been aware that grieving is a part of the divorce process. For death, there is a set ritual, with a funeral, a casket, and acceptance that grieving is important. For divorce, there is no prescribed ritual other than the court hearing, and grief is often not acknowledged or accepted. But the death of a love relationship is more than enough cause for us to grieve.

The Many Faces of Grief

Many forms of loss occur when we end a love relationship. Most obvious, of course, is the loss of the love partner, which many people do grieve. There are other losses: the *future plans* as a pair; the love *relationship* itself; the *role* of husband or wife or lover; the *status* associated with being a couple. Many changes occur as one progresses through the transition from being married to being single. For some people, the loss of the relationship is as important as the loss of the partner.

There is the loss of the future. When you were married "till death do us part," there were plans, goals, joint careers, and a house that had become a home. Now all of these future parts of your life are no longer there. The future is a very difficult loss to accept, and many will need to grieve that loss for a long time.

The pain of ending a love relationship often forces us to look at past pain. Many people have not properly grieved a loss in the past, such as the death of a loved one. Reexperiencing a past pain intensifies the grieving process. For those who carry an unresolved loss from the past, divorce grief will be especially painful and difficult.

Similarly, a history of unfulfilled emotional needs—perhaps childhood deprivations—may become prominent during divorce grief. Dan reported that he dreamed frequently about childhood experiences on the farm while he was working through his divorce. As he talked about his divorce grief, he realized that he was grieving the unhappiness he experienced during his lonely childhood.

Many divorced people are forced to move from the house they lived in while in the love relationship, and they may have to grieve the loss of that house. Single parents may have to grieve the loss of children when they are with the other parent. And the children must also grieve the loss of a house, a parent, a family—which are all part of the divorce process.

A Fable of Grief: The Check Mark

A favorite device of Bruce's, useful in understanding grief, is the fable of the "check mark." It goes like this:

Once upon a time, there was a little creature called Jot, living a good life, oblivious to the Black Cloud hovering over it. Suddenly, the Black Cloud let loose, and Jot's lover went away. In the anguish of lost love, Jot tumbled down a huge slide so long that Jot could not see the bottom of it. There were no handles to hold on the way down the scary slide, and the ride was painful, but Jot finally landed on a soft rainbow. Looking around, Jot spied stairs that led up into the sunlight again. The stairs were very difficult to climb at first, but they became easier and more exciting as Jot neared the sunshine and began to feel completely renewed.

You might like to know what Jot's trip was like, since you will have to take the grief trip someday.

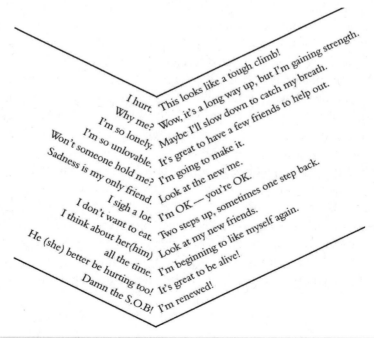

Some of Jot's companions on the grief trip see a mean Giant Dragon with fangs that's breathing fire at the top of the slide. The Dragon frightens them right past the slide. They bury their heads and imagine that the Dragon is wearing a T-shirt that says such things as: don't go down the slide...you must control your emotions...don't cry or show weakness...you aren't strong enough to take any more pain...you may end up crazy. So they stay in this self-chosen hell until they somehow muster the courage to confront the Giant Dragon, only to discover that the sayings on the Dragon's T-shirt are only myths. At last, Jot's companions risk the slide, and they, too, discover the steps leading to the warm sunshine.

Are you willing to risk the slide into pain, like Jot? Or do you see a scary dragon in your path? What do you see on the dragon's shirt?

The check mark fable offers a good perspective on the divorce grief process, illustrating many of our fears about grieving. An intellectual understanding of the grief process may help us to emotionally understand our feelings as well. Eventually, however, each of us must allow ourselves to experience grief, not just talk about it.

Symptoms of Grief

Let's see what we can learn from a head trip. As a beginning, a list of the grief symptoms commonly felt during divorce will help you see that your feelings are much like those of others.

Many people talk continuously about their situation until they drive away their friends and then need to seek new ones (the "verbal diarrhea" stage). The grieving person needs to stop talking about irrelevancies and begin to express their genuine feelings of grief. (If you find—or friends tell you—that you continually repeat yourself, this is a likely indication of a need to *express* your feelings rather than talking *about* them. Later in this chapter, you'll find some help with this.)

Grief has a *push-pull effect*. Having been hurt, you have a big, empty feeling in your gut, and you expect friends to help you fill it. You try to talk with friends and get close to them, but at the same time, this empty feeling—like a big wound—is very vulnerable to being hurt again. When people get too close, you tend to push them away to prevent further emotional pain. Thus, you pull people toward you emotionally, but you push them away when they get too close. Quite a mixed message for your friends!

With grief, *feeling emotionally drained* and *not sleeping* are frequent problems. Many grieving people have trouble falling asleep at night without using drugs or alcohol. They often wake up very early in the morning, unable to go back to sleep, yet too tired to get up. At a time when sleep is needed most, they have difficulty sleeping, and the hard emotional work has them tired all day long. Grief is hard work, and you will likely feel tired continuously until you have finished your grief process.

Eating is another problem during grief. You may have a feeling of tightness in your throat and find swallowing difficult. Sometimes your mouth will be very dry, also making eating difficult. You may not have any appetite and have to force yourself to eat. You may have an empty feeling in your stomach as though you were hungry, but you do not feel hungry. For these and other reasons, most people lose a great deal of body weight during the grief process (although a small percentage may actually gain appetite and weight). During a break in one divorce seminar, several participants were comparing their loss of body weight during divorce grief. Of the six people present, all had lost at least forty pounds! While the amount may not always be so dramatic, the unanimity is not surprising.

One of the most useful questions on the Fisher Divorce Adjustment Scale asks about *sighing often*. People are often not aware that they are sighing, but it is an indication to others that the person is grieving a great deal. Not only does a sigh release body tension, but the deep breathing of a sigh seems to "carry feelings from the gut" that need release.

Rapid mood changes are typical during divorce grief. Even after you have moved from the black pits of grief and are finally starting to feel good again, you may suddenly—without apparent reason—feel out of control emotionally, unable to keep from crying. The mood swing may have been triggered by something a friend or acquaintance said to you or did for you. You were feeling fine and in control until then. Your return to the depths of grief leaves that person confused and sad, not understanding what he or she did to upset you. For your part, the downer is made even worse because you feel bad about feeling so out of control. The incident is a clear sign that you have not completed your grief work yet.

There may be a sense of *loss of reality*, of being in a daze, in an unreal world. You observe the environment as though watching a movie, remote and detached from the events happening around you. You are unable to wake up from this dream into the real world.

You may experience a period of *lack of contact with your emotions.* You are afraid to trust your feelings because of your inability to control them. The emotional pain is so great, you have to protect yourself from feeling too much by deadening your emotions. You may sense an emotional "numbness."

Many people experience quite a bit of *fantasizing* during grief. You may fantasize that you see your former love partner or that you hear his or her voice. You may fantasize that a part of your body is missing, as though your heart were removed, symbolizing the loss of the other person. This fantasizing may be frightening if you do not recognize it as a normal part of grief.

Loneliness, lack of concentration, weakness and helplessness, depression, guilt, lack of interest in sex, and perhaps even a *feeling of impotence or frigidity* may accompany grief. *Self-criticism*—a need to continually question your errors and how you would relive the past differently—persists.

Anger is a part of grief that results from the apparent unfairness of the loss. Anger directed toward the former love partner may approach rage in its intensity. We will look at this in detail in the next chapter.

Suicidal feelings are common during divorce grief. Approximately three-fourths of the participants in the Fisher divorce seminars admit to having experienced some suicidal thoughts during their grief periods. Research indicates a much higher than normal rate of suicide among people engaged in the divorce process.

All of these feelings can be overwhelming. *Uncontrollable mood swings, loss of reality, fantasies, depression, suicidal feelings…*one may wonder fearfully, *Am I going crazy?* For most people, this is a difficult fear to discuss. And holding that fear inside makes it even scarier, even more crazy feeling. The "craziness" is a real feeling, but it is related to the situation rather than to a permanent psychological diagnosis. You may well be experiencing a normal grief reaction if you feel like you are going crazy.

These grief symptoms may be handled by acknowledging them, accepting that they indicate grief work to be done, and allowing yourself to feel the pain without denial. Crying, shouting, and writhing are other nondestructive actions to express your grief. Make a decision to manage the grief by deciding on an appropriate time and place to do grief work. On the job, for example, is not the time to cry and grieve. At work, you must put the grief aside—"on the shelf," so to speak—and concentrate on your job. Because you have set aside time to grieve, your emotions become easier to control at other times, and you do not become caught in the grieving. But be sure you do grieve during the time you have set aside for grieving! If you do not manage the grief; it will manage you.

If you do not do your grief work, your body may express the feelings of grief in symptoms of illness. You may have simple ailments like headaches, or you may develop, such as ulcerative colitis, arthritis, or asthma. Unresolved grief puts a great deal of stress on your body and may increase your medical and hospital bills.

Often people are reluctant to participate in the seminar or another divorce recovery program because they do not want to experience the pain and crying of grief again. This reluctance may be translated as their need to complete grief work. Somewhere deep inside, you will know when the grief work is completed because of the feeling of letting go that you'll experience. You cannot be pulled down into the grief pits again!

Stages of Grief: The Work of Elisabeth Kübler-Ross

During this part of the climb, it is helpful to identify the five stages of grief identified by Dr. Elisabeth Kübler-Ross. An overview of her fine work will help us to work through the five stages emotionally.

Stage 1: Denial. The first reaction to the sense of loss is to *deny* it: "This isn't happening to me. If I just wait a while, everything will be okay and my lover will come back." There is often a state of emotional shock, numbness, and a lack of acknowledgment of any feelings. One may enter into a robot-like phase, acting as though nothing is happening. Best manners are extended toward the former love partner, in the hope that it is all a bad dream and that person will not really leave. No one wants to tell friends and neighbors that a love relationship is ending. Indeed, we don't want to tell ourselves.

Stage 2: Anger. As one gradually begins to move away from denying the ending of a love relationship, a feeling of *anger* develops. The anger that was initially turned inward is now turned outward, toward others. Expressing the anger feels good, but there is also concern that the other person will not return because of the anger, thus there is some guilt and ambivalence.

The frustrations that have existed in the relationship for years begin to come out. Friends may wonder how you have tolerated that person when you have been so emotionally upset in the love relationship for so long. In turn, you may go to great lengths to convince others how terrible your former partner was, resulting in a lose-lose situation. If you talk about how good that person is, how do you stay angry? But if you say how terrible that person is, then the question becomes why you chose to love such a terrible person in the first place!

You have started working through the grief process when you admit and express the grief anger.

Stage 3: Bargaining. Beginning to face the fact that the love relationship is ending, yet reluctant to really let go, one may start *bargaining*: "I'll do anything if you'll just come back. I'll change my ways and put up with anything. Just take me back!" This stage is dangerous in the divorce process because many people do get back together, for the wrong reasons—to avoid the loneliness and unhappiness of ending the love relationship. They are not choosing to live successfully with the former love partner, but rather choosing the "lesser of two evils."

Stage 4: Depression. The fourth stage of grief is, in a sense, the darkness before the dawn as one moves toward *letting go* of the relationship. The depression of this stage is different from the sadness that often occurs during the denial stage—it's a "blah" feeling: "Is this all there is?" There is much internal dialogue about the meaning of life: "Why am I here on earth? What is the purpose of my life?" Despite the deep depression that can take hold here, this is a stage of personal growth to build a stronger identity, to find a deeper purpose for living, and to make life more meaningful.

A number of people feel suicidal during this stage: "I've tried so long and worked so hard, and here I am down in the pits again. I don't want to let go!" Because this stage sometimes comes so long after the actual separation, people are surprised to feel so depressed again. It is discouraging to have worked so hard but to feel so little progress. People who are aware of this stage tend to get through it much more easily. They are comforted to realize that there is a purpose for the depression they are feeling, that it will not last long, and that it is different from that of early-stage grief.

Stage 5: Acceptance. The grieving divorced person who has dealt with the painful issues of denial, anger, bargaining and depression is ready to *accept* the loss of the love relationship and to move on. At the final stage of the grief process, the person begins to feel free from the emotional pain and the need to invest emotionally in the past relationship. Now one can continue to move up the mountain toward fuller personal freedom and independence.

It is critically important to work through these five stages of grief before one enters into another love relationship.

Allow the Children to Grieve

Children, too, must grieve an important loss, although sometimes it is difficult for parents to let them do the grieving they need to do. When we see them in tears over the loss of the marriage or because they miss the other parent, we want to just take away the pain and reassure them, "Now, now, don't cry, it'll be okay.... Daddy will be back.... You'll get to see Mommy soon."

Reassurance is not necessarily what kids need; rather, they need to come to some sort of acceptance: "I know you feel very sad that your father isn't living here anymore. It must be so hard living away from him when you love him so much." It is easy for us to get our own emotions and guilt involved instead of allowing the children to express their feelings and emotions. Children tend to cry and grieve more naturally than adults unless we take away permission to do so and start interfering with the process.

The same can be true with the anger stage of their grief. Children may get very angry about being separated from a parent and having to undergo a lifestyle change. But when they start expressing that anger, parents often make the mistake of trying to take it away by saying things like, "Well, you're just going to have to grow up and understand. Someday you'll see that we made a choice that's better for everyone." It's important to allow your children just to experience their anger, acknowledging their emotions: "I can see that you feel very angry about our divorce."

Children will go through Kübler-Ross's five stages of grief as well. They will start out by denying that their parents are separated and believing they'll get back together. As they proceed through the stages of anger, bargaining, and depression, children need to be *allowed* to work through all five stages. All of the information in this chapter, plus the checklist at the end, can be very helpful for children as well as for adults.

Obviously, there is a difference between your child's loss and your loss: the child isn't being divorced. The parent-child relationship will persist, it is hoped, although in many cases, the child doesn't see one parent as much—and in some cases, unfortunately, not much at all.

As with all other feelings, a parent who *shows* the child how to grieve is far more influential than a parent who *tells* the child about grieving. Children will emulate a grieving parent and will gain much from experiencing that healthy and needed release.

Working Through Your Grief

Many people are afraid of the grief process because it can seem to bring out signs of weakness or maybe even of "going crazy." It is reassuring to find that other people experience many of the same feelings and symptoms of grief. You can effectively work through the grief stages, overcome your fear of grief, and come out on the other side of your grief work feeling safer and on more solid ground.

Take time now to get out your handkerchief and see if you can let go of some more grief while you rest on the trail. Now that you understand the grieving process and have permission to grieve as a mentally healthy activity, you may feel freer to do some needed grieving (perhaps over a past loss as well). Call upon a trusted friend, family member, clergyperson, or counselor to provide support (without interference) while you allow yourself to express the depths of your grief.

As you do so, a homework assignment you may find helpful is to write a "good-bye" letter to what you're letting go. It may be your home, your relationship, or a long-ago loss. This is a difficult assignment, so you might want to start with something more superficial. Eventually, you'll grow ready to say good-bye to major aspects of your life. The letter may or may not be mailed to another person; it is really for your own benefit. In most cases, you will not want to share the letter with the person you are grieving.

On the following page is an example written by a woman who attended a Fisher divorce seminar. It will give you insight into her thoughts and feelings, maybe help stimulate what you'd like to write. Read it thoughtfully, then begin work on your own letter(s).

goodbye

goodbye to the New House that I spent endless afternoons and weekends looking for—making sure that it met all the rigid requirements. I'll probably never find another house like that again. It was so much more than a house—it represented an end to looking, an achievement of a goal, a new beginning of the beginning. So very far away from that place I'd worked so hard to get to. God, I was so tired of searching and so grateful to have found it, and now I've lost it all.

goodbye to the home we were making for our future. goodbye to the tulips we planted in the fall but that we never saw together in the spring when it came time for them to bloom. goodbye to the plans we made for the nursery and fixing up the old cradle for the baby we never had.

goodbye to all that potential our new beginning was bringing us.

goodbye to the confidence and satisfaction I felt as "your mate"—the well-defined role; knowing what was expected of me.

goodbye

I've wanted so badly to say goodbye. To let go of you, to push you swiftly and completely from my life as you have done with me.

What is it that I'm holding on to?

Promises

    the good old "as-soon-as-we" promises...

        degrees...

        travel...

        jobs...

        honeymoon...

        money...

funny how they changed to "as-soon-as-I" promises.

I loved you because you were the other half of a marriage that I needed very badly in order to feel whole; because you were the future father of our family; because I needed someone to care for, to nurture, to parent; you made me feel needed.

I guess I've already said goodbye in more ways than I would have thought possible. You've been gone for a year and a half. Somehow I'm still here, all here; and nowhere, not even on the final decree, does it say that I am now only half a person with only 50 percent of the purpose, of the value that I once had. I am not trying to say goodbye to my self-worth or dignity—I've not really lost that—but rather, I am trying to say goodbye to my need for your credibility stamp on those feelings in order to make them valid.

The last goodbyes are the positive ones. For they are goodbyes to the negatives.

goodbye to the feelings of enslavement

goodbye to the picky little dislikes:

> onions, mushrooms, olives and
>
> my flannel nightgown and
>
> getting up early and
>
> Joni Mitchell and
>
> my friend Alice and
>
> going to the zoo.

goodbye to your lack of direction and

> your lack of creativity and
>
> your lack of appreciation and
>
> your lack of sensitivity.

goodbye to your indecisiveness and

> your stifled, dried-up emotions and
>
> your humorless sense of humor.

goodbye to feeling ashamed of getting angry and showing it,

feeling embarrassed for being silly,

feeling guilty when I knew the answer and you did not.

> goodbye
>
> Trisch

Now, dry your eyes and read on. As before, please be sure you have dealt thoroughly with this rebuilding block before you go on. Grief is a tough and painful stage. Do not just bury it! And do not try to get through it in the time it took you just to read this chapter. Use your lifeline friends (see chapter 6) for help as you work through your grief. The mountain will still be yours to climb when you are ready.

How Are You Doing?

Here again is a checklist for your review. Take a few minutes to consider these statements honestly and to consider how much grief work you may have to complete before you move on up the mountain.

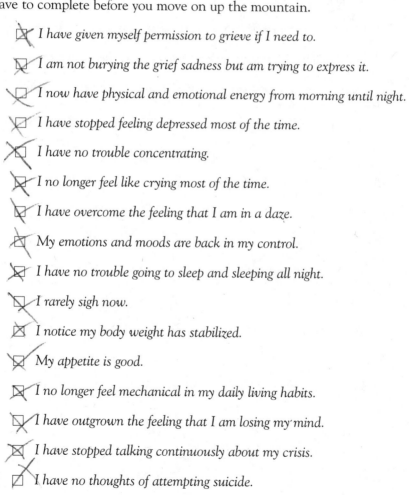

- ☒ *I have given myself permission to grieve if I need to.*

- ☒ *I am not burying the grief sadness but am trying to express it.*

- ☒ *I now have physical and emotional energy from morning until night.*

- ☒ *I have stopped feeling depressed most of the time.*

- ☒ *I have no trouble concentrating.*

- ☒ *I no longer feel like crying most of the time.*

- ☒ *I have overcome the feeling that I am in a daze.*

- ☒ *My emotions and moods are back in my control.*

- ☒ *I have no trouble going to sleep and sleeping all night.*

- ☒ *I rarely sigh now.*

- ☒ *I notice my body weight has stabilized.*

- ☒ *My appetite is good.*

- ☒ *I no longer feel mechanical in my daily living habits.*

- ☒ *I have outgrown the feeling that I am losing my mind.*

- ☒ *I have stopped talking continuously about my crisis.*

- ☒ *I have no thoughts of attempting suicide.*

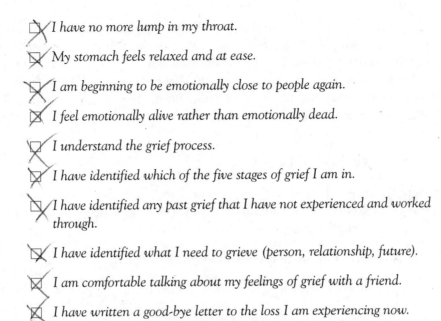

☒ I have no more lump in my throat.

☒ My stomach feels relaxed and at ease.

☒ I am beginning to be emotionally close to people again.

☒ I feel emotionally alive rather than emotionally dead.

☒ I understand the grief process.

☒ I have identified which of the five stages of grief I am in.

☒ I have identified any past grief that I have not experienced and worked through.

☒ I have identified what I need to grieve (person, relationship, future).

☒ I am comfortable talking about my feelings of grief with a friend.

☒ I have written a good-bye letter to the loss I am experiencing now.

CHAPTER 9

Anger

"Damn the S.O.B.!"

You'll feel a powerful rage when your love relationship ends, whether you're the dumpee or the dumper. Those angry feelings are a natural, healthy part of being human. How you express them makes all the difference. Don't bottle your feelings up inside, but you needn't get aggressive either. You can learn to express both your divorce anger and your "everyday" anger constructively. And you can learn to reduce your anger altogether.

I don't know what came over me. I saw his car in the parking lot and I knew he had met his girlfriend and left in her car. I went over and let the air out of all four tires. Then I went behind the building and waited until they returned so I could watch them find his car with the tires flat. I watched them trying to solve their problem and I felt so good. I've never done anything like that before in my life. Guess I didn't know how angry I could get.

—Jean

You're approaching a point in the trail where fire is a very real danger. The hazards of anger are great during the divorce process, and if you don't deal with it effectively, your anger might start a fire that can spread to the other rebuilding blocks and keep you from making progress on the trail.

In this chapter, we'll take a close look at two types of anger: the extreme anger that is such a common feeling among people going through divorce, and the everyday anger we all experience in response to irritating life events and encounters with other people.

Divorce anger is extreme. Rage, vindictiveness, and overpowering bitterness are common feelings when a love relationship is ending. It is a special kind of anger that most of us have never experienced before. Married friends don't understand the strength of it unless they, too, have ended a love relationship.

Everyday anger, while less intense than divorce anger, is just as important to deal with over the long haul. Somebody treats you unfairly. You're stuck in traffic. The plumbing fails twenty minutes before your dinner party. The children are driving you nuts. Your boss gives you a project five minutes before closing. Your neighbor's dog barks all night.... The list goes on.

Let's begin our exploration of this "hot" topic by recognizing that anger is a feeling (an emotion), not a behavior, and it's one we all experience, though each of us responds in our own way. When you get angry, your body knows it, even if you don't (consciously). Although you may not be conscious of them, anger events have physical, psychological, and social elements. Your heartbeat and breathing speed up, your muscles tense, your thoughts focus on "what (or who) went wrong," and you may express your angry feelings in words or actions that involve other people.

A lot of angry folks—maybe you?—try to keep their anger inside and not express it, and one school of thought suggests that you may become depressed as a result of buried anger. The divorce process can be pretty depressing anyway, and people who fail to express their anger during the early stages of divorce often get even more down. Others view anger and depression as separate emotions. What's important here is the point both views agree on: like other emotions, *anger needs to be dealt with in healthy ways.*

Dumpers tend not to express anger because they feel so guilty, and dumpees don't express it because they fear the other person won't come back if they do. Both are "nice" for a while, and both feel a lot of depression during the breakup.

Anger may be expressed in violent ways, of course. Given the opportunity while they are at their angriest, some people do commit acts of violence during the divorce process. You're lucky if you are able to restrain yourself and find more suitable methods of expressing these feelings of rage and vindictiveness.

The Three Phases of the Anger Rebuilding Block

The anger rebuilding block falls rather naturally into three phases.

The first phase is learning to *accept that it's okay to feel angry*—it's part of being human. There are many myths in our society depicting anger as weak, childish, destructive, immoral.

Many of us learned growing up that it's not permissible to feel angry. Now we have to relearn that it is okay after all. This may be easy to do in your head, but it is much more difficult to do emotionally. The strong emotional reactions of others when you become angry may make you very reluctant to accept your angry feelings now. Just remember there is a difference between your *feelings* of anger and the way you act to *express* them.

The second phase, after acknowledging that you're human and can feel anger, is to *learn as many positive ways of expressing anger as possible*— ways that will not be destructive to yourself or to those around you. We will explore in this chapter a number of those ways, including humor, physical exercise, assertive communication, and other methods.

Let us add a note of caution here about one of the most destructive ways people express anger at their exes during the divorce process: using their children as a vehicle. Corinne, for example, tried to turn the children into spies during visits with their dad, expecting them to report back to her when they came home. Annette would not allow Russ to see the kids until he paid child support; Russ would not pay child support until Annette allowed visitation. We forget about what's best for the children because we are so intent on "getting back" at that other person. Getting back through the kids is hitting below the belt.

For the sake of the children, if for no other reason, learn constructive methods of dealing with your anger.

The third phase of anger rebuilding is to *learn forgiveness and other ways to minimize your anger.* Those of you in the first two stages may react emotionally with a big outburst now: "I will never forgive!" Well, it's not just forgiving the other person that's important, but learning to forgive yourself as well. It will also help to discover the triggers of your anger, practice effective relaxation responses, and develop calming messages to say to yourself. You'll cut your stress a lot if you reduce your anger.

Whose Anger Is It, Anyway?

"You make me so mad!" How often have you heard—or said—those angry words? But it's not so. Nobody makes you mad. You get angry because something happened or someone did something you didn't like, but you are responsible for your anger; it's your feeling. Blaming someone else for your anger is a mistake we all make, and learning to take responsibility for your anger is another important goal for rebuilding your life.

There is a powerful anger statement in the Fisher Divorce Adjustment Scale: "I blame my former love partner for the ending of our love relationship." People who have not yet dealt with their anger will completely agree with that statement. Those who have done sufficient rebuilding work to have dealt with their anger begin to realize that failure, blame, and responsibility are two-way streets. What happened was part of a complicated interaction that did not work, not the fault of one person.

Taking responsibility for anger takes a long time for most of us. It requires a great deal of maturity and strength to do that. It's so much easier to blame the other person! The stage of forgiveness is actually about learning to forgive yourself and letting go of your anger. A key step in that learning is to discover the triggers of your anger.

Push-Button Anger: What Triggers Yours?

A helpful exercise when exploring anger is to identify and list the "triggers" of your anger. Some of the life events that trigger anger include unrealistic expectations, frustration, delays, interference, disrespect, abandonment, rejection, and discrimination, among many others. When you get really angry, can you tell which of your buttons someone has pushed? What are some of the things that set you off? It is worth a break on the trail to think about it for a time.

Elaine was so angry about Steve's efforts to gain custody of the children because she was doubting her own abilities as a parent. Charles was so angry about Marie leaving the marriage because it reignited the feelings of abandonment he experienced in the past when his mother died.

Dumpees, as we have discussed, tend to feel more anger than dumpers. When relationships end, most of the power is in the hands of the dumpers. They hold the cards, and the dumpees have to take whatever hand is dealt. It is frustrating to feel out of control, and frustration can lead to anger.

How about rejection? Dumpees are usually still in love, and they suddenly find out that the people they love don't love them anymore. Such deep rejection often leads to anger.

The future can be another push-button issue. Dumpees thought their future was all planned. Then suddenly they're alone (and lonely), forced to develop a brand-new life plan. This step is often accompanied by worries of making it financially, which is very difficult and frustrating to face. The dumpee feels afraid—often *really* afraid. Anger can seem an effective way to fight that fear, to get the adrenaline going to overcome it. Dumpees thus tend to feel more anger, and their scores on the Fisher Divorce Adjustment Scale tend to reflect that.

Appropriate vs. Inappropriate Anger

Have you thought about how appropriate it is to feel very angry when your love relationship ends? "What," you may ask, "is *appropriate* anger?" Anger that is in proportion to the present situation is appropriate. Harry was mad because someone ran into his new car; Jan felt angry because someone said something mean to hurt her; Sharon got quite frustrated when she was unable to accomplish a simple task, such as threading a needle. Appropriate anger is realistic for the situation—the feeling fits the event.

Inappropriate anger is out of proportion to the event. When Bea is driving and the light turns red, she also turns red. A chance remark causes Bart to start a fistfight. These excessive responses are not consistent with the importance of the event. Of course you feel angry when your love relationship ends. It's not only appropriate, it's beneficial and productive. "What?" you say. "Anger is beneficial?" Yes, because anger helps us to let go and become emotionally distant from the former love partner. People who are unable to express anger will prolong the letting-go process. They often experience a great deal of depression, stay stuck, and are unable to end the strong feelings they have for the former love partner.

Why Do You Bury Your Anger?

Many people find that obstacles from the past block the trail for them in this stage of rebuilding, keeping them from learning about the positive aspects of anger. Theresa had been badly abused as a child and had accumulated a great deal of childhood rage. In trying to help her express her anger, she was asked what she thought would happen if she expressed her feelings with her therapist. Theresa was silent for a long while, and then she admitted that she was afraid the therapist would hurt her. The fear of retaliation keeps many of us from expressing anger.

Anthony came into the office with a "Buddha smile" on his face. His son was flunking out of school by doing nothing, and his daughter was running away. An always-smiling face is often a mask for anger. Anthony, a self-ordained minister, was unable to express his anger because he had an image to maintain: "Preachers don't act angry" was his motto. But his anger came out with his children through physical abuse. His children reacted to the divorce with appropriate angry *feelings*, but their *behavior* was harmful and not constructive. The children needed to learn positive ways of expressing anger, but emotionally, they were learning from Anthony to abuse their future children instead. We often learn to express anger the same way our parents did.

Sometimes it is a reaction to our parents' anger that we learn. Jim saw his father throwing temper tantrums and acting childish, and as a result, he decided that he would never be like his father by acting childish around his children. So when he felt angry, he became stoic, putting on a stone-faced mask, like Anthony's always-smiling mask. His face would look like granite, and he would never admit that he was feeling angry.

If your angry feelings were validated when you were a child, if you were taught to express your angry feelings freely and in constructive ways, you're not likely to accumulate and "sandbag" anger. But if your anger was punished, if you weren't allowed to express anger in constructive ways (such as those described later in this chapter), or if you grew up among very angry people or others who pushed your normal frustration up to abnormal levels, you probably accumulated what might be called "childhood rage."

Anger that accumulates unexpressed may lead any small event to trigger inappropriate behavior. You won't have to think very long to imagine someone you know whose anger expression is always out of proportion. Look out for such people during the divorce process. They sometimes do violent things, like run over people with cars!

Scapegoats, Martyrs, and Anger

Some families need someone to blame for everything that goes wrong. They find a *scapegoat* and dump all of the blame upon that person. A person who has been the scapegoat in his or her family (were you?) will have great difficulty expressing anger. This person will have a great deal of childhood rage.

Perhaps it's not surprising, then, that scapegoats are prone to divorce. They have to do a great deal of emotional relearning before they can overcome the feeling that they are too worthless to have the right to be angry. Being the scapegoat is so harmful that professional counseling may be needed to heal from this destructive role.

And let's not forget the *martyr*. Almost every divorce seminar we've conducted has either a martyr or an ex-partner of a martyr in it. Martyrs try to live through other people. They sacrifice themselves to "helping" others, seemingly without limit, at great personal cost to themselves. The feeling behind martyrdom may well be genuine, but the giver is not giving because he or she cares, but because there is a fear of losing the other person or because giving as a way of connecting was learned at an early age. Perpetual giving, for selfish reasons, will eventually cause resentment in the martyr's partner. But the partner will find it very difficult to express this resentment because the martyr's self-denying style generates a nurturing response.

Martyrs try to find their identities through other people, and living through others makes the martyr relationship destructive to both people in it. (Chapter 15 contains an exercise that may help clarify the martyr role.)

How do you escape being a martyr if you are one yourself? Or how do you help another person to escape being a martyr? The martyr who doesn't have an identity of his or her own needs to work at finding that identity; to stop giving exclusively and learn to take and accept from others as well; to feel good about himself or herself; to establish his or her own activities, interests, goals; and to escape the martyr role.

If you're a martyr or the partner of a martyr, find a friend or therapist to talk to so you can begin to work through your feelings.

Venting Divorce Anger vs. Expressing Everyday Anger

It's important to emphasize again the difference between the special *divorce anger* you may feel about your dissolution and your *everyday anger* in connection with other life situations: Divorce anger needs to be *released* (by yourself or in therapy) in nondestructive ways. Your goal is to get over it. Everyday anger—in relationships with friends, family, lovers, children, coworkers—needs to be *expressed constructively*, directly, firmly, and honestly. Your goals are to encourage communication, to develop deeper relationships, and to move on.

Let's take a look at some methods for constructively expressing divorce anger, then we'll examine ways for you to deal with anger whenever it occurs in your everyday relationships.

What Can You Do with All That Divorce Anger?

It is tempting to act on your strong desire to take your divorce anger out on your former spouse directly. Most of us want to call up the ex and do what we can to hurt, get back, be vindictive, and vent our anger directly. *This is not helpful.* When you throw a few logs on the divorce anger fire, your ex will likely throw a few logs back in retaliation. Pretty soon, the fire is consuming both of you. It's better to express your anger in other ways, such as those suggested here, rather than taking it out directly on your former spouse.

Couples who have learned to express anger to each other in their relationships often are able to continue to express this anger as they go through the divorce process. However, if you—like most of us—had trouble expressing anger in your marriage, you're not likely to find it any easier during the adversarial and often inflammatory divorce process. We hope the ideas in this chapter will help.

Humor can be a very effective way of expelling angry feelings. Harriet became the "comedian" of one seminar group. "I don't know what to tell people when they ask me where my ex is," she told the group. "I don't want to tell them that he's off with another woman." One week she arrived with a big smile. "I finally decided that the next time a person asks me, I'll tell them that he croaked!" She laughed, the whole group laughed, and everybody was able to vent at least some of their angry feelings temporarily through laughter. A sense of humor is always valuable in life, but it is especially valuable in dealing with anger.

Another effective way to express anger is to *call a friend* and say, "I need to talk about this anger that I'm feeling toward my ex. I know I may not make sense sometimes. I know that I may become very emotional. And I know that some of the things that I say may not be what I'm really feeling all of the time. But right now, I'm feeling really angry, and I need you to listen to me talk about my anger." A lifeline support friend who will help you through these times is one of your best tools for dealing with anger.

Many people who experience intense divorce anger are able to use *fantasies* to help them express it. Sandy was an expert at conjuring up scenarios like this: "I go to the garden store and buy a sack of hot lawn fertilizer. Then, in the middle of the night, I go over to my ex's house and write obscene four-letter words with the fertilizer all over his front lawn. Every time he has to mow the grass all summer long, he'll read them!" We have to keep in mind, of course, that fantasies are just that and should not be acted upon! If you're someone who doesn't have much self-control, you probably shouldn't try this tactic, because acted-out fantasies are likely to be destructive.

Physical exercise of any sort is usually helpful for a time. Physical games, jogging, housecleaning, beating a rug, or anything like that is especially useful. Anger is a source of energy, and it's healthy to use up that energy. Physical activity is a good way to do that. You can be more effective in expelling anger through physical exercise if you use other techniques along with it. For example, when you play a game of golf or tennis, you can fantasize that the ball is your ex's head. If you add some grunting and groaning, using your voice along with your muscles, that would be even more effective. When you go jogging, you can mentally picture your ex's face on the ground in front of you, then pounce on it with every step.

If you feel comfortable using *cuss words*, this can be an effective way to vent strong feelings of divorce anger. Using your vocal cords provides a vehicle for getting your gut feelings to literally come out your throat and mouth and be expelled from your body.

Try getting your feelings out by *screaming*. Most of us would not be comfortable screaming with people around, but maybe you can find a place to go and scream alone. Charlene was able to do this by driving her car to a private place. Then she would park for a while and scream, cry, and yell, which she found so helpful to get out her anger. Her kids became aware of it, and when they saw her getting upset, they would say, "Mom's about ready to go to her screaming place again!"

(Keep in mind that the purpose of your cussing and/or screaming is to get your feelings out, not to attack the target of your anger.)

Tears are another way to express divorce anger. Crying is a positive, honest expression of feelings. Many people, especially males, have difficulty crying. Give yourself "permission" to cry—it will help you feel better. Crying is a natural body function for expressing sadness or anger.

Yet another effective way of getting divorce anger out is to *write a letter* saying all of the things that you would like to say to your former love partner. Write it in really big or bold letters, maybe using crayon or marker, to show your anger. But after you have written the letter, *do not mail it.* Instead, take the letter to the fireplace and burn it up. In this way, you will have both expressed your anger and symbolically burned it up.

You may find the *empty chair technique* to work for you. Imagine that your former love partner is sitting in a vacant chair in front of you, and say everything that you would like to say to that person. If you're good at this kind of thing, you can even switch chairs and say the things that you imagine the person would say back to you. Then go back to your chair and continue the dialogue until you've adequately expressed your emotions.

As you can see, there are many ways for you to vent your divorce anger. You will not find all of these ways helpful—in fact, you may have a great deal of resistance to some and be completely unable to use them. But you are limited by only your own creativity, ingenuity, and inhibition in finding ways to vent your divorce anger.

Keep in mind, as you consider and perhaps try the divorce anger expression methods noted above, that venting, while it can be healthy if handled constructively, is not a cure for anger. Again, your goal is to get over it, to get it out so you can let it go.

Incidentally, some people are not able to express anger because of a need to "keep" it, like a security blanket. If you let go of that anger, you will not have it as a tool for punishing the other person. So you may get some sort of payoff or reward for holding on to your anger. The question for you to think about is: What kind of person would you like to be? Do you like being an angry person, or would you like to let go of the anger?

And once again, remember that these are ways to release some of your divorce anger. We do not recommend any of the above methods as healthy ways to express everyday anger. That's coming up next.

Beyond Divorce: Expressing Your Everyday Anger

As we begin this discussion of everyday, garden-variety anger—the kind we all experience in response to the ups and downs of daily life, we encourage you to keep in mind that how we act (our behavior) is not the same as how we feel (our emotions). Feelings and behavior are really two different parts of who we are.

Anger is a *feeling*. Assertion and aggression are types of *behavior*. Remember Jean from the beginning of this chapter? She's the one who let the air out of her ex's tires. Jean was feeling such strong anger that her behavior was definitely aggressive. It would have been possible for her to express her anger in other ways. For instance, she could have been even more aggressive and acted in some violent way toward her ex—maybe by physically attacking him. Or she could have expressed her anger by confronting him directly and telling him exactly how she felt: "I'm so mad at you, I feel like letting the air out of your tires! You've been unfair and unreasonable!" You get the idea: angry *feelings* can be expressed through many different behaviors. Put yourself in the following situations:

You have been waiting in line for concert tickets for two hours. Two "friends" of the man in front of you walk up and say, "Hey, Joe, how about letting us in here?"

The child support check is two weeks late, and you really need the money to buy clothes for the kids before school starts next week. When you call your ex, the answer is, "Well, I had a lot of expenses from my trip to Hawaii, and I won't be able to pay you until next month."

You read in the newspaper that your state legislature has just voted itself a 20 percent raise—and voted to cut support for schools by 10 percent.

Angry? Well, you should be! These situations and a thousand other examples of unfairness, abuse, thoughtlessness, and other mistreatment are good cause for anger. Never mind what you were told as a child—anger is natural, normal, healthy, and human! We all feel it at times. (If you think you *never* get angry, maybe you have already forgotten the difference between feelings and behavior. Go back and reread the paragraphs above.)

The question now is, "What *do* I do about my anger?" We have already discussed some ideas for releasing the strong feelings of divorce anger—humor, fantasies, exercise, screaming, crying, and others. These ways are helpful while you are getting rid of that powerful anger toward your former partner. But they do not give you much help for dealing with your anger in everyday situations because they are designed to release anger about a situation you are no longer in. We need methods to use in situations involving ongoing relationships.

Taking Responsibility with "I-Messages"

One of our favorite communication techniques is the use of I-messages, first introduced years ago as a part of the Parent Effectiveness Training programs of psychologist Thomas Gordon. As mentioned in chapter 4, I-messages start with the word "I" and place the responsibility for your feelings on you, rather than blaming the other person for your anger. I-messages allow you to get anger and other strong feelings out of the way so that closeness, intimacy, and love may come into the relationship. I-messages also help you identify what it is you are feeling, rather than covering up your feelings by blaming the other person.

Learning to use I-messages will help you communicate with all of the loved ones around you—lovers, children, friends, relatives. Start practicing I-messages as a way of improving your interactions with others and as a way of expressing anger constructively. A simple example: instead of "You *make* me mad!" try "I *get so mad* when you..." The difference may seem subtle, but notice that, when you say "I get so mad," you accept responsibility for your own feelings. And you take back control over your feelings rather than giving that power to someone else.

(Note that I-messages are great for expressing *positive* feelings as well!)

Expressing anger constructively is probably as important as anything you can do to make your love relationship productive and keep it clear of all the garbage that accumulates. (That garbage is another cause of divorce—how many is that now?) Talking out anger is the relief valve that keeps the relationship from exploding. And talking out anger usually leads to intimacy (and often to good sex). It is worth it!

Assertive Anger Expression

Anger expression has been a special interest of Bob's for many years. His best seller *Your Perfect Right: Assertiveness and Equality in Your Life and Relationships*, coauthored with Michael Emmons, offers a system for positive, constructive anger expression. It takes some effort, but you and your relationships will benefit a great deal if you follow the steps below, adapted from the book.

Before you get angry:

- Get to know yourself and the attitudes, environments, events, and behaviors that trigger your anger.

- Don't set yourself up to get angry.

- Reason with yourself.

- Learn to relax.

- Save your anger for when it's important.

When you get angry:

- Develop several coping strategies for handling your anger (relaxation, physical exertion, counting to ten, calming self-talk).

- Take a few moments to consider if this situation is really worth your time and energy, along with the possible consequences.

- Decide if you want to work it out with the other person or resolve it within yourself.

- Express your anger assertively. (Be spontaneous; don't let resentment build; state your anger directly; use honest, expressive language; let your posture, face, gestures, and voice convey your feelings; and avoid sarcasm, name-calling, put-downs, physical attacks, one-upmanship, hostility.)

- Express concern verbally. ("I'm very angry"; "I strongly disagree"; "That's unacceptable to me.")

- Schedule some time to work things out.

- State your feelings directly and accept responsibility for them.

- Stick to specifics and to the present situation.

- Work toward resolution of the problem.

Forgive and Forget

As noted earlier, not all anger is justified (appropriate), and not all anger must be expressed. Sometimes an act of forgiveness is the healthiest thing you can do. We're not saying to "turn the other cheek" all the time, nor are we going back on our advice to express your anger and keep your life clear. What we're saying here is that you must make a choice as to where you're going to expend your energy.

You can't address all the wrongs in the world, not even those in just your own life. Sometimes, as the old saying goes, discretion really is the better part of valor. Take a moment to decide if a situation is worth making the effort to express your anger. If it is (as when someone has treated your child unfairly), then by all means do so assertively. If not (as when someone has cut you off on the freeway), take a deep breath and get on with your life.

"Smoke Gets in Your Eyes"

Don't stop climbing when you feel the fires of anger starting within you. This chapter has given you permission to feel angry and has offered you ways of expressing anger positively and constructively so you can work it through until there's nothing left but ashes. The fire may smolder for a long time, but it is better to let it burn out so that you can be free. Take your time on this part of the trail, with forest fires raging around you, and be careful. It is important that you get through without destroying the people in your environment or destroying yourself. Uncontrolled anger can be very destructive.

Our research indicates that the average person going through the divorce process stays angry at his or her ex-spouse for three years. How long will you choose to be angry at your former partner? Who is being hurt by your anger, and what does it accomplish?

Only You Can Prevent Relationship Fires

Anger is one of the most important rebuilding blocks because it spreads to the feelings in the other blocks. If the fires of divorce anger are burning out of control in you, then you will have trouble working your way up the trail until you get them under control.

A great sense of relief will result from working through your anger until there is nothing left of it but ashes. This will free energy for other areas in your life. You can forgive yourself and your partner for the love relationship not working out. You can stop blaming yourself, stop feeling like a failure; you can find the internal peace that comes from letting go of painful things. You will then be able to talk to your ex in a calm and rational manner without becoming emotionally upset. Now you can deal with friends—either your partner's or yours—without becoming irritated. You suddenly wake up and find there is sunshine back in your life instead of the stormy cloud of anger. You realize that things just happened the way they happened and that there is no point in blaming somebody.

Zack, a seminar participant, picked up a slogan that is very useful when working through the divorce process: "It just doesn't matter." So many things that seemed important to us before just are not anymore. Once you reach the stage of forgiveness, you'll no longer feel the need to punish or be vindictive toward your former partner.

Children Get Angry Too

Children of divorce experience the same type of extreme divorce anger that their parents do. The daughter of one divorced parent became uncontrollably angry at her father in the swimming pool one day. She screamed at him about some very minor oversight. The anger was far stronger than the situation warranted and was apparently a direct result of a feeling of abandonment, for which she blamed her father.

It is very easy for divorced parents not to allow their children to be angry. The custodial mother will many times try to establish a good relationship between her children and their father, even though he has not kept visitation appointments and appears to be involved in activities without the children much of the time. The mother may try to help the children to accept their father without being angry. But it is appropriate for children to be angry at the noncustodial parent who lets them down.

It is also easy for us to withdraw love when our children express anger. We may be so emotionally uptight ourselves that when our children get angry, we immediately become unaccepting: "Go to your room until you can learn to behave properly!" We need to find that extra energy to listen to and accept our children's anger. But we also need to see to it that they do not become aggressive, have temper tantrums, or break things. Allow your children to express their anger in the same positive, constructive ways explained in this chapter. When they express that they are very angry at their father or mother for not showing up, just accept that and say, "I think it's right for you to feel angry in this situation, and when you get over it, you'll feel better."

Most of us learned our emotional blocks for expressing anger through some interaction with our parents. We were punished for being angry, or we were not allowed to be angry, or we were sent to our rooms for showing anger, feeling rejected and unloved because of it. It is far better for children to learn that anger is part of being human and that it is okay to express anger in a positive way.

How Are You Doing?

Check up with yourself with these statements before you go on. Remember to be honest with yourself!

I can communicate with my former love partner in a calm and rational manner.

I am comfortable seeing and talking to my former love partner.

I no longer feel like unloading my feelings of anger and hurt on my former love partner.

I have stopped hoping that my former love partner is feeling as much emotional pain as I am.

I no longer feel so angry at my former love partner.

It is not important anymore that my family, friends, and associates be on my side rather than on my former love partner's side.

I have outgrown the need to get even with my former love partner for hurting me.

I no longer blame my former love partner for the failure of our love relationship.

I have stopped trying to hurt my former love partner by letting him or her know how much I hurt emotionally.

☑ I have overcome my anger and have begun to accept the things my former love partner has been doing.

☑ I am expressing my anger in a positive manner that is not destructive to me or to those around me.

☑ I am able to admit it when I feel angry rather than denying my angry feelings.

☑ I understand the emotional blocks that have kept me from expressing anger in a positive manner.

☑ I am able to express my anger constructively rather than venting it inappropriately.

☑ I am reaching a stage of forgiveness instead of remaining angry.

CHAPTER 10

Letting Go
Disentangling Is Hard to Do

You need to stop investing emotionally in your dead love relationship. It is easier to let go if your own life bucket is full rather than empty. Dumpers tend to let go more quickly, often because they let go even before they left. Failure to let go may be a sign that you are not facing some painful feelings within yourself.

Stella: "Harry left me four years ago, and he immediately remarried."

Counselor: "I notice you are still wearing a wedding ring."

Stella: "Yes, it's very important to me."

Counselor: "And you wrote me a check for the therapy with Harry's name still on the bank account."

Stella: "I guess I just can't let go."

Did you ever get a song in your brain that you keep humming over and over? How many songs can you think of that have to do with letting go? Here are a few to get you started:

"Hello," Adele

"Yesterday," Beatles

"Nothing Compares 2 U," Sinead O'Connor

"Somebody That I Used to Know," Gotye

"You'll Think of Me," Keith Urban

"He Stopped Loving Her Today," George Jones

Most of us have ended a love relationship at one time or another in our lives, even if it was when we were teenagers and dating. It is interesting that this common phenomenon has been researched so little. We seem to depend a lot on poets and songwriters to teach us about ending a love relationship.

What Is This Thing Called "Disentanglement"?

Let's start with a clear idea of just what letting go is. Try this: Clasp your hands together with the fingers loosely intertwined, then pull your hands apart while you continue to clasp. That gives you an experiential description of what we mean by "disentanglement." It involves the painful letting go of all your strong emotional feelings for that other person.

The feeling of being in love is not the only thing that's hard to give up. There are also feelings of anger, bitterness, and vindictiveness. Someone who still talks about the former love partner a great deal, whether in endearing or in angry terms, has not let go of strong feelings for that person.

It's common for people to claim during the "honeymoon period" of the divorce process that they want to continue being friends. Then when the dumper guilt and dumpee anger set in, the desire to stay friends begins to disappear. But many people strive so hard to remain friends that they fail to let go—and fail to allow the anger to come and help them do it. Because of this, it is advisable not to maintain the friendship during that early stage; wait until after you have disentangled. Trying to be friends may prolong the process and even endanger the possibility of being friends later on. (That doesn't mean you shouldn't be civil, or even cordial, just not friendly.)

Another aspect that needs to be mentioned is "runaway syndrome." Most divorced people at some time in the process have a strong urge to run away. They want to move to a new community, away from where the former spouse is living, to avoid the pain of running into the former spouse or mutual friends.

Coleen had been married to a college professor who left her when he became involved with a young student. Driving her car down the street one day, Coleen saw him in his car with the younger woman. Before she could even pull over, she vomited. Needless to say, it is very painful to see the former love partner with a new mate.

If you are running *toward* something, such as a new job, a former home with a support system of family or friends, or anything that is an advancement in your life, maybe a move is advisable. But if you are running *away* from dealing with the unpleasant situation, you should reconsider. You are already under a stressful situation, and a major move will only add to the stress.

Difficult as it will probably be, there are advantages to staying in your present community and dealing with the painful feelings of seeing your former spouse and his or her friends. ("So you were married to the president of the chamber of commerce? I know him well.") People who move may just be burying and denying the process of letting go. Those who stay and tough it out will likely be able to see and talk with the former spouse sooner without becoming emotionally upset. They will have dealt with the disentanglement rebuilding block more effectively by confronting it.

There appears to be a connection among three key rebuilding blocks: *denying* that the love relationship is ending; *grieving* the loss; and *letting go* of the dead relationship. As we climb the trail, we may be working on all three interconnected blocks at the same time.

Don't Drag It Out

Let us talk to you dumpers for a moment. (You dumpees may listen in if you want, because we'll be talking about you!)

Dumpers often want to "be kind" to the dumpee to avoid feeling guilty, but this only prolongs the process. If you are going to be a dumper, do it with strength, courage, and firmness. It is far kinder than being timid about dumping.

Richard thought he would be a kind dumper, making it a point to take Barbara (the dumpee) out to dinner every week, supposedly to make her feel better. But each time he did it, it was like throwing a few crumbs to a hungry cat. It kept the cat from finding other places to eat, and it kept the cat at a starvation level. Barbara failed to let go as long as there seemed to be some hope of reconciliation. Bluntness may be far kinder than "kindness" to the dumpee. Richard was being "kind" only to himself—easing his guilt feelings.

There are other situations that prolong letting go. Lengthy court hearings will drag things out. Children and pets that have to be exchanged at regular intervals may prolong the process, as may continuing to live close to each other. (The same town is okay; next door is not!) A joint business that forces you to keep dealing with each other is another delaying factor. (Business matters often do make disentanglement more difficult; weigh carefully any decisions in this area. You'll want advice from your attorney and tax advisor.)

Another problem in letting go has to do with in-law relationships. Divorce usually includes separation from the ex-partner's family as well. While in most cases, the ties with in-laws are broken or much loosened at the time of divorce, the breakup may have the opposite effect. In some situations, the in-laws' emotional ties remain stronger to their son- or daughter-in-law than to their own son or daughter.

All fifty states have laws that give grandparents visitation rights with their grandchildren regardless of who has custody. However, it's not a sure thing. In 2000, the US Supreme Court overturned a Washington State law that granted grandparents broad visitation rights. Currently, about twenty of the states have statutes that restrict visitation, usually under "best interests of the child" criteria. Even in states with more permissive laws, grandparents may have to petition the court to gain access to their minor grandkids if the parents object. It appears likely that grandparents' rights will be more clearly defined—and perhaps more limited—in the future. In the meantime, we advise grandparents to view visitation as a privilege, not a right and, if this is an issue in your family, check out the current law in your state.

Disentangling Is Hard Work

With or without all of these complications, the big question remains: *How do you let go?* For many of us, "How do I stop loving that person?" is the tough issue. It is much easier to let go, of course, if you have other things going for you. A good job, a good support system, friends and relatives who are helpful and supportive, some sort of internal fullness rather than emptiness—all of these will help fill the void created when the beloved person is removed.

There are some specific things you can do to help yourself let go. Start by going through the house and removing all of those things that tend to keep you thinking about your former love partner. Pictures, wedding gifts, birthday gifts, and similar mementos can be removed so that they are not a constant reminder. You may need to rearrange the furniture in the house, perhaps even make the house look as different as possible from the way it was when you were living there as a married couple. The marriage bed is often an especially important symbol. You may need to get a new spread, move the bed to a new spot in the bedroom, put it in another room, sell the bed, or even give it away.

You may want to make a collection of all those reminders of your former love relationship and store them in a box in the garage or basement. Some weekend you may choose to do some *implosive grieving*, bringing out all of these mementos and setting aside a period of time to grieve as heavily as possible. This heavy grief period will probably be very depressing, and we suggest you have another person around for support. Becoming as out of control as possible in your grieving may help you to let go more rapidly. By increasing the intensity of the grief, this implosive grieving may shorten the number of weeks or months it takes you to let go fully.

Another area that is a problem for many people is dealing with phone calls, letters, and visits from—or for—the former love partner. If it is evident that he or she is hanging on, you may feel irritated. But the fact that you keep allowing it to happen may indicate that you have not let go either. It takes two to keep this game going. If you simply refuse to play the game, it will be easier on everyone in the long run. You will have to become assertive, perhaps hanging up the phone or returning letters unanswered and unopened.

You also can make a decision to control your thinking and fantasizing about the former love partner. Whenever you find yourself weeping about that person, think about something painful or something unpleasant in the love relationship. That will lead you to stop thinking about the person. As an alternative, you may simply choose another image or subject to concentrate on, instead of focusing on the past love.

Letting Go of Your Fears

There is a more abstract answer to the problem of letting go. Often a pattern of behavior has at its core a specific feeling—such as guilt, fear of rejection, fear of being unlovable, or low self-worth and lack of confidence. It is surprising how often we set up our lives to feel the feeling we are most afraid of! If we fear rejection, we either consciously or unconsciously set ourselves up to be rejected. If we have a need to feel guilty, we set up situations that make us feel guilty.

When Teresa and Patrick came for marriage counseling, his pattern of behavior was to seek rejection, and hers was to feel guilty. Their neurotic needs fit together perfectly. They went through years of marriage with her feeling guilty because he felt rejected. She set up reasons to feel guilty, thus feeding his feelings of rejection.

When love relationships end, we tend to respond with the feeling that is at the root of our behavior. If it is rejection, we feel rejected; if guilt, we feel that. Unfortunately, such a feeling may be so great that one is not strong enough to endure it and let go at the same time.

If you are having a difficult time letting go, ask yourself, *What feeling would I feel the strongest if I did let go of my ex-love?* Maybe your reluctance to let go is actually covering up your inability to face yet another painful feeling. For instance, you may be afraid to let go because it will force you to deal directly with your fear of being alone. So you avoid feeling alone by not letting go. You will probably have to face that feeling directly before you will be able to let go. Get help from a lifeline friend or a counselor if you feel the need for support.

Invest in Yourself

The goal of working through this rebuilding block is to emotionally invest in your own personal growth instead of in the dead relationship. There is no return on an investment in the relationship's emotional corpse. The greatest possible return comes from investment in yourself.

Helping the Children to Let Go

Children of divorce deal with this rebuilding block by letting go of their past concept of the two-parent family. Suddenly, it is a one-parent family, with a custodial and a noncustodial parent. Even if there is joint custody, the children still have to deal with two different lifestyles in two different homes. It is hoped that the children will not have to let go of the *quality* of their relationships with both parents.

Children may have difficulty, however, in dealing with their parents' ability to let go or not. This may become an important rebuilding block for children if they continually hear from one parent about all of the good things (or bad things) the other parent is doing. If the parents have not let go of the relationship, the children will tend to get caught in either the positive or negative feelings between the parents. This will prolong the adjustment process for the children.

How Are You Doing?

Take time on the trail now to stand still and shake off those feelings from the past that keep you investing in the dead relationship. Jump up and down to feel strong inside, shake off the heavy burden you have been carrying, and find the free feeling that comes from not carrying that dead love relationship on your back.

Finally, check yourself out on the items listed below. Have you really let go?

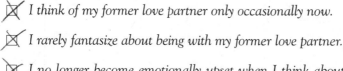

- ☒ *I think of my former love partner only occasionally now.*

- ☒ *I rarely fantasize about being with my former love partner.*

- ☒ *I no longer become emotionally upset when I think about my former love partner.*

- ☒ *I have stopped trying to please my former love partner.*

- ☒ *I have accepted that my former love partner and I will not get back together.*

- ☒ *I have stopped finding excuses to talk to my former love partner.*

- ☒ *I rarely talk about my former love partner with friends.*

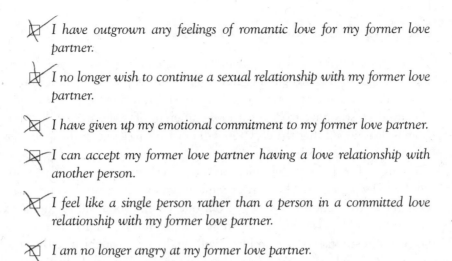

☒ I have outgrown any feelings of romantic love for my former love partner.

☒ I no longer wish to continue a sexual relationship with my former love partner.

☒ I have given up my emotional commitment to my former love partner.

☒ I can accept my former love partner having a love relationship with another person.

☒ I feel like a single person rather than a person in a committed love relationship with my former love partner.

☒ I am no longer angry at my former love partner.

CHAPTER 11

Self-Worth

"Maybe I'm Not So Bad After All!"

It is okay to feel good about yourself. You can learn to feel better about yourself and thus gain strength to help you adjust better to a crisis. As you successfully adjust to a crisis, you will feel even better about yourself! If you are experiencing a personal identity/rebellion crisis, you may be seriously straining your love relationship.

When I was a child, my father continually warned me about getting a "big head" and becoming "stuck on myself." Then I went to church and learned that I had been born sinful. At school, it was the jocks and the brains who got all the attention. Finally, I married so there would be someone who thought I was worthwhile. It made me feel good that someone cared. But then she became a pro at pointing out my faults. I finally reached a point where I began to believe I was truly worthless. It was then that I decided to leave the marriage.

—Carl

Wow! This self-worth portion of the trail is crowded with people who appear unable to continue the climb. Some sit on rocks, dejected, without energy left to climb. Some are lying on the ground like doormats, expecting everyone to walk on them. The faces of some show the effects of criticism and feelings of worthlessness. Some seem almost invisible, as if a shield surrounds them, blending them into the background.

Notice those people who are followed everywhere by a black cloud! Rain falls on them, but not on those around them. That woman over there seems to have misplaced her black cloud for a while. She is anxiously peering over her shoulder, stumbling over rocks—can she be searching for the lost cloud? Sure enough, the cloud has caught up with her and is raining on her again, and she actually seems more content now.

The Importance of Self-Worth

In this portion of the climb, learning more about self-worth and ways to improve it are our main concerns. Self-worth—also known as "self-concept" and "self-esteem"—refers to the way you see yourself, your core beliefs about your value as a human being. Heavy stuff.

Growing up, Bruce thought he alone suffered from an affliction called an "inferiority complex," never realizing that the term was used so often because many others feel inferior. (Indeed, hasn't everybody at some point?)

When Fisher divorce seminar participants are asked to raise their hands if they want to improve their self-esteem, *all* hands usually go up. Do you see how important this rebuilding block is?

Have you ever wondered whether self-concept exists at birth or if it is learned later? These days, psychologists believe it's about fifty-fifty. Apparently, we are born with certain tendencies, and then we learn much of how we feel about ourselves during the early years from the significant people around us, including parents and siblings, teachers, coaches and counselors, and relatives. This basic level of self-concept is later influenced strongly by peers—especially during the teen years. As an adult, a love partner becomes a primary source of validation and feedback, greatly affecting one's feelings of self-worth.

Many marriages that end in divorce developed a pattern of interaction destructive to the self-concept of one or both of the parties involved. In fact, some become so destructive that the parties may not be able to end the marriage: "I don't even deserve a divorce!" For example, a battered wife may think she *deserves* to be emotionally and physically abused. She may be unable to risk leaving the marriage because she's convinced she would not be able to make it on her own. Many people suffer serious erosion of their self-esteem in bad marriages before finally seeking relief in divorce.

But when the physical separation comes and the love relationship ends, self-concept hits an all-time low. So much of a person's identity is involved in the love relationship that when the marriage fails, the identity suffers.

Bruce once had a group of separated people complete the Tennessee Self-Concept Scale (a paper-and-pencil psychological test designed to measure feelings of self-worth). It would be hard to find another group of people whose average score was as low as theirs. Ending a love relationship can be devastating to self-concept. In fact, feelings of self-worth at this time may be the lowest ever experienced. A low self-concept immobilizes some people emotionally, making them unable to function in their jobs, in their parenting of their children, or in their interaction with others.

Further study of the self-concept scores of this same group of people showed that those with a good self-concept were better able to adjust to the ending of their love relationship. The research confirms what our common sense tells us: a good self-concept makes adjustment to a life crisis easier.

Obviously, feelings of self-worth are very important to the way we live. Since ending a love relationship is usually detrimental to selfconcept, most of us need to improve our feelings about ourselves after experiencing a major life crisis such as this. It is reassuring to know that self-concept can be enhanced. That is an exciting and optimistic viewpoint—you can relearn, grow, and change! You don't have to be saddled with old feelings of low self-worth.

Eleven Steps to Greater Self-Esteem

During the course of the ten-week Fisher divorce seminar, changes in self-worth are among the most significant outcomes for participants. What techniques are used? How do people make such big changes? Let us share with you some tools you may use to improve your own self-esteem. These are not magical, and your attitude toward yourself will certainly not change overnight, but we hope you'll try them. We think you'll be pleasantly surprised.

Step 1: You must make a decision to change. This step seems obvious, but it is often overlooked. Years ago, it seemed that several of Bruce's clients were being followed by little black clouds—like the woman we met earlier on the trail. When there was progress in therapy, these folks would become uncomfortable, look for the cloud, and expect rain to fall.

Frustrated, Bruce decided to take a solitary hike up Big Thompson Canyon in the Rocky Mountains. Near the top of the trail was a little sign pointing out a Douglas fir tree uprooted by the wind. The tree had been lying on the ground long enough for the end of the trunk to bend around and continue growing toward the sunlight—about twenty feet of new growth was pointing toward the sky, in fact. Because the old trunk's roots were mostly out of the ground, you have to wonder how the tree could keep growing for so many years! Besides the trunk, several branches also reached from the upper side of the trunk to the sky, one more than thirty feet high.

"I thought to myself," Bruce recalled, "as I studied this tree, that it was uprooted in its life just as a person's life is uprooted by a crisis such as a divorce. The tree sought its own fullest potential, continuing to grow and reach for the sky. I was greatly moved by the sight of this tree. I realized that there is a force within each of us that will help us to reach our full potential after a crisis has uprooted our lives. The tree's continuing reach for the sky led me to develop my belief in changing self-concept."

We need to find and listen to that inner source of emotional energy that encourages the development of our potential. If you get in touch with that source—whether it's called a religious "soul," a psychological "ego," the "inner source," or the "life force"—you will be capable of making the changes you desire. Look within yourself for this source of strength, and use it to become the person you would like to be.

If you make a decision to improve your self-concept, almost everything in your life will be affected: your work; your relationships with other people; the way you parent your children; your choice of a partner in a future love relationship; and, most of all, the way you feel about yourself. Enormous changes may occur in your personality and your life if you proceed to improve your self-concept. The decision is the first and perhaps the most difficult step. If your commitment is firm, the steps that follow will come much more easily.

Step 2: Change the way you look at yourself. Most people can easily list twenty things they do not like about themselves. Why not make a list of twenty things you *do* like about yourself? When this assignment is given in the Fisher divorce seminar, there are groans and comments such as, "How about two instead of twenty?" One late-night phone call from a class participant started with, "Damn you! I came home from teaching school and started the list of things I like about myself. It took me an hour to come up with the first one. It took almost that long for the second one. Now it's eleven p.m., and I only have five things on my list!" That was the most important homework for him in the whole ten weeks.

This is an important task; take the time to do it. Be sure to write out your list so you can complete the next step.

Step 3: Read these positive things about yourself aloud to others. It's easier to silently write down good things about ourselves than to say them out loud, because all the old messages inside start screaming, *Don't act stuck up and conceited!* Ignore those messages. Take your list and share the comments with a friend. Get your courage up and break the negative pattern. It is *okay* to make positive comments about yourself. It does take courage to say them out loud. Remember, changing your self-concept is *not* easy!

Those voices inside us are especially loud if a critical person influenced us when we were growing up. Russ resisted doing this step, explaining that his parents had often warned him "not to get a big head." He had been a good athlete in high school and might have built up his confidence that way, but his parents' voices were louder than his desire to feel good about himself. He had learned to be "humble." As an adult, he could not say good things about himself out loud because he still feared his parents' displeasure. That may sound ridiculous to you, but it wasn't to Russ. He was finally able to read his list aloud to his seminar group—although with a pained look on his face—and when he finished, everyone applauded. "Boy, I feel good!" he said.

Step 4: Reexamine your relationships with others and make changes that will help you break destructive patterns and develop the "new you." This is a tough one.

Much of your self-concept is validated by feedback you get from others. Take a hard look at your relationships. Which are constructive for your self-concept? Which are really more harmful than good? If you see that some of your relationships with other people are destructive to your self-concept, choose either to end those relationships or to make them more productive and positive for you. Old and established patterns of interaction are hard to change. Nevertheless, to remain in a comfortable relationship that reinforces a poor self-concept is to choose to keep a major obstacle in your own path of growth.

As a probation officer, Bruce often heard people say that any given juvenile in trouble needed only to "find a new peer group" or "stop hanging with the wrong crowd" to solve all that kid's problems. In reality, it's not that simple. Troubled teens generally need to change both their peer group *and* their feelings about themselves. They tend to seek feedback from others that basically agrees with their own self-concept. Peer group relationships powerfully reinforce the present level of self-concept. This happens partly because the group was chosen as a reflection of the self-concept: "I really feel at home with these people."

Changing your relationships may be very difficult due to your tendency to follow old patterns and seek relationships that reinforce your present level of self-esteem. But if you sincerely want to feel better about yourself, you will need to invest in positive relationships—those that help you feel good about being you!

Step 5: Get rid of the negative self-thoughts in your head. We all hear messages playing in our heads. Much of this self-talk may have originated from parents or from teachers or other significant adults: "Don't get too big for your britches…. You're being selfish…. You think you're so smart, don't you?" Such messages are destructive and prevent you from improving your self-concept. They were originally designed to discipline and control you. Unfortunately, they turn out to be neither helpful nor productive.

As adults, we choose whether we want to continue to listen to those messages or not. Recite your own "tapes" out loud and record them or write them down. Think about whether they are appropriate. Analyze these "parental" or "childish" messages from your adult point of view to see if they are rational and healthy at this time in your life. Then rid yourself of those that prevent progress toward feeling better about yourself.

You may need to express these feelings of not being okay in a counseling or therapy session, with lifeline friends, or perhaps in self-introspection. You need to somehow "carry out the emotional garbage of the past" so you can stop letting it control and burden you now. Allow yourself to air, ventilate, express, and verbalize those old messages of inadequacy. Then let go of them—move them out of your path toward improving your self-concept.

Step 6: Write positive notes to yourself and post them up around your house in prominent places, like on a mirror or on the refrigerator.

These notes might be compliments, such as *You have a pretty smile*. The notes could come from the list of twenty positive things that you like about yourself. This may sound like a silly activity, but it worked for Tammy.

Tammy came to a weekend seminar and was like an emotional corpse. She had a great deal of difficulty paying attention, but for some reason, this exercise rang a bell for her. She reported the following week that she had written about a hundred notes to herself, even placing one on the toilet! She became a different person; her self-concept improved almost miraculously. Writing notes to herself appeared to make a big difference. Such a dramatic change is rare, but it shows the potential power of *active effort*.

Step 7: Open yourself up to hearing positive comments from others. People tend to hear only what they want to hear. If you have a low sense of self-worth, you will hear only the negative comments that other people make. When somebody praises you, you deny it, ignore it, or rationalize it by saying, "Oh, they're just saying that. They don't really mean it." Some people protect themselves from hearing anything positive because such comments do not align with their basic self-concept.

The next time someone praises or compliments you, try to let it soak in rather than defending yourself against hearing it. This may be hard for you to do. But it is very important to break your pattern of hearing only the negative. When you allow yourself to hear positive comments, you will feel better about yourself.

Step 8: Make a specific change in your behavior. Determine a part of your personality that you want to change. Maybe you would like to say "hello" to more people, or to be on time to work or school, or to stop putting off small jobs, like making your bed each morning. Decide to change that behavior every day this week. Make the change easy so that you can accomplish it and feel successful. Don't set yourself up for failure by deciding to make an impossibly big change the first week.

Each day that you meet your goal, perhaps you'll want to make a check mark on the calendar to reward yourself a little and track your progress. At the end of the week, you can look back and say, "I accomplished it! I've changed something! I'm different *in this particular area* of my personality." After you've made this first change, pick another one for the following week. If you do this several weeks in a row, you will notice that you can make significant changes that will improve your self-esteem.

Step 9: Give and get more hugs! This step is a fun one. Yet there is great reluctance in our society to touch others to show affection, probably for a variety of reasons, such as fear of rejection, worry about invading another's personal space, and an overemphasis on sex. Many people are not aware of the difference between affectionate touching and sexual touching, so they avoid touching and hugging altogether. Other societies never had or have overcome this hang-up and are more comfortable with affectionate touch.

A warm and meaningful hug from a friend reinforces far more than spoken words can. A hug helps heal emotional wounds and can help improve self-concept rapidly. It frees us, warms us inside, heightens our feelings of self-worth. "I'm worthwhile enough to be hugged!" may be one of the nicest messages we can hear. If you can overcome any fear you have of touching and even ask for a hug when you need one, you will make a big step toward improving your regard for yourself—and you will enjoy the process as well!

Step 10: Work hard at meaningful communication with another person. Some of the most significant growth people experience after divorce is accomplished while communicating with close friends. Ask for and give honest feedback about each other. Say things that you never said to anyone before. Call it as you see it. Such a dialogue provides a mirror for you to see yourself as others see you.

Step 11: Find a licensed professional therapist if you need extra help to enhance your self-concept. Therapy is a safe place to talk about anything you want to. Guidance from a professional therapist may shorten the time it takes to change your self-concept.

If you work diligently at all these steps, you are likely to make significant improvements to your postdivorce self-esteem. All you have to lose is your poor view of yourself. Make this part of the trail an important facet of your growth. This rebuilding block will probably affect more aspects of your overall life than any of the others.

Children Have the Most Fragile Self-Concepts

Be aware that divorce can be very damaging to a child's self-concept also. Suddenly, life has been uprooted. Children feel rejected, lonely, alienated, and perhaps guilty, wondering what they did wrong that contributed to their parents' divorce.

Children's adjustment to divorce may be further complicated by growth stages they are going through, which are themselves threatening to self-concept. As a prime example, there is some evidence that the junior-high years are the most difficult for most children in terms of growth and development. Over the years, we've heard many adults talk about the painful difficulties of their junior-high years. Puberty brings dramatic changes in the body: height, weight, sexual characteristics, body hair, and voice. Suddenly, an adolescent's identity—who they *thought* they were—comes into question. They experience new attitudes and feelings, such as attraction to the opposite sex. Relationships with peers become much more important. This rapid period of change is a real strain upon a youngster's self-concept, even under the best of conditions. So when tweens or young teens who are going through these extreme changes in themselves are simultaneously faced with the stress of their parents' divorce, their self-concepts are more likely to be affected.

So share the steps in this chapter with your children. Doing the exercises together is not only a good way to increase family communication, but as you follow the steps toward improving your self-concept, you can assist them in improving their own as well.

How Are You Doing?

Here is your checklist for this portion of the trail. Once again, allow yourself adequate time to deal with this important area. When you are comfortable with most of these items, you are probably ready to resume the climb. Take care!

☒ *I am willing to work hard to improve my self-concept.*

☒ *I want to improve my self-concept even though I understand that it will change many aspects of my life.*

☒ *I like being the person I am.*

☒ *I feel I am an attractive person.*

☒ *I like my body.*

☒ I feel attractive and sexually desirable.

☒ I feel confident most of the time.

☒ I know and understand myself.

☒ I feel good being a woman/man.

☒ I no longer feel like a failure because my love relationship ended.

☒ I feel capable of building deep and meaningful relationships.

☒ I am the type of person I would like to have for a friend.

☒ I'm attempting to improve my self-concept by following the eleven steps presented in this chapter.

☒ I feel what I have to say is important to others.

☒ I feel I have an identity of my own.

☒ I have hope and faith that I can improve my self-concept.

☒ I am confident that I can solve the problems facing me.

☒ I am confident that I can adjust to this crisis.

☒ I can listen to criticism without becoming angry and defensive.

CHAPTER 12

Transition

"I'm Waking Up and Putting Away My Leftovers"

Early experiences are extremely influential in our lives. The attitudes and feelings you developed in childhood—and in relationships with family, friends, and lovers—are bound to carry over into new relationships. Some of these attitudes and feelings are helpful; others are not. Common "leftovers" that cause problems in adulthood include an unresolved need to rebel against prior constraints (such as parental rules) and power struggles over control. Recognize the valuable leftovers, so you can keep and nourish them; work at changing those that get in your way.

When I was a child, I spoke as a child, I understood as a child, I thought as a child; but when I became a man, I put away childish things.

—Saint Paul (1 Cor. 13:11)

W e are well over halfway up the mountain now, and it's time to make a careful inspection of our packs before we proceed on the climb. Many of us may be carrying extra, unneeded weight. Bob remembers his first backpacking trip, when he carried a quart of water to the campsite at 11,000 feet in the Sierra Nevada Mountains in California. When he arrived at the top, he realized that he had been carrying an extra two pounds of water while climbing through five miles of snow!

Are you lugging an unnecessary load of leftovers from earlier days? You may have extra weight from your past marriage or perhaps from relationships with parents, school friends, or others while you were growing up. It's time now to put away those unneeded burdens. In this chapter, we'll take a look at the most common leftovers, where they come from, and how to deal with them.

We've observed that most divorced people don't recognize the importance and power of these four key leftovers from the past: (1) family of origin issues; (2) influences of childhood experiences; (3) the confusing period of rebellion; and (4) the frustration and hopelessness of the power struggle. These factors often contribute directly to the ending of a primary love relationship.

The four influences overlap and are difficult to separate from one another, but we can divide them roughly this way: Events that happened in your parental family before you were born are *family of origin* influences. Events that happened from the time you were born until you moved away from your parental home are *childhood influences* (these include events happening outside of the home, such as at school, at church, and in society). Your attempt to find an individual identity separate from the expectations of family and society is the period of *rebellion*. The *power struggle* is a combination of all of the unresolved issues from all of these areas.

Family of Origin Influences

Your *family of origin* is the family in which you grew up. Your parents, siblings, grandparents, aunts, and uncles—all were important influences shaping your view of "how a family should be." Most of the ideas you gained during those years were probably healthy; some were not.

Now think about the beginning of your own love relationship. If you could imagine the bride's "significant parent" married to the groom's "significant parent," you would have an idea of what your marriage would be like in later years. (For example, Bruce imagined his father married his ex's grandmother. They never met, but if they had, it would have been disastrous!) There is hope: we can grow beyond our family of origin patterns of interaction. But some of you will be able to see that it's your parents in you and your partner who are divorcing.

Bruce asked people from many different countries, "How many of you would like to have a marriage basically like your parents' marriage?" Less than 5 percent raised their hand. So, if we don't want a marriage like our parents', what kind of marriage do we want?

Some of the family of origin influences are easy to see and understand. We tend to belong to the same political party as our parents, to join the same religious organization, to live in the same community. Some of us rebel, striking out on our own and choosing a completely separate path. Even in rebellion, however, the family of origin is an important element.

There are many other subtle influences from the family. Bruce observed: "My love partner came from a family of powerful females; I came from a family of powerful males. One of our family of origin issues was to make a compromise as to which gender was going to be the boss. (She says I won, and I say she won.)"

Another issue is how you handle money. Again, here's Bruce's experience: "My mother came from a family where the males were very irresponsible in handling money. She learned to be the saver and controller of money. She, of course, lived out her family of origin influences by marrying a man who was, like the men she grew up with, underresponsible in handling money." Many people marry thinking they are escaping family influences only to discover they have perpetuated them.

"That doesn't seem to fit," you may say. "If the father was the dominant and stronger personality, why was the mother the one who controlled the money?" The answer shows up in sociological studies of families, and may have been true in your house as well. The "woman of the house" was often more powerful than it appeared, but *she exercised her power in a subtle and indirect manner.* In other words, Dad appeared to be in charge, but Mom held the purse strings.

It can be confusing—thinking you married the father or mother you didn't have, then ending up playing the role of father or mother to your spouse. Do you recall the explanation for this in our discussion of adaptive behavior patterns in chapter 4? Most of us learned to adapt when we didn't get all of our needs met in the formative childhood years. Often the adaptive behavior was to become a "father" or "mother," which resulted in giving to others what we were hoping to get ourselves.

Skeptical about family of origin influences? Here's an exercise you'll find helpful: Make a list of the ways your most significant parent dealt with various human emotions: anger, guilt, rejection, loneliness, fear, intimacy. Then make a similar list for yourself. When you compare the lists, you'll have a better idea of just how independent you are from the influence of your significant parent. Until we question and grow beyond the influence of our families of origin, we tend to deal with emotions in much the same way as our most significant parents.

Incidentally, when people who've made such a list are asked to identify their "most significant parent," those who are in the process of divorce quite frequently list an adult other than mother or father. When one parent was not there physically or emotionally, many of us found a "pseudoparent" to compensate for the loss.

Those of us who didn't receive enough good parenting tend to make our partners responsible for making it up to us. There is a part in each one of us that wants our love partner to provide the parenting we didn't receive from our mothers and fathers. For some, this part is large; for others, it is small. When this happens in a love relationship, it often contributes to the demise of the relationship. Few love partners are happy to make up for the parenting we didn't receive when we were little.

Family of origin issues are, of course, extremely complex and pervasive in our lives. A full discussion is beyond the scope of this book. Such issues as birth order, scapegoating, boundaries, family triangles, rituals and traditions, secrets, substance abuse, and many others are powerful influences on who we are and how we relate to our love partners. For now, let's agree that we all need to wake up to the important effects of these family of origin leftovers and learn how to deal with them in our future relationships.

Healing the Influences of the Family of Origin

Linda offers one typical example of an unresolved family of origin issue. When she began to realize she married Noah because he was like the parent she had not finished making peace with, it was the beginning of the end of the relationship. This concept can be expressed in one of two ways. Linda might have married someone like her disliked parent because that relationship was comfortable and familiar, even though it was stressful and painful. Or perhaps she did *not* marry someone *like* the parent, but when she began the process of healing that parental relationship, she put Noah on the stage so she could work through the unfinished business. She told him, "You're always telling me what to do, just like my father did." It may not be true, but her old anger at her father for being so domineering made it *seem* to her as if Noah was bossy also.

When one or both partners begin waking up and realize the marriage is much like their parents' marriages, they have a problem. Either they have to accept their parents' marriages (instead of disdaining them), or they have to change their own marriage into what they want it to be. Without one or the other, they'll probably feel their marriage is a failure. (Actually, the *marriage* didn't fail; the process of healing family of origin influences was not successful.)

Childhood Influences

In the first years of life, we adopt many beliefs about ourselves, about the world, and about relationships. We learn how we feel about ourselves and our self-worth. We learn whether the world is safe and whether we can trust the people around us. We learn to feel loved, and when we don't feel loved enough, we learn to adapt. We may develop fears of rejection and abandonment. We learn if we are "okay" or "not okay."

Have you ever tried to compliment a not-okay person, one with low self-esteem? It usually goes like this:

"I like your hair."

"Oh, I just washed it and can't do a thing with it."

"That was a nice thing you just did."

"No, no, not really. Anyone would have done the same thing."

Complimenting such people causes them discomfort because their inner child does not agree. They've adopted, at an early age, a belief that they are "not okay."

At some level in your adult relationships, you will attempt to grow through any part of your growth and development that you didn't complete during your formative years. People who learned low self-worth at an early age want to improve their feelings of self-worth in their marriages. But they prevent learning what they want to learn because they don't believe the partner's positive view of them: "You tell me you like my hair, but you're just saying that to make me feel good."

It takes more than a few compliments to change a person's "inner child" beliefs. If low self-esteem is a central theme of your inner child, we hope you paid special attention to chapter 11. You may want to go back to that point in the trail and do some more work. (And we urge you to carry out the homework assignments.)

Another example of a lasting childhood influence is the emotional bonding that ideally takes place in the first year of an individual's life. Parents who are comfortable being intimate and who are able to continually hold their babies closely and look them in the eyes help their children learn to be intimate. Those who didn't learn early to bond emotionally often are attempting to finish the process with adult love partners. But they may not even be aware of what emotional bonding is and may actually distance partners who attempt to become intimate. They want intimacy, but they "check out"—one way or another—when they begin to experience it.

Healing the Influences of Childhood

There are many examples of attempts to heal negative childhood influences. A man who has remained childlike and underresponsible may resent his partner's parental behavior; he finds another relationship or starts having an affair. But when you look at the situation closely, he found in his marriage another mother figure to serve his need for the mothering he didn't receive as a child. The third-party relationship is not likely the solution for him. The inability to heal the unmet needs of his inner child is where this man needs to focus.

If you'd like to learn more about how family of origin issues and early-childhood experiences influence the adults we become, we strongly recommend Virginia Satir's classic book, *The New Peoplemaking.*

Rebellion: The Rocky Road to Adulthood

One of the most common leftovers we carry from our earlier experiences is the unresolved need to establish ourselves as independent people by rebelling against our parents and their rules for us. If you or your partner carried that particular burden into your love relationship, it may have seriously jeopardized your chances of success.

There is a period of rebellion in each teenager's growth when the not-quite-adult is seeking an individual identity. Although it is a necessary part of young adult development, it causes a tremendous strain in the family relationship. Let's take a look at these key developmental stages we all must grow through on our journey toward independent adulthood, which we've labeled as the "shell stage," the two-component "rebel stage" (external and internal), and the "love stage."

The Shell Stage

This stage occurs when we are young, conforming and trying to please our parents. During these years, children have the same moral and political values as their parents, follow the same societal patterns, and more or less behave in ways expected of them by their parents. The child in the shell stage is basically a reflection of the parents, similar to the egg that is laid by a chicken, with no identity of his or her own.

Vocabulary in the shell stage is full of inhibitions: "What will people think? I must be careful to do what I'm supposed to do. I should follow the rules and regulations of society. I must conform to what's expected of me."

In the teen years (sometimes later), a period of rebellion begins, with the individual breaking out of the shell. This process includes changing behavior patterns, doing what one "should not" do, pushing against the limits, and trying to find out how far one can go. It is a very experimental stage, filled with trying out different kinds of behavior. The little chicken inside is growing, beginning a life of its own, and starting to pick its way out of the shell.

The vocabulary at this point leading up to the rebel stage is "I've got to do it on my own. I don't need your help. If it weren't for you, I would be able to be the person I want to be. Please leave me alone!" The actual rebellion occurs in two ways: externally and internally.

The Rebel Stage: External

The rebellion identity crisis usually begins when the person starts feeling overwhelmed by internal pressure and stress—the point at which the burden of carrying around the "shoulds" from family of origin, childhood, and society becomes too great. Having learned such behaviors as overresponsibility, perfectionism, people pleasing, or the avoidance of feelings, the person is like Atlas carrying the world on his shoulders: tired of the whole situation. The love partner in the external rebellion stage wants to run away and may act like a defiant teenager, searching for an identity separate from the one given by parents and society.

The behavior of people in rebellion is predictable. (Isn't it interesting that nonconforming rebellion is so predictable and conforming?) Here are some of the behaviors typical of external rebellion:

- These people feel unhappy, stressed, smothered, and caged in. They believe their partners are responsible for their unhappiness, and they reflect that by saying things like, "As soon as you change, I will be happy." They project their unhappiness onto others, especially their love partners.

- They like doing all the things they didn't feel comfortable doing before. They start having fun and don't understand why people don't appreciate the things they are doing, because it feels so good to be doing them. Their partners say, "This isn't the same person I married."

- They like being underresponsible after feeling so overresponsible all of their lives. They take less responsible jobs or quit work if possible. One partner of a person in rebellion said, "I have four kids, and I'm married to the oldest one."

- They find people—perhaps just one person—they can talk to outside of the marriage. They tell their partners, "I could never talk to you. But I found this person who understands me and really listens to me." Such people are usually younger and potential love partners. It looks like an affair, but those in external rebellion will usually deny having an affair. Although others may believe it is a sexual relationship, it is quite often a platonic one.

- The vocabulary of external rebellion often goes like this: "I care for you, but I don't love you. I thought I knew what love was, but now I don't know. I'm not sure I ever did love you." ... "I need to be out of this relationship so I can find myself. I need emotional space away from you. I need to find my own world, and I don't want to continue to be sucked into your world. I want to be me.".... "You remind me of my parent, and I don't want to be around anyone who is parental. I can smell a parent a mile away."

If all of this behavior is happening in a love relationship, is it any wonder that the relationship ends? Partners of those in rebellion usually buy into each one of the behaviors above, take it personally, and get bent out of shape emotionally and psychologically. What they need to do instead is sit back and watch the show and become aware of how much change may be taking place in their mates. They need to realize their mates are going through a growth process that has very little to do with them. The rebels are trying to get rid of people and relationships from the past, but they often dump their love partners in the process.

The Rebel Stage: Internal

If people in the process of rebelling gain enough courage and insight to take a real look at themselves, they will move into the phase of internal rebellion. This is when they realize that the battle is actually within themselves, a battle between what they "should" do and what they "want" to do. They realize that they are trying to separate from the expectations of their family of origin and society, that their resistance isn't really against their love partners and other parental figures.

The partner of someone in rebellion often decides to wait the situation out, believing the rebel will "come back to sanity" and that the relationship will then work again. The partner considers the rebel to be a "patient" and doesn't accept any responsibility for finding a remedy for the difficulty.

On the other hand, partners of rebels can become emotionally drained by their mates' trying behaviors, assigning the rebels all the blame. They don't recognize that the love partnership is a two-way system and that they share responsibility for its problems. People who adopt this attitude usually don't have the courage and emotional strength to do the personal work needed to save the relationship.

Rebellion is not an accident. The partner of a person in rebellion is usually "parental." The partner has, at some level—maybe unconsciously—found a mate who needs parenting: "I know what's best for my partner, if he would only listen!" Their need for control makes it difficult for these folks to accept the rebel when he or she seems "out of control."

Instead of just waiting for the storm to blow over, the partner of a person in rebellion also needs to look inward, to take this opportunity to experience as much personal growth as possible.

The Love Stage

Eventually, rebels begin to gain an individual identity. This leads to being able to make life choices based on love instead of on what they think they "should" do. They feel more self-love and love for others, especially their parents.

The vocabulary of the love stage includes words of acceptance and understanding: "My parents did the best they could. They made mistakes, and many times I was angry and upset with them, but they've tried hard and I understand and accept them for who they are."

This period of adulthood is called the "love stage" because the person now has an independent identity and is capable of loving another person as an adult rather than as someone with childish expectations.

In the shell stage, one does what one *should do*; in the rebel stage, one does what one *should not do*; and in the love stage, one does what one *wants to do*. Many times, behavior in the love stage will be similar to behavior in the shell stage, but the motivation behind it is entirely different. Instead of trying to please somebody else, the person is trying to please himself or herself now.

Shell, Rebel, Love: A Summary

Figure 12.1 is a summary of the progression through these three stages. The chart shows some typical characteristics of the stages: vocabulary, behavior, and growth steps one may find helpful. Please recognize that these are highly individual. Although some patterns exist, each individual's experience will be unique.

		SHELL	REBEL	LOVE
Vocabulary		"What should I do?" "I'll do whatever you want." "Take care of me." "You're everything to me." "I only want you to be happy."	"If it weren't for you ..." "I don't need your help!" "Leave me alone!" "I'll do it anyway." "If it feels good, do it!"	"I've considered the alternatives." "I'll take responsibility for my choice." "It may not work, but I want to try." "You and I can both enjoy ourselves."
Behavior		Compliant, obedient. Caregiving [obliged]. Consistent, predictable. Careful, nonrisking. Obligations, not choices.	Self-centered, selfish. Irresponsible, blames others. Erratic, unpredictable, careless. Childish, "plays" with young people. Sports cars, flashy clothes, sex.	Self-enhancing, respects others. Responsible, flexible, open. Willing to risk, learns from mistakes. Makes choices based on facts.
GROWTH STEPS	**Self**	Begin to trust self. Begin to take risks. Begin to communicate openly. Begin to accept responsibility. Begin to try new behavior.	Try positive growth activities: classes, recreation, exercise, friendships, hobbies, community. Enter therapy (perhaps with spouse). Talk to spouse, friend, therapist. Maintain moral, ethical balance.	Work at self-awareness. Work at self-acceptance. Work at open, honest communication. Develop close, nonromantic friends. Express anger assertively. Maintain balance of independence and interdependence in close relationships.
	Partner	Encourage partner's growth. Lessen dependence on partner. Cooperate in therapy if needed. Prepare for turbulence when "rebellion" starts.	Maintain stability, patience. Allow partner to grow up. Be available to talk with partner. Encourage joint therapy. Recognize rebellion is against shell, not you!	

Figure 12.1. Becoming an Adult in Three Not-So-Easy Stages

Over the years in the Fisher seminars, we've witnessed many examples of this three-stage phenomenon. Eloise, for example, came to class one night very angry because her ex, Larry, was going through the rebel stage and causing her a lot of unhappiness. Larry had been a school principal when he was in the shell stage; but because he was looking for less administrative responsibility, he'd returned to full-time teaching. He developed a relationship with a woman involving "a lot of communication," helping him to find out "who he was." Larry, of course, was very excited about this new relationship. After his young son came to visit, Larry sent him home with a suitcase full of clothes and a note explaining to Eloise how great his new relationship was. Needless to say, this made her extremely angry. As it happened, we were discussing the rebel stage that week in the seminar. Eloise began to understand what was happening with Larry and his attempt to grow up and leave behind some of his old leftovers. She was able to let go of some of her anger as she gained an understanding of what was happening.

Gretchen became very excited as the concept was explained in class. Her husband had been a college professor and had proceeded to run off with one of his students while he was in the rebel stage. The whole thing seemed insane to her, until she heard the shell/rebel/love theory of growth and development. When she recognized that Charles was trying to get free from past expectations and establish his own identity, Gretchen was able to see that there was some sanity in what had appeared to be insanity. (It didn't save the marriage, but at least she felt she understood what had happened.)

Bill told the group that his marriage had suffered a crisis three years earlier while his wife was going through the rebel stage. When he and Charlotte went for marriage counseling, the therapist put a damper on the rebel stage and pushed Charlotte to "behave as she should"—in effect telling her to remain in the shell stage. Bill said he felt this was a mistake at the time. The marriage lasted another three years until, suddenly, Charlotte's growth pressures and need to rebel surfaced again, and she became "completely irresponsible," leaving the marriage and the home without even taking any clothes. Bill did not hear from Charlotte for three weeks. Looking back on those painful events, Bill observed that maybe people need to be concerned about what stage of growth and development their *therapists* are in!

Many people ask, if so many marriages end when one person is going through the rebel stage, is there any way to have the relationship last when a person is going through the rebel stage? The rebel who can focus inward and realize the internal interaction going on between him or herself and the parental figures of the past may be able to deal directly with the *shoulds*, the *oughts*, and the expectations. To talk about one's rebellion rather than acting it out will be much less destructive to those near and dear in the present.

It is possible for a person to find the emotional space *within* a marriage to rebel, perhaps by becoming involved in therapy, college classes, community service, recreational or sports programs, or other creative activities. The rebel needs opportunities to experiment with behavior, to try new styles of relating, and to interact with people other than the spouse. If the couple can understand directly what is happening—that the rebel is working on an internal conflict that has little to do with the spouse—it can free the work of growth and development to be done within the person, rather than strain the love relationship.

Rebelling love partners need to accept that their process of rebellion is an internal one and not the responsibility of other people. Their partners need to work on healing their own "inner child," because their parenting and controlling behavior patterns result from unmet needs.

The Stormy Seas of the Power Struggle

Many couples find themselves arguing over the correct way to squeeze the toothpaste tube and which way to unroll the toilet paper. And the issues they argue over never become resolved, even if they think they do. Each person feels he or she has no power or control in the relationship. Both feel hopeless, helpless, and tired of fighting. The war may be a hot war, with a lot of shouting, anger, and verbal abuse. Or it may be a cold war, with the silent treatment, walking out, pouting, and other such passive ways of attempting to gain control and power.

The two people involved have stopped talking about or sharing feelings. Instead, they send "you-messages" to each other. They have given up on finding any intimacy other than the pseudointimacy they feel while fighting. Neither wants to lose, so both use any method they can to win the war.

The power struggle is like a pot of stew boiling over on the stove. The ingredients in the stew are all of the unresolved issues within each partner that are projected out into the relationship. The heat under the stew is the belief that someone else is responsible for one's happiness or unhappiness. The two people married with the belief that they would live happily ever after. It worked fine as long as the honeymoon lasted and they were happy. But when the honeymoon was over and they sometimes were less than happy, the person who was responsible for their happiness is now responsible for their unhappiness. They gave away their power when they began to believe someone else was responsible for their happiness or unhappiness.

Calming the Rough Seas of the Power Struggle

The power struggle changes into growing pains when each person takes ownership for the unresolved problems within them. These problems may involve the shell/rebel/love stages discussed above, but the unresolved issues can come from anywhere in their lives or their personality. It is truly an internal power struggle projected out upon the relationship. The problems each person is unable to face and overcome become projected out into the relationship, and the pot keeps boiling over.

The power struggle is diminished when:

- Each person learns to talk about feelings.

- Each person starts using I-messages instead of you-messages.

- Each person takes ownership of unresolved problems.

- Each person looks at the other person as a relationship teacher.

- Each person works at learning more about herself or himself, instead of projecting the hurt and blame upon the other person.

Leaving Leftovers Behind

As with any life transition, this stage of the climb is very uneven and quite difficult. Waking up and understanding why your past relationship died is usually not an easy process. It may even be quite painful: it is much easier for me to see the splinter in your eye than it is to see the log in mine.

When Bruce was a juvenile probation officer, he typically referred one family a week for family counseling. When family members went to counseling to discover what they could learn and change about *themselves*, the counseling was usually helpful and successful. But when each person in the family went to counseling believing *others* in the family needed to change, counseling was usually unsuccessful.

Next time you see a person on the trail acting like a teenager, rebelling and always angry at authority figures, you can be understanding. You'll know that the rebel is trying to grow up emotionally, to gain an independent identity, and to become free from past expectations and controls. Even though you may want to become parental and tell the rebel how to behave, maybe you'll back off, remain adult yourself, and say, "I think that's probably the best thing for where he or she is right now." Indeed, perhaps you are still in the shell stage yourself, needing to start some rebellion of your own to improve your sense of self-worth and to find a better identity.

Do you notice that you are really making progress in the climb up the mountain? The fact that you are able to face and deal with leftovers is an indication that you are getting a much broader perspective of life and yourself. You probably could not have done much about carrying out the leftovers when you were at the bottom of the mountain trying to survive emotionally.

Children and Transition

Most children will have some difficulty with their parents' leftovers: family of origin issues, childhood experiences, rebellion, and power struggles. A child's view of the actions of others is based on only a few years of life and a limited repertoire of experience.

A very strong influence on children during this process is the feeling of internal pain. Growing children will interact with other significant adults as they learned to do with their parents, until some healing learning takes place. (Children are, after all, going through their own family of origin and childhood experiences.) If a new stepparent comes into the picture, for example, the child will tend to have the same problems with that stepparent that he or she had with his or her natural parent. This will change only when the child learns—perhaps with loving support from understanding adults—how to deal effectively with those old emotions (without destructive adaptive behaviors) and how to develop new ways of relating to adults.

Homework to Ease Your Transition

- Describe what a relationship between your ex-partner's most significant parent and your most significant parent would be like. Was your past relationship anything like that imaginary relationship?

- How did your family of origin influences affect the ending of your love relationship?

- Make a list of the ways your family of origin reacted to anger, love, fear, guilt, rejection, intimacy, and conflict. Make a list of the ways you react to these same emotions and situations.

- Do you perceive your former love partner to be like one of your parents? Did your marriage begin to resemble your parents' marriage? Do you want a marriage that is different from your parents' marriage? How would you go about creating such a marriage?

- Do you believe you really bonded emotionally with your parents in your childhood? Are you comfortable being intimate with another person? Did you develop good feelings of self-worth in your childhood? Did you have a good relationship with both of your parents? Is your relationship with your love partner anything like the relationship with one or both of your parents?

- This chapter identified the stages of rebellion as the shell stage, the rebel stage (external and internal), and the love stage. In which of these stages are your parents? Your former love partner? You?

- Did the process of rebellion have anything to do with your love relationship ending?

- Were you and your partner in a power struggle when you ended the relationship? Did you believe that when you married, you would live happily ever after? Do you believe someone else is responsible for your happiness or unhappiness? Have you identified any of the unresolved issues within you that contributed to you and your partner having a power struggle? For example, did you start standing up to your husband as you wished you had stood up to your father? Did you start being responsible for yourself instead of letting your partner smother (mother) you?

- What did you learn in this chapter that you need to work on before you can create a healthy relationship in the future?

How Are You Doing?

Once you make sure you are ready by responding to the checklist below, go on to the next part of the journey. After a discussion of the importance of open and honest communication, we will take a look at that elusive but ever-present phenomenon, love.

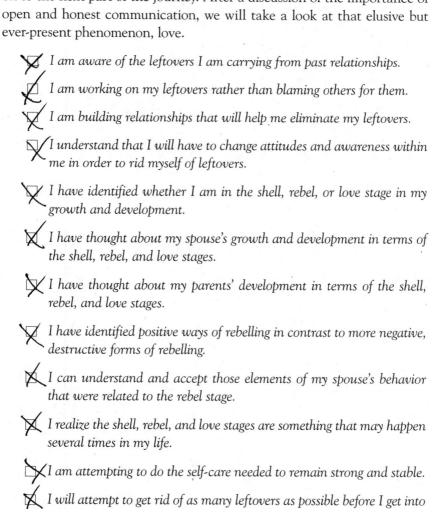

☒ *I am aware of the leftovers I am carrying from past relationships.*

☒ *I am working on my leftovers rather than blaming others for them.*

☒ *I am building relationships that will help me eliminate my leftovers.*

☒ *I understand that I will have to change attitudes and awareness within me in order to rid myself of leftovers.*

☒ *I have identified whether I am in the shell, rebel, or love stage in my growth and development.*

☒ *I have thought about my spouse's growth and development in terms of the shell, rebel, and love stages.*

☒ *I have thought about my parents' development in terms of the shell, rebel, and love stages.*

☒ *I have identified positive ways of rebelling in contrast to more negative, destructive forms of rebelling.*

☒ *I can understand and accept those elements of my spouse's behavior that were related to the rebel stage.*

☒ *I realize the shell, rebel, and love stages are something that may happen several times in my life.*

☒ *I am attempting to do the self-care needed to remain strong and stable.*

☒ *I will attempt to get rid of as many leftovers as possible before I get into another long-term, committed love relationship.*

CHAPTER 13

Openness

"I've Been Hiding Behind a Mask"

A mask is a false face—a feeling projected to others that's different from what you're really feeling. Some masks are appropriate; others are inappropriate. Masks may protect you from emotional pain you feel or fear, but wearing masks takes a great deal of emotional energy. Masks distance you emotionally from others, keeping you from building intimate relationships. When you remove your mask appropriately, you find intimacy, rather than emotional pain.

After my divorce, looking for ways to meet new people, I took a small part in a little theater production. One night at rehearsal, I suddenly realized that's what I'd been doing in my marriage: reciting lines. I wasn't myself; I was a character in a romantic comedy-tragedy.

—Scott

At this point in our climb, most of us have learned a lot about ourselves and our former love relationships. You probably have a good idea of what happened, and we hope you're starting to think about how you'll avoid similar mistakes in the future.

One key element in successful love relationships is *openness*. Were you really honest with your partner? Are you really even honest with yourself? Or do you often hide behind an "everything is okay" mask?

Masks and Openness

All of us wear masks at times. Sometimes you just don't want others to know what you're feeling, and a "mask" is a convenient way to hide what's going on inside—a protective shield. So the mask projects a different attitude or feeling on the surface, protecting you from the pain underneath. The pain may be fear of rejection, fear of somebody not liking you, fear of feeling inadequate, or maybe just a feeling that nobody really cares.

Young children don't wear masks as adults do—that's one of the reasons it's enjoyable and delightful to be with them. We develop our masks as we mature and become "socialized." It's not a conscious effort to deceive; the idea is simply that the masks will help us to interact with people more effectively.

However, some masks are not productive in helping us to connect with others. Instead, they keep us at a safe emotional distance from others. Openness, after all, can be pretty scary at times.

What Color Is Your Mask?

What are some examples of the masks we're talking about?

There are some people who, as you become emotionally close to them, immediately start making jokes and cracking humor—the *humor mask*.

A similar mask is the *Barbie-doll face*. Whenever you start getting real with such a person and start talking about something important, you immediately see the happy, smiling, unchanging face that looks like a Barbie doll.

Many people going through divorce put on the *strength* mask. They project an image that says, "I'm so strong"—in control at all times and never showing any weakness—but underneath lies the real turmoil of confusion and helplessness.

Like nearly all divorced people, Connie had been close to the fire of emotional intimacy. When she was married to Chris, he made her feel really warm. Then she was burned by the fire, and she grew afraid to become emotionally close to warmth from another person again. Now she distances other people emotionally in all kinds of sophisticated ways. Her "don't mess with me" *angry* mask has a reputation for miles around; it's very effective in keeping others at arm's length.

Who's Masking What from Whom?

Some masks are not very productive. In wearing them, we fight against the very things we long for: closeness, intimacy, a feeling of being safe with another person. But because we've been hurt, we're also afraid of that same intimacy and closeness.

Marian projected a mask and thought she was fooling people; that they didn't know what she was really feeling. She learned, however, that not only did others see through the mask, they saw her more clearly than she saw herself. That's one of the strange things about masks: we often fool ourselves more than we fool other people. The mask Marian thought nobody could see through allowed others to know—better than she knew herself—the pain she was feeling underneath.

A mask may keep you from getting to know yourself, rather than keeping somebody else from getting to know you. When you wear one, you are actually denying yourself your own hurt. It's kind of like the ostrich: with his head in the sand, he thinks no one can see him just because he can't see them.

Masks Can Be a Burden

Sometimes we invest a great deal of emotional energy in wearing our masks.

You're carrying around a great big burden all the time by trying to act the way you think you "should" act instead of just being yourself. The emotional energy that is put into carrying a mask is sometimes almost overwhelming. You spend more energy carrying the mask than you do learning about yourself, achieving personal growth, or doing anything more productive.

Think about how lonely it is behind a really big, thick mask. A person is more or less living in his or her own world, and there is no one else who really knows and understands that person deep underneath the big mask. Often the more lonely you feel, the more of a mask you create around that loneliness. There seems to be a direct connection between the amount of loneliness you feel and the thickness of the mask you're wearing.

Anybody who has been carrying around a really heavy mask and then takes it off—in counseling or in sharing and talking with a friend—discovers a great feeling of freedom after unloading the burden. It leaves a lot more energy to do other things in life.

Jeff started wearing a mask as a child. He learned early that he had to exhibit certain "acceptable" behaviors in order to get the love or the strokes or the attention that he needed. He learned to take care of other people when he really wanted to be taken care of himself. He learned to excel in school, even though he really didn't care whether he got A's or not. He learned to keep all his feelings inside rather than open up and share himself with others. Jeff grew up with the idea that love was not related to being himself. It came to him when he wore his "good boy" mask. He sure learned well not to value openness.

We develop most masks because we have not felt loved unconditionally just for being ourselves.

"Let's Do Lunch: My Mask Will Call Your Mask"

Imagine somebody trying to kiss you when you have a mask on. That's a good image for how hard it is to get close to another person when either of you is wearing a mask. It gives an idea of what a mask does for the communication between you and another person. Think of all the indirect and devious messages that are sent because of our masks. So much for openness!

There are appropriate masks and inappropriate masks, of course. An appropriate mask is one that you wear at work while dealing with other people. You project the feeling of efficiency, of competence, of "I'm here to serve you"—an evenness and a calmness that makes your work with other people more effective. But when you get off work and go home to be with a friend or a loved one, the same mask becomes inappropriate. It emotionally distances you from your partner, prevents straight communication, kills openness, and doesn't allow either of you to be yourselves. That could be appropriate when you need time just for yourself, but it's tough on intimacy!

A Matter of Choice

A mask that *you choose* to wear is probably an appropriate mask, but the mask that *chooses you* is probably inappropriate. It chooses you because you are not free to expose the feelings that are underneath. And in that sense, the mask controls you. Many times, you are not aware that you're wearing a mask that controls you.

Are You Ready to Take Off Your Mask?

How does one decide to take off a mask? At some time during the divorce process, it becomes appropriate to take off some of the masks you've been wearing—to try openness instead. Is that time now?

What would happen if you took your mask off? Why not try it with some safe friends? Take off a mask and see how many times you find acceptance from those friends rather than the rejection you expected. See how many times you become closer to somebody rather than being hurt. See how many times you feel freer than you felt before.

Here's an example of how to take off a mask with a friend you can trust. You might say something such as this: "You know, there have been times when I've not been very honest with you. When you come close to me, I become a joker. The 'joker mask' is a defense I use to protect myself from getting hurt. When I'm afraid or feel that I'm about to get hurt, I start making jokes. When I make jokes at inappropriate times, it keeps me from knowing you and you from knowing me. I want you to know about my mask. When I tell you about it, it destroys some of the power of the mask. I'm trying to take off the mask a bit by sharing this with you." (Later in this chapter, we'll give you an exercise in "lifting the mask.")

Some friends may hurt you when you take the mask off. Those people are not able to handle the feelings you've been covering up with the mask. But if you had your choice, which would you choose? To continue to wear the mask and not get to know that person? Or to take off the mask, be open, and risk being hurt or rejected? If you are at a point emotionally where you can think ahead to a possible love relationship in the future, what kind of a relationship would you like to have? One that would include openness, intimacy, and trust? Or one in which both of you wear masks of one kind or another? You *do* have the choice!

If you are wearing a mask to cover up pain, then part of removing the mask must be to deal with that pain. As counselors, we prefer to help our clients try to get in touch with the pain behind the mask and to express and verbalize it.

When Sharon was going through a divorce, she was trying to be the strong person, always in control. Her therapist encouraged her to talk about the pain and confusion she was feeling underneath, and she did, hesitantly. She learned that maybe it is appropriate to be confused when going through a confusing situation and that taking down the mask and dealing with that confusion is productive. It took her several sessions in therapy to fully acknowledge her pain and to build some constructive coping strategies that allowed her to keep the mask off.

Many who have been hurt at the end of a love relationship put on more masks than they were wearing before. Part of climbing this mountain we've been traveling is learning to take off some of the masks you may have put on to cover the pain of ending your love relationship.

Your Self Behind the Mask

We all have a distinct self inside us—not yourself, but your *self*—the real person deep down inside. We all develop our personalities—the face we show to the rest of the world—around this essence of self. We communicate outward from that self down inside, through the personality, to the people around us. Ideally, the communication is two-way, from one person's self to another's.

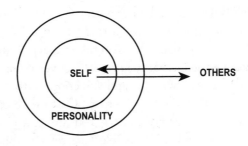

When you develop a thick shell or facade to "protect" your inner self, your communication is blocked by that mask. Instead of messages going from self to other back to self, they go from mask to other back to mask. (Of course, the other person may be wearing a mask also!)

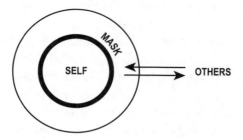

In this situation, your self is not really involved in the communication. If you keep the mask on, your inner self becomes starved and never sees the sunshine and never finds anything that will help it grow. Your inner self becomes smaller—or at least less influential—until it is so small that you may not even be able to find your own identity. Meanwhile, the shell around you grows thicker and harder all the time.

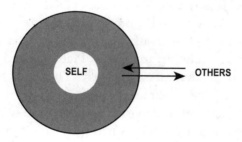

There's another variation on this theme: you may mask certain areas of your personality but not others. In the diagram below, there are barriers to parts of your personality that prevent communication through them, but there are other parts of your personality through which you do communicate to other people.

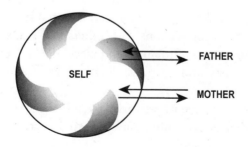

To take another example from Bruce's probation officer days, he found some juveniles very easy to work with, while others were very defensive around him. After a while, he noticed a pattern: A juvenile who was easy to work with usually had a good relationship with his father. He was able to communicate well with his probation officer, who was somewhat of a father figure. But a young man who felt uncomfortable relating to Bruce probably also was uncomfortable with his father. He had developed a powerful protective mask that prevented communication between his inner self and adult males in authority. This same juvenile might find it easier to work with a female probation officer, particularly if he had learned to relate well with his mother.

Who Are You?

Do you know yourself? Are you pretty sure of your own identity? Many people use masks because they lack a sense of identity. They can't be open because they don't know who they are or what they're really feeling. They start wearing masks, and the masks begin to get thicker and thicker and the self inside gets even harder to identify. Pretty soon, these people have lost touch with their identities completely. They lack the support and encouragement needed for their identities to grow.

If you want to take off your masks, then you need to get as many feelings as possible out into the open. When you share things about yourself that you have not shared before, you are actually taking down a mask. And when you ask for feedback from other people, you often find out things about yourself that you did not know before, and this, too, takes down one of the masks that you have used to keep from knowing your self.

To get rid of some of the inappropriate and unproductive masks that you are carrying around, begin to open yourself up as much as possible to other people. Develop some relationships with other people that have a great deal of open, *meaningful* communication (not just talking about yourself endlessly). These connections with others will help you take off the masks, allow your inner self to grow, and place all your relationships on a foundation of honesty and openness—with yourself and with those you care about.

There are many people whose little boy or little girl inside is extremely frightened and fearful of coming out. If you're experiencing that kind of fear, you'll find it helpful to enter into a professional counseling relationship. Counseling is a safe place to let your scared little boy or girl out—to get open with yourself.

Homework to Help You Move from Masks to Openness

- Sit down and make a list of all of the masks you wear. Examine these masks and determine which are appropriate and which are inappropriate. Identify the masks that you would like to take off because they are not serving you well.

- Focus deep inside yourself and try to get in touch with your feelings. See if you can locate the fear or pain underneath the masks you wear. Why is it important to protect yourself from intimacy with others? The masks are probably hiding fear of some sort. Look at those fears and see if they are rational or if they are perhaps fears you developed from interacting with other people in unproductive ways.

- Find a friend or a group of friends with whom you feel safe—friends you can trust. Describe this exercise to them and let them know that you are going to try to share some of your masks with them. Explain that by revealing your mask, it will not have the same power over you as it did before. Share with these friends some of the fears that have kept you from being open and honest and intimate with others. Ask the other people to do the same thing with you. Open, meaningful communication between you and your friends will help you get free from the masks you've been carrying around and will help you recover some of the emotional energy they've required.

The Masks of Children

How open and honest are you with your children? Have you shared the important things happening in your relationship that directly affect them? How did you tell your children when you were ready to separate from your partner? How consistent have you been with them? Can they depend upon you to do what you say you will? In short, can they trust you?

In one workshop we conducted for children of divorce, a thirteen-year-old girl was asked what kind of an animal she felt like. "That's easy," she responded. "When I'm with my dad, I am one person. When I'm with my mom, I'm another person. I try to please both of them so they won't be upset. So I'm a chameleon."

It is so hard for us to really listen to our children when we are caught up in our own pain. We can easily be hurt and upset by their comments. No wonder they walk around on thin ice, being careful what they say and do. They often feel so responsible for us, so sympathetic with us, so afraid they will upset us even more.

Children should be encouraged to speak their truth and their thoughts and feelings, even when it's hard for us to hear. If you can't listen without judgment or criticism or getting upset, help them find another person—someone more detached and more objective—they can talk to.

Their whole world has been shattered. They wonder what will happen next. When they have open and honest communication with their parents—or at least with one understanding adult—they begin to feel a part of the solution instead of part of the blame.

How Are You Doing?

Before you go on to the next portion of the climb, ask yourself if you can agree with the following self-evaluation items:

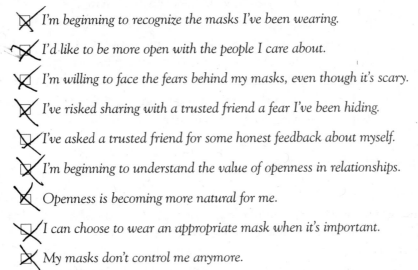

☒ *I'm beginning to recognize the masks I've been wearing.*

☒ *I'd like to be more open with the people I care about.*

☒ *I'm willing to face the fears behind my masks, even though it's scary.*

☒ *I've risked sharing with a trusted friend a fear I've been hiding.*

☒ *I've asked a trusted friend for some honest feedback about myself.*

☒ *I'm beginning to understand the value of openness in relationships.*

☒ *Openness is becoming more natural for me.*

☒ *I can choose to wear an appropriate mask when it's important.*

☒ *My masks don't control me anymore.*

CHAPTER 14

Love

"Could Somebody Really Care for Me?"

Many people need to relearn how to love, in order to love more maturely. Your capacity to love others is closely related to your capacity to love yourself. And learning to love yourself is not selfish and conceited. In fact, it is the most mentally healthy thing you can do. There are a number of specific steps you can take to increase your self-love.

Love is like a bouquet of roses: you don't remember the work to get them; you only remember the love in her eyes when she received them.

Love is like sitting with my back to the fireplace. I can feel the warmth without ever seeing the fire.

Love is the greatest gift you can receive. But you have to give it to yourself.

—Ed

As we make our way up the mountain, we observe graffiti on the rocks, written by poets commenting about love. Most of what we learn about love is from the poets. Who had any homework in school concerning the nature of love? Would you take time right now to do some "homework?" In the space below, write your definition of what love is. (We are talking about love between two people in a romantic relationship, not about parental love, spiritual love, or love for humankind.)

Love is:

We've asked thousands of people to complete this exercise, and what we discovered is that although it's a difficult assignment for anyone, it's particularly difficult for divorced people. A typical comment is, "I thought I knew what love is, but I guess I don't." Many people feel inadequate defining love. But love is like a diamond, with a multitude of facets. You can view it from many different directions, and there is no right or wrong way to define it. There is only the way you feel about love.

In our society, many people have stereotyped love to be something you do for somebody or to somebody. Very few people have learned that love is something that should be *centered within you* and that the basis for loving others is the love you have for yourself. Most of us recognize the biblical injunction to "Love thy neighbor as thyself." But what if you don't love yourself?

Here is a somewhat cynical definition upon which many relationships are based: "Love is the warm feeling that you get toward somebody who meets your neurotic needs." This is a definition of neediness rather than love. Because we are not whole and complete people, but have emotional deficiencies, we try to fill those emotional deficiencies by "loving" another person. What we lack in ourselves we hope to find in the other person. In other words, many of us are "half people" trying to love someone in order to become whole. Love coming from a whole person is more mature and more likely to be lasting.

Falling in Love with Love

Perhaps you have heard the expression "warm fuzzies with a fishhook in them." A "warm fuzzy" is a nice gesture that you give somebody, such as saying "I love you." Unfortunately, many of us are still struggling to fulfill *ourselves*. If your own life bucket is nearly empty when you say "I love you" to another person, it probably means, "Please love me." The other person finds the warm fuzzy, swallows it, and is hooked. Saying "I love you" from an empty bucket tends to be manipulative, while love from a full bucket allows others to be themselves and to be free.

Another problem with love in our society is that falling in love is the most acceptable reason for getting married. However, "falling in love" may have more to do with loneliness than with warmth toward the other person. Falling in love to overcome loneliness is not actually love. Rather, it is a feeling of warmth that comes from breaking down the barriers that have kept us from being intimate with other people.

Sometimes one does not love the other person, but instead loves the idealized image of that person. When the difference is realized, one becomes disillusioned, falls out of love, and the relationship is dissolved. If a couple can grow past the stage of loving their idealized images of each other, there is a possibility that they will be able to love in a more mature manner. For some, this growth will occur in the love relationship, and their love for each other will mature. For others, maturity comes only after dissolution of an immature relationship.

We see many people loving with an immature love: love means doing something to somebody or for somebody; love means taking care of someone; love means achieving; love means always being in control; love means "never having to say you're sorry"; love means always being strong; love means being nice.

Shirley believed that always being nice equated to love, so she was trying to improve an unhealthy love relationship with niceness. Ken asked her why this didn't seem to be working for her. Shirley replied, "I guess I just wasn't nice enough."

Unconditional Love: "Warts and All"

Many (most?) of us did not receive enough *unconditional* love while growing up—love given by parents or others just because we were, not because we earned it by being "good." We thus adopted *immature* forms of love toward others because we were not loved unconditionally. That's a tough history to overcome. Nevertheless, we can come to realize that mature love equals loving yourself for being who you are and, likewise, loving others for who they are. When we can feel such unconditional no-matter-how-you-act love, we have learned *mature* love. Mature love allows you to be fully yourself with your loved one.

For many people, it is difficult to give up immature forms of love. That is the way they have always received their strokes, attention, and good feelings. Eventually, though, they recognize that they have to keep striving harder and harder to earn the love they are seeking. It is like settling for second best, taking whatever strokes we can, rather than going all the way to get really good strokes by learning to love ourselves.

The need to be loved unconditionally is not met very often. To children, parental love can be seen as unconditional. After all, most parents are able to provide the basics of food, clothing, shelter, care, and physical affection. The child's limited awareness makes this seem like unconditional love. The child has no question that this love is infinite and omnipotent.

However, with age, maturity, and awareness, one recognizes that any human being may at any point stop loving another for any reason. Or the love may be ended by death. For adults, it is difficult emotionally to accept *unconditional* love.

Perhaps you can attack the problem from another direction: by learning to love yourself unconditionally. Sound like "pull yourself up by your bootstraps"? Actually, it is simply an acceptance of yourself for who you are: a unique individual, with no one else like you. You can begin to feel that you are an okay person and begin to feel love for yourself.

It is difficult to love yourself if you were not loved as a child. For many people, belief in a supreme being or higher power who offers the unconditional love they have difficulty giving themselves can bring great benefits. Feeling loved for what you are—not for what you do to or for somebody—can give you the potential to love others in the same way.

The widespread problem of mental illness in our society gives us yet another perspective on love. One way of looking at mental disorders is that they are all ways of compensating for lack of unconditional love. If we could peel all of the psychological diagnoses down to the heart and core, we would find that many emotional problems stem from lack of loving and being loved.

We tend to teach our children the same concept of love that we learned ourselves. Thus, if you have developed an immature form of love, your children may tend to develop an immature form of love also. If you want to teach your children to love in a mature way and to make them feel loved unconditionally, you will have to learn to love yourself! Then you can develop the capacity to love your children so that they feel loved unconditionally.

We are emphasizing unconditional love so strongly because it is such a vital quality for human growth. To know that you are valuable enough—just because you are you—to be loved regardless of how you act, that's the greatest gift you can give yourself and your children.

(Please understand that we are not advocating irresponsible or antisocial behavior; rather, we are acknowledging our universal humanness and imperfection, and urging you to learn to accept yourself fully, "warts and all.")

As You Love Yourself

Look at the definition of "love" that you wrote at the beginning of this chapter. Most people include in their definition something that makes the love other-centered—centered in the other person rather than within themselves. Many people write that love consists of caring and giving and making that other person happy. Very few people include in their definition of love a mature idea of self-love.

Let's examine that. If the center of your love lies in your partner and the relationship dissolves, the center is suddenly removed; as we considered earlier, this makes divorce even more painful. What might it be like if you had become a whole person and learned to love yourself? If divorce came, there would still be pain and trauma. But it would not be so devastating; you would still be a whole person.

Divorce is especially traumatic for those who have not centered their love within themselves and learned to love themselves. They end up feeling unlovable or that they are incapable of loving another person. Many spend a great deal of time and energy trying to prove to themselves that they are lovable. They may search for another love relationship immediately, because that helps to heal the wound. They may become sexually promiscuous, developing all kinds of relationships with anybody who comes along. Many of these people have confused sex and love, feeling that if they go out and find sex, with it will come the love they have been missing and needing. It sometimes seems it would be more appropriate for them to say "I sex you" rather than "I love you"!

As we discussed in previous chapters (particularly in chapters 2 and 6), it is wiser to go easy on love relationships during this difficult time. Invest in friendships instead until you have made good progress learning to love yourself. (More on this in chapter 16 also.)

So many people have never really learned to love and to be loved. Sometimes it seems easier to love others and not allow yourself to be loved. By "wanting to love another person," you may really be hiding your own need to be loved.

How Warm Is Your Love?

Bruce recalled something that happened when he was working through his own divorce process:

> I was taking part in a meditation exercise. We sat with our eyes closed and meditated to bring a flow of energy through the different levels of our bodies until it reached the tops of our heads. I was able to follow this meditation and feel a warm flow of energy within me, gradually rising higher in my body. When the guided fantasy had reached the level of our chests, the leader said, 'Many of you at this point will be feeling that the flow of energy is leaking out the front of your chests. If you are feeling such a leak, then imagine a cover over the front of your chest so that the warm flow of energy will not leak out.' She was describing exactly the way I felt! I was amazed!
>
> After the guided fantasy was over, I asked, 'How did you know how I was feeling when I was sitting there with my eyes closed, not talking?' She replied that many people have the feeling that the flow of energy is leaking out the front of their chests. She related it to the belief that love is doing something to somebody or for somebody, that it is other centered rather than centered within ourselves. Thus the flow of energy leaks out toward others. We emotionally drain ourselves by putting the love into others, rather than filling our own bucket of life.
>
> I thought about this a great deal and decided that my goal was to learn to love myself in a more adequate manner. I decided that

I would like to have my love be a warm glow, burning within me, warming me and the people with whom I came in contact. My friends would be warm without having to prove that they were lovable. They simply would feel warm by being close to my fire.

Since a special, committed love relationship involves being very close, that special person gets an extra flow of warmth from my fire.

How about you? Do you have a fire going within you? Or has your fire gone out? It is important for us to care for the fire within us and make sure that we have a glow that warms us and also allows the people around us to be warm.

Styles of Loving

Our lives express our definition of love. If we believe that love is translated as making money, then that is how we spend our time. We act out our definition of love in our behavior. How have you been acting out your definition of love? What has been the important priority in your life? Are you satisfied with the definition of love you show by your behavior, or do you want to change? Think about it.

An interesting paradox exists about the way we love others. While each of us has a unique style of loving, each person tends to believe that his or her style is *the only way there is* of loving! It is difficult for us to see that there are styles other than our own.

When you enter into a love relationship, it's important to be aware of your own style and that of the other person. Perhaps by examining some of these styles, we can better understand ourselves and others. We're impressed with the work of University of Toronto sociologist John Alan Lee, who has researched the subject rather thoroughly and identified nine "types of love." We've simplified his list a bit to offer the following six types for your thoughtful consideration:

1. The *romantic* style of loving has a lot of warmth, feeling, and emotion. It is the "electricity" type of love, sending all kinds of tingly feelings through your body when you see the beloved person (there actually are physiological changes in the body, such as increase in heart rate and body temperature). This tends to be an idealistic type of love, leading you to search for and find the "one

and only" person for whom you can feel it. Many popular songs refer to this style of love. The romantic lover tends to love deeply and to need a sexual relationship along with romantic love. Withholding sex from a romantic lover is sometimes compared to withholding food from a baby. It is an important part of this style of loving. Because it is so loaded with feeling and emotion, romantic love may not be as stable as some of the other styles of loving.

2. *Friendship* love is not as loaded with emotion and feeling. The relationship starts with a liking for each other, and then the liking "just sort of grows" into something more, which might be called "love." It is cooler, lacking the passion of romantic love. Sex is not as important to the friendship lover, often developing long after the relationship has started. This is one of the most stable styles of loving, and it is not unusual for people who get into this style of loving to remain good friends even if they divorce. Their love was based upon mutual respect and friendship rather than strong emotional feelings.

3. *Game-playing* love regards the love relationship as a game with certain rules to follow. Game players are not as interested in intimacy as romantic lovers are. In fact, they may carry on several love relationships simultaneously in order to *avoid* closeness and intimacy. Game-playing love is represented by that old song lyric, "When you can't be with the one you love, honey, love the one you're with." Game-playing lovers tend to make up their own special rules, and their sexual relationships will follow whatever rules are most convenient.

4. There is a *needy* style of loving that tends to be full of possessiveness and dependency. This style of loving is very emotional, and the need to be loved makes it very unstable. The people involved tend to have difficulty maintaining the relationship; they feel a lot of jealousy, possessiveness, and insecurity. Many people who have been through divorce adopt this style of loving because it reflects the neediness resulting from the divorce pain. It's especially typical of the first relationship after the separation: "I've got to have another love relationship in order to be happy." This is an immature style of dependent and possessive love.

5. The *practical* lover takes a realistic look at the love partner and decides, on a rational and intellectual basis, if this love is appropriate. This type of person will make sure that there is similarity in religious beliefs, political beliefs, ways of handling money, views on raising children.... The lover may look into deficiencies in the person's family by considering socioeconomic status, characteristics, and genetic makeup. The practical lover will choose to love someone it "makes good sense" to love.

6. There are *altruistic* lovers, who may be somewhat other-centered and very willing to meet the needs of the other person. Carried to the extreme, the altruistic lover may become a martyr, trying to meet his or her own "empty bucket" needs. There is, however, an authentic altruistic lover: a person who has a full bucket and enough inner strength to be able to love another person in a very unselfish manner.

One couple in marriage counseling had a great deal of difficulty because he was a friendship lover and she was a romantic lover. She felt that his cool love was not love, and he felt that her romantic love was unstable. His style of loving was to take care of her, provide for her needs, and stay with her in the marriage, and he felt that this was proof of his love for her. Her request was for him to say, "I love you" and to express different forms of romantic thoughts that would make her feel loved and romantic. His friendship love was not a good mix with her romantic love. They had difficulty in communicating and understanding each other's viewpoints because their basic beliefs about what love was were not compatible.

Each person obviously is a mixture of these styles, and there is no one style that fits anyone at all times. Understanding your own mix of styles is very important when you get into a love relationship with another person.

Learning to Love Yourself

As people move up the trail of the divorce process, the question often arises, "How do we learn to love ourselves?" As we have seen, the answer is not easy. Here is a specific exercise that will *help* you learn to love yourself.

Think of a time in your life when you started to make changes. It may have been when you first had difficulties in your marriage, when you first separated from your beloved, or perhaps when you started reading this book. Make a list of the changes that you have made, the personal growth you have experienced since that time, and the things you have learned about yourself, others, and life. Consider the feeling of confidence you have gained by learning these things and getting more in control of your own life. That confidence is what gives you the good feelings. The length of your list may surprise you.

The late esteemed psychotherapist Virginia Satir devised another method of helping people learn to gain more self-love, which we recommend you do at this point in your journey. Make a list of five adjectives that describe you. After you have listed these adjectives, go through and put a plus or minus sign after each word to indicate whether you think it is a positive or negative trait. Then analyze those you marked with a minus sign to see if you can find anything positive about each of these qualities or aspects of your personality.

One woman listed the adjective "bitchy," noting that was what her husband often called her. As she began to talk about it, she realized that what he called "bitchiness," she recognized as *assertiveness*—a positive way to stick up for herself. Once she understood that difference in labels, she was able to accept that as a part of herself and feel good about it.

That's what self-love is: learning to accept ourselves for what we are. As renowned psychologist Carl Rogers observed, when you learn to accept yourself as you are, that gives you permission to grow, change, and become more the person you *want to be*. But as long as you don't accept a part of who you are, you will have trouble changing that part. Does that sound like a strange paradox?

We all need to discover that "it's okay not to be okay" in certain areas. We have all had traumatic experiences that have left us wounded someplace, incidents when we did not feel loved, experiences that have left us less than whole. But those experiences are part of life and part of living. We are not perfect; we are human beings. And when we can learn to accept some of the not-okay things about ourselves, then we can begin to feel more okay. And that's a step toward self-love.

Have you thought about how we learn to love another person? What causes the feelings of love for that other person to begin suddenly—or slowly? Perhaps it was a kind and thoughtful deed he or she did; maybe by doing something that met your needs, she or he helped you feel good.

What would happen if you did kind and thoughtful deeds for yourself? If you set aside a period of time tomorrow to do something that feels really good and makes you feel okay about yourself? That could be a way of learning to love yourself more fully and more completely. After all, it would be you who was capable of doing something kind and lovable for you!

Perhaps the most important method of learning to love yourself is to *give yourself permission* to love yourself. If you can decide that it is okay, and not selfish or self-centered, to love yourself, maybe you can allow yourself to go ahead and have feelings of self-love.

The growth you have achieved is something that no one else has done for you, so no one can take it away from you. Your life is in your control, through knowledge of yourself and others. To that extent, you are not at the mercy of others anymore. Let the good feelings of your growth soak into your body, and let yourself feel the warmth of what you have achieved. Let yourself feel love for yourself for a while. It is okay to love yourself. No, it's more than okay—*it is the way life is meant to be!*

Let Children Know They Are Loved

While everyone is concerned about what love is, children may feel somewhat unlovable because one parent has left. Many suffer from the fear of losing the other parent as well. At the very time children need a great deal of parental love, parents are undergoing their own trauma and often are incapable of giving as much love to the children as they would like. Awareness of this problem and special efforts to overcome it—especially through much honest conversation with youngsters about what is going on and reassurance that they are much loved by both parents—are what is needed at this crucial time.

A mother told a delightful story, one of those little vignettes in life that seem to make everything worthwhile. Her three-year-old son came downstairs one morning and sat on the sofa. He was just sitting there, presumably thinking, and suddenly came out with, "What do you know? It seems like everybody loves me. Isn't that nice!" Moments like that are special in life. As parents, a major goal for us should be to try to help all children of divorce feel that same way, even though we are going through a period of feeling unlovable ourselves.

How Are You Doing?

Check out your own level of self-love before you proceed to the next chapter:

- ☑ I feel I am lovable.
- ☒ I am not afraid of being loved.
- ☒ I am not afraid of loving another.
- ☑ I have an understanding of what I believe love is.
- ☒ I am living a lifestyle that is congruent with my definition of "love."
- ☑ I feel comfortable, rather than selfish, meeting my own needs.
- ☒ I am able to accept love from others.
- ☒ I am able to express love to others in a way that makes them feel loved.
- ☒ I am able to love myself.
- ☒ I have experienced a great deal of personal growth since my crisis began.
- ☒ I am trying to develop my immature, needy, dependent parts of love into a more mature style of loving.

CHAPTER 15

Trust

"My Love Wound Is Beginning to Heal"

If you say, "You can't trust men (women)!" you are saying more about yourself than about the opposite sex. Love relationships after divorce are often attempts to heal your love wound, so many of them will be transitional and short-term. In your new relationships with others, you may be reworking and improving the way you got along with your parents. By building a basic level of trust within yourself, you can experience satisfying emotionally close and intimate relationships.

I was doing just fine and enjoying myself. Then he said, "I love you." I panicked and told him to get up, put on his clothes, and go home.

—Ann

On this trust part of the trail, you will notice people who walk some distance away from members of the opposite sex. They are like wild animals that come close, hoping to get some food, yet run for cover the minute you move toward them. These people talk about relationships a great deal of the time, and they seem to want to date. But as soon as someone makes a move toward them, they run and shout, "Stay away!" They wear T-shirts declaring "You can't trust men!" (or "You can't trust women!"). They have severe *love wounds*.

A love wound is the internal pain felt after the end of a love relationship, but it may originate much earlier in life. Many of the juveniles Bruce worked with earlier in his career suffered from love wounds. They had learned that "love equals getting hurt." If they were put in a warm, loving foster home, they would run away. People who have painful love wounds will hold others at a distance emotionally until the love wound is healed. It may take months or even years for some people to heal—to be able to be emotionally close again.

There Are Relationships...and Then There Are Relationships

Relationships are important to people after divorce. When seminar participants are asked what topics they want to discuss, every group picks "relationships" as the top choice.

(Have you ever noticed at a gathering of singles how often the word "relationship" is used? One woman suggested that the word be censored with a *bleep*, she was so tired of hearing it! We use it a great deal in this book simply because we don't know of a better one that carries the same meaning.)

It is often assumed that the only way to prove that you're doing okay after a breakup is to become involved in another love relationship. In fact, some experts in the divorce field consider remarriage an indication of divorce adjustment. A research study using the Fisher Divorce Adjustment Scale demonstrated the inadequacy of that assumption. A large number of remarried people have not adjusted to the past divorce.

The idea that another relationship will "prove you are okay" leads many people to immediately start seeking out a new "one and only." We urge you not to go there. The healthiest early relationships after divorce have the goal of healing the love wound. They are *transitional*—rather than long-term, committed—relationships. (More on this in chapter 16.)

You may have heard the saying, "You have to kiss a lot of frogs before you find a prince." It would be healthier to reword that as, "You have to kiss a lot of frogs before you *become* a princess (or prince)." If you can make this transition in your thinking, you can free these early relationships from expectations, pressures, and a futuristic outlook. Consider this: instead of asking yourself, "Can I live with this person for the rest of my life?" try instead, "Can this person and I benefit from some time together?"

Allow your new relationships to flow in the present and to help heal your love wound (and perhaps the other person's love wound as well). Sit back and enjoy the sunsets each day, stop to "smell the roses," let yourself heal, and realize that many of these early relationships will be short-term because they are built during a needy time in your life. Let these early transitional relationships help you clear the confusion. You will have plenty of time later to build another permanent relationship when you have rebuilt a good foundation within yourself.

The divorce adjustment process may be viewed in two major steps. The first is *learning to be a single person*, ready to face life alone, with the rubble of the past cleared away. The second step is *learning to love again* after you have rebuilt your strength to carry the burden of a long-term, committed relationship. If you complete step one first, step two will be easier!

Styles of Relationship: A "Body-Sculpture" Exercise

Here is an exercise that will help you examine your own style in relationships. It is derived from Virginia Satir's body-sculpting work, and you'll need a friend to help out. The diagrams below illustrate different body positions that show various types of love relationships people have. Let's look at the body sculptures and consider the feelings underneath each style:

A-Frame Dependency Relationship

In the dependency relationship, two people lean on each other. Dependency upon another person sometimes feels good, but it's somewhat confining. When one person wants to move, change, or grow, it upsets the other, who is leaning on him or her. Try this sculpture pose with another person and then put into words some of the feelings that you have while you are assuming this position.

Smothering Relationship

Here is a position quite frequently seen in teenage relationships. The vocabulary for this relationship is "I can't live without you. I want to spend the rest of my life with you. I will devote myself completely to making you happy. It feels so good to be close to you." Many lovers start out by smothering, then gradually release the stranglehold on each other to allow more room for growth. This smothering pattern may be particularly significant during the honeymoon stage of a new love. The smothering relationship feels good for a while, but eventually, the partners begin to feel trapped.

Pedestal Relationship

This "worshipful" relationship says, "I love you not for who you are, but for who I think you are. I have an idealized image of you, and I'd like to have you live up to that image." It is very precarious on top of the pedestal because there are so many expectations to live up to.

You can see the problems of communication here. In love with the person's idealized image, the worshipper is looking up to and trying to communicate with that image instead of with the real person. There is a great deal of emotional distancing inherent in this relationship, and it is difficult for the two people to become close.

Master/Slave Relationship

The master acts and is treated according to these ideas: "I'm the head of this family. I'm the boss. I'll make the decisions around here." Do not assume that this relationship necessarily places the male as the boss and head of the family. There are many females who are masters, making all of the decisions for their families.

In most relationships, one of the partners has a personality that is at least a little stronger than the other's, and that is not necessarily bad. It is when a relationship becomes rigid and inflexible, and when one person is set up to make virtually *all* of the decisions, that emotional distancing and inequality take place. Maintaining one person as master and the other as slave tends to take a great deal of emotional energy and often results in a power struggle that interferes with the communication and intimacy of the relationship.

Boardinghouse: Back-to-Back Relationship

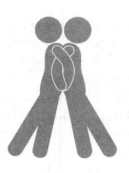

Linked by their elbows, these two have some sort of contract or agreement that they are going to live together. There is no communication in this relationship. The typical thing is for people to come home and sit down and watch TV while they are eating, then retire to their own living habits for the remainder of the evening. There is no expression of love toward each other.

Notice as you try this position that when one person moves forward (that is, changes, grows, matures), the other person is linked to that movement. A back-to-back relationship is very confining. Many people recognize this as the pattern that existed just before their relationship ended.

Martyr Relationship

Here is the person who completely sacrifices by trying to serve others. Always doing things for other people, never taking time for self, the martyr goes about "asking" to be stepped on. But don't let the lowly posture fool you! The martyr position is very controlling.

Note that when the person lying down moves, the other person—who has a foot on the martyr—is thrown off balance.

How does the martyr gain control? You guessed it: through guilt. How can you be angry at a person who is doing everything for you, who is taking care of you completely? The martyr is very efficient at controlling people. It is very difficult to live with a martyr, because you feel too guilty to express your own needs and angry feelings. Perhaps you have a martyr parent and can recognize ways of dealing with that parent by understanding the martyr relationship.

Healthy Love Relationship

Two people who are whole and complete have happiness within themselves. Standing upright, not leaning on or tangled up with the other person, they are able to live their own lives. They have an abundance of life to share with the other person. They choose to stay together because they are free to be individuals who are sharing their lives together. They can come close together and choose the smothering position temporarily; they can walk hand in hand as they might do in parenting their children; they can move apart and have their own careers, their own lives, and their own friends. Their choice to stay together is out of love for each other rather than needing to stay together because of unmet emotional needs. The healthy love relationship gives both people the space to grow and become themselves.

Again, we urge you to try these different positions with a friend and see how you feel in each instance. Talk or write about the feelings you experienced in each body position. Which of these positions describes your past love relationship? Don't be surprised if you relate to more than one—many people feel that their love relationship went through almost all of the unhealthy body positions at one point or another.

Did you learn more causes of divorce from the exercise? The unhealthy relationships seem to suggest a half person looking for another half person. As you become more of a whole person (do we ever become completely whole?), your chances of developing a healthy, healing relationship are greatly increased.

Feelings into Actions

We tend to act out our internal feelings in our relationships. If you are angry, you probably express anger in your love relationship. If you are lonely, you probably tend to be possessive in the relationship in order to keep the other person from leaving you and making you lonely again. If you are in deep emotional pain, you'll likely have a relationship full of pain. If you have a love wound, you will emotionally distance the other person to avoid exacerbating your wound.

Many of us seek relationships with people who have qualities we are missing in ourselves. If you are introverted and want to be more comfortable around people, you may get together with an extravert. If you lack confidence, you'll be attracted to someone who exudes confidence. And if you need to feel guilty, you'll develop a relationship with someone who makes you feel guilty.

Of course, the coin also has a positive flip side. If you feel happy, confident, and lovable, you'll act out those feelings in your relationship. We can learn much about ourselves by looking at our relationships. What feelings are you expressing in your relationships? Is there a pattern? (For example, do you always bring home stray cats?) Do your relationships reflect good feelings within, or do they reflect neediness?

Is Your History Repeating Itself?

Another major factor in relationship styles is one we've mentioned before: the interaction we had with our parents. Each of us learned how to respond to love, anger, rejection, and intimacy from our own parents. If your parents fought, then you are likely to have a very tough time with fights. If your parents were cold and untouching, then you may find it difficult to touch and to handle warm emotions. Many a marriage is not satisfactory because the partners are interacting just like their parents did.

Jeff put it this way: "Marriage is like a favorite recipe. If you don't make it right the first time, you keep doing it over until you get it right. In my first marriage, I was acting out the unproductive patterns I learned as a child. I didn't change internally after my divorce, so I continued to act out those patterns in my second marriage."

If you can use each relationship to learn about yourself and how you are acting out your internal feelings in your relationships, you can then use each relationship to become more the person you want to be. It is possible to grow from each relationship, and that is a positive way of looking at having had more than one marriage.

After divorce, we often interact the way we did earlier in life. This can be positive: becoming a healthy person emotionally is like climbing a slide on the playground. You progress up so far, then lose your grip and slide back down. The next time you try, you are able to climb to a higher point. Although each relationship that ends might find you back down at the bottom of the slide, when you climb again, you know how to climb higher and become more healthy. In their relationships after divorce, many people are reworking the patterns of interaction they learned from their parents in order to make those patterns more productive.

We hope the discussions in this chapter of various concepts of relationships are helping you carry out the rubble and make room to rebuild yourself. The problem of trust is largely internal rather than external, and understanding your past is helpful in understanding where you are now. The first step of growth is to become aware of ourselves, our patterns of interaction, and our methods of relating with others.

Enough of carrying out the rubble—let's start rebuilding!

"Where Do I Meet Someone?"

This is one of the questions formerly married people ask most frequently. The simple, almost absurd, answer is, "Right where you are!" People go to bars, singles groups, and ceramics classes (it's amazing how many once-marrieds do that) in their attempts to meet people. We don't quarrel with going places where single people gather. But take care. The "bar scene," for example, typically includes many lonely people who can't relate until they are slightly under the influence. And bar hoppers are often game players out to practice and improve their games of interaction, with sex frequently being the goal of the game.

The question "Where do I meet someone?" often indicates that the asker is looking for a committed, long-term partner. Perhaps somewhat desperate and thus sending out desperate vibrations with body language, vocabulary, and "the look in their eyes," these people tend to drive others away. Others fear that they will become sucked in by the neediness; some even call the needy ones "vacuum cleaners"!

How often have you heard it said, "There ain't nothing but turkeys out there"? Of course, that's partly true. Many formerly married people are hurting and are therefore not especially attractive dates during the rough periods. But have you thought about what you would do if an eagle landed near you? You would probably run like mad! A person who is eligible and looks like a possible marriage partner scares the hell out of you if your love wound is still fresh. Maybe you are looking for turkeys because they are safe? Maybe you are still hurting and more or less a turkey yourself? Turkeys do tend to hang together, you know. Maybe, if "there ain't nothing but turkeys out there," you haven't rebuilt yourself yet to the status of an eagle.

When you have blinders on and see only potential marriage partners, do you realize how many people you are not seeing out there? When you start becoming interested in getting to know the people around you, then you will start making friends. And some of those friends might become lovers, but *looking* for lovers keeps both friends and lovers away.

It bears repeating: Your goal (for now) is to get acquainted and develop friendships with the people around you. Pay no attention to whether or not they are "eligible singles"; notice only if they are *interesting people* you would like to get to know. Develop as many positive relationships with people of both sexes as you can. You can get to know these potential friends wherever you are. When you go to the grocery store and send out positive vibrations and act interested in others, you attract people like flies to honey. At parties, if you forget about trying to find a bed partner or someone to go home with after the party, you might get to know a number of interesting people. If you've found happiness within and send out those vibrations, people will enjoy being with you.

There's a difference in the numbers of formerly married males and females, and the ratio is unfair: US census statistics for recent years show that women make up well over half of unmarried adults. Women live longer than men; for each year of life, there are more females than males living. Also, there are many males who remarry someone much younger, often a woman not married before. (It may be small compensation to women, but it is true that women adjust to living alone much better than do men.)

Ginger posed another issue frequently discussed by recently divorced people: "Every time I go to a singles gathering, it becomes a game of 'my place or yours?'" There are many singles who have not learned to deal with the opposite sex other than sexually, but that doesn't mean you have to narrow yourself the same way. Keep developing your personality and broadening yourself. The more interests you develop, the more interesting people you will find. And keep in mind that you can always say, "No thanks!"

Rebuilding Trust

Some ideas that have grown out of the Fisher divorce seminars may help you overcome problems of trust.

Try this one: *be really honest the next time you go out.* If you are hurting over a painful love wound, explain to the person who seems interested in you that you want to spend time with him or her, but you fear you'll be a wet blanket. Don't try to put on a mask of "cool and sophisticated" when in reality you're scared to death. When you explain your fears to others, you might be surprised to learn they're feeling or have felt the same way. After all, we're *all* human. And you'll both be relieved to be able to be yourselves instead of some "Joe Cool" you thought you had to be.

Have you thought about learning to trust with friends rather than lovers? If you find someone of the opposite sex with whom you can be friends, that person is much safer for you than a lover. When you add romance to the ingredients of a friendship, it adds instability to the relationship and makes it harder to take risks and learn to trust.

We project our lack of trust onto others. Many parents believe that their teenagers are not to be trusted. Valerie's parents, for example, feared she would become pregnant, so they wouldn't allow her to date, even though she was a junior in high school. It turned out that her mother had become pregnant as a teenager and was projecting her lack of trust in herself onto Valerie.

A similar event often occurs in marriage counseling. Tess admitted that her husband, Andre, kept checking on her to make sure she was not having an affair. Then she discovered that Andre was having the affair and projecting his lack of trust onto her! Like so many other feelings, lack of trust may become a self-fulfilling prophecy. Valerie said she felt she *should* become pregnant because that was what her parents seemed to believe was going to happen. And Tess felt she *might as well* have an affair if that was what Andre suspected anyway!

A severe love wound leads to fear of trusting. As appealing as the warmth may be, to become close is to risk being burned again. Relationships after divorce are controlled by this lack of trust. The purpose of these relationships ought to be to learn trust again and to heal the love wound. Again, this is why many such connections are short-term. Trying to make them into something long-term often does nothing but aggravate the love wound and prolong the adjustment process.

We have all learned how to interact from our love relationships and from our parents. As adults, we may choose to improve the styles of interaction that we learned. Becoming aware of one's style is an important first step. It may also take several friendships and love relationships to help one develop healthier styles.

We have to take risks to learn to trust. Risks may backfire and lead to rejection or misunderstanding, but they're necessary if one is to become close and experience intimacy again. The rewards are worth the risks.

Trust and the Children

The problem of trust is especially difficult for children who were not made aware of what was going on with their parents' divorce. Children have trouble adjusting to the sudden absence of a parent with whom they had little or no direct communication. If the mother, for example, leaves the household without communicating to her child why she is leaving or the problems she was having in the marriage, the child may feel deserted and in turn have trouble trusting that parent.

Kids really are tougher than you think, and they can handle an awful lot of reality if parents would just take the time and find the courage to communicate directly with them. Parents who hide their heads in the sand or feel they cannot share the truth of their situation with their children often create mistrust in the children and lose a potentially valuable source of love and support in the process. It is a very unusual—or very young— child who does not figure out that the parents are going to get a divorce before the parents tell the family. The more you can communicate and level with your children, the more they will trust what you say.

How Are You Doing?

Here are some items to help you see how you are doing and if you are ready to continue the climb. We are nearing the top, so take care not to rush here—this rebuilding block must be securely in place before you proceed.

- I can trust members of the opposite sex.

- I have begun to understand that men and women are much more alike than different in their responses to feelings such as love, hate, intimacy, and fear.

- I can trust myself and my feelings.

- I trust my feelings enough to act on them.

- I am not afraid of becoming emotionally close to a potential love partner.

- I am aware of the ways in which I distance people.

- I am building relationships that will help me heal my love wound.

- I am building healing and trusting relationships with friends of both sexes.

- I communicate with others about where I am emotionally rather than giving mixed messages.

- I understand that not everyone is capable of being trusted.

- I am capable of trusting someone when it is appropriate.

- I want to heal my love wound and experience intimacy.

- I am trying to live in the present in my relationships.

- I realize that many of the early relationships after divorce may be short-term.

- I am taking risks in my relationships by exposing my true feelings and thoughts.

- I am truly interested in the friends around me rather than desperately seeking another love relationship.

CHAPTER 16

Relatedness

"Growing Relationships Help Me Rebuild"

It's okay to have an important relationship after your primary relationship has ended. You need support, companionship, and feedback from others to help yourself rebuild. These relationships are often short-term, so you need to learn how to bring about "healthy termination." You need to take credit for creating these relationships as part of your growing process. And you need to become aware of how you can make these relationships as growth-oriented and healing as possible.

Have I had a growing relationship? Not one, but four. Each seemed healthier than the one before. I guess I learned something from each one.

—Susan

I had one with a woman who had a great built-in crap detector. When I was sorting through my stuff, I could bounce off her and she would tell me what parts of me were authentic and what parts of me were crap. I think I found the perfect partner to have a growing relationship with.

—David

M any people climbing the mountain decide to pair off, to help support each other in the difficult climb. They appear to enjoy each other's company very much for a while, but often they part ways and continue the climb alone.

It helps to have another person's support for a while, but sooner or later, one or both of them realize they need to make this climb alone. When they part, one or both of them feel very sad for a while. They often have to rework some of the blocks they had already gone through, such as grief and anger. Both appear to make rapid progress while they are together, but when this new relationship ends, their progress slows down considerably.

What Is a Growing Relationship?

We call these unions "growing relationships." Other professionals have variously labeled them "transitional relationships," "rebound relationships," "experimental relationships," and "healing relationships." Psychiatrist Martin Blinder, for example, in his book *Choosing Lovers*, describes the various types of this relationship in some detail and asserts that each type is unique, meeting particular needs of the partners. Later in this chapter, we'll discuss a couple of the more common types.

Growing relationships, because they help folks manage the climb better for a while, can be very healthy for both partners. But it's not enough just to let them "happen." It's important to understand them and how they work, so they can be made longer-lasting and more growth-enhancing, and—just maybe—so they hurt less when they end.

Among the typical characteristics of growing relationships:

- They often occur after a marriage or love relationship has ended, but they can occur at any time.

- They are often with a potential love partner, but they can be with a friend, a family member, a therapist, or even with your primary love partner.

- They are usually temporary, but they can become more permanent, long-lasting relationships.

- They are usually very healing, but they can be destructive.

- They usually occur when you are in a personal growth or transformation period in your life.

- They are an attempt to find new ways of creating and building relationships with yourself and with others.

- They can end with a "healthy termination," rather than the painful, destructive endings you may have experienced in the past.

- They typically involve good communication. Usually, the two people spend a great deal of time talking with each other about important topics, such as personal growth and the meaning of life.

- These relationships are based upon honesty and openness—with each other if not with their primary love partners—and the people often share themselves in ways they have never shared before. Instead of "dressing up and putting on good clothes"—to put on their best facade for the new partner (as most of us did in the old "courting" system)—these people strip down to the bare emotional essentials, so they can present their true essence in ways that allow them to feel excited about their new behavior.

- They are growth-oriented, not stagnant. There is a difference between this type of healing relationship and one that is simply a summer rerun of an old show. The male who needs mothering is often married to an enabler/overresponsible person. He often leaves that relationship and marries another enabler/overresponsible person (often with the same or a similar first name!). The female who needs to take care of someone may marry another "stray cat" so she can continue her old pattern. In contrast, the growing relationship is dedicated to developing a new and different relationship—a laboratory for personal growth—not to perpetuating old patterns.

Are We Talking Affairs Here?

Sometimes a person in a primary love relationship has a third-party relationship and deems it a growing relationship. Such a union can take the form of an affair. We've worked with clients who have been able to make their third-party relationships into healing experiences, using them to enrich their primary relationships and make them stronger. That usually is possible only if the new pairing is a *friendship* rather than a romantic affair. Romantic third-party involvements typically have long-term consequences and make it difficult for the people involved to heal the pain of the affair.

The old parental tapes from childhood about sex and marriage come back and say, "When you talk about relationships outside of marriage that may include sex, aren't you encouraging affairs or promiscuity?" Not necessarily; these relationships don't have to be romantic or sexual. If your values—religious or moral—are such that you don't want a relationship that is sexual outside of marriage, you can still learn and heal tremendously by having a nonsexual friendship.

A growing relationship must fit your moral values while it focuses on the lessons that you need to learn.

Why Are Some People More Likely to Create Growing Relationships?

There are certain groups of people who are more likely to have growing relationships:

- Dumpers after a divorce will tend to get into other relationships quicker than dumpees.

- Men will tend to get into other relationships more quickly after a divorce than women.

- Women are more likely than men to create a growing relationship with a friend.

- Extraverts are more likely than introverts to use the growing relationship to heal. Research with the Myers-Briggs Type Indicator (a psychological test that describes people by personality types) reveals that extraverts heal better with other people, whereas introverts heal better by themselves.

- People who are able to be emotionally open and vulnerable will more likely create a growing relationship than emotionally closed-down people who can't talk about their feelings.

- People in rebellion will usually have a growing relationship. (See chapter 12 for more on rebellion.)

- Younger people are more inclined to develop growing relationships than older people.

- People who are involved in some sort of divorce recovery therapy or support group will almost automatically develop growing relationships with the other participants in the group. This is one of the great "side benefits" of group participation. The friendships you make will probably last for a long time, maybe for the rest of your life. And the friendships will be more healthy and growing than many of the relationships you have had in the past. Remember that you can create the same kind of relationships outside of the group that you have created within the group.

Many people will not want to start such a relationship because it could become more than they can handle. They want something safe that won't become long-term. It's important to be clear and communicate your intentions, needs, and desires directly and openly with a potential partner. You can decide how to control your future involvement and not let the relationship become more than you want it to be.

Interestingly, 15 to 20 percent of the participants in the Fisher divorce seminars don't enroll after their marriage has ended. They enroll *after* their growing relationship following their divorce has ended. The first relationship after a marriage has ended usually doesn't last very long, but the emotional pain is often greater when this relationship ends than when the marriage or primary love relationship ended.

Growing relationships appear to be one of the myriad social transitions that take place in society. Learning more about these types of relationships will increase the chances of them becoming more healing. Toward that end, let's take a look at two of the most common types of growing relationships: the *passionate* and the *therapeutic*.

Passionate Emotional Relationships

Perhaps the most common of the several types of growing relationships that occur after a primary love relationship has ended is the passionate type, with its emphasis on romantic love. Here at last—or so it seems—are all of those qualities that were missing in the late marriage: passion, honesty, good communication, empathy, understanding. No wonder the new partners want it to last forever, hang on to it tightly, and talk about their future together.

But commitments for the long term might not be healing for either party at this stage. Let's consider some of the potential pitfalls and benefits of the passionate emotional relationship:

Pitfall: *There are risks in making the other person responsible for your excitement and passion.* Have you made this new attachment too important in your life? It feels so good when you are on the rough seas of your transition that you want to make it last forever. You think you can't live without this exciting new partner. What you need to remember is that *you're in the process of recovery.* Take responsibility for creating this relationship yourself. You have just begun to be the person you want to be; give yourself the time it takes to finish the job. It does feel good to be with that other person. But don't give away all your power by making another person responsible for your happiness.

Benefit: *Your personal growth is an important reason for this relationship.* The lesson for you to learn in this relationship is to heal, to become, to be free, to be yourself. Take advantage of the lesson, and take credit for what you are learning. You have created an environment in which you can grow.

Pitfall: *Idealizing your new partner is short-sighted.* That mistake will almost surely limit the healing potential of this relationship. Remember the "pedestal relationship" from the previous chapter? Try this exercise with your new partner: Have your partner stand on a chair, stool, or small table while you stand below on the floor. Talk to each other. Give each other a hug. Become aware of how the dynamic feels. The partner on the pedestal usually feels lonely, precarious, and uncomfortable.

Pitfall: *Focusing too much on the future limits healing.* Because the relationship feels so good, you start thinking about the future, what it would be like to be married to this person forever. Living in the future inhibits healing, while living in the present maximizes healing. Living in the present is an indication of a self-actualized person. You need to enjoy the sunset each day in this relationship. You need to live each day as though it were your last. You need to communicate about everything you are feeling now and let go of dreaming about the future or how long this relationship is going to last.

Benefit: *Communication is usually good in such a relationship.* You often share things about yourself and become more vulnerable than you have ever been. You treasure being open, vulnerable, and intimate. Realize that an important lesson in this relationship might be learning to be intimate and vulnerable. Remember that the communication skills and the feeling of vulnerability you are learning in this relationship will always be available to you in other relationships.

Pitfall: *You believe you'll never have another relationship with such a wonderful person again.* Part of the reason you hang on to this relationship so tightly is that you see this person as your "one and only" (a societal expectation perhaps?). Anyone else will seem dull and unexciting after this person. There is some truth in this. But the excitement you feel is not because of the other person. It is because of your own process of growth. You are living in the present, being vulnerable, feeling new feelings. Much of the excitement you feel is because you are coming out of your shell, finding yourself, "coming home" emotionally.

While you may never feel this same exuberance again—becoming free of your shell—you do have the potential of experiencing the joy and excitement of intimacy, being emotionally close, and feeling loving and being loved in your future relationships. And these future relationships may be more meaningful than this relationship now, when you are just coming out of your shell.

Benefit: *You discover how good it feels to be healthy.* As you grow and become you, you can allow yourself to be vulnerable, which results in more intimacy and feeling more secure in your own identity. The really important point for you to learn here is that *you can feel this way in many relationships and with many people.* So stop believing this is the only person you can have such a relationship with. You will be able to have other healthy relationships if you choose, because you are learning to have a better relationship with yourself. True, later relationships may not feel as intense, but that's because you won't be as needy.

Benefit: *A healing relationship allows you to experiment with growth.* Recall the themes from chapters 4 and 12—family of origin and childhood influences. You can rework and relearn the things you learned as a child. This relationship might be as good a "laboratory" for growth as any relationship you have ever had or will ever have. This new relationship is very likely much different from the relationships you built with your family of origin and with your ex-partner. This may partly explain why this relationship feels so good.

Pitfall: *There may be an imbalance in your emotional investment.* It is very easy to invest 80 percent or more of your emotional time and energy into this relationship and neglect investing in yourself. That inhibits your healing and your growth, contributes to the relationship ending, and makes it much more painful when it does end. If you want to maximize the healing potential in this growing relationship, discipline yourself to keep investing as much in yourself as you are in the relationship. This will help you keep your individual identity rather than losing it in your exciting, new, passionate love relationship.

Keep track of your time. How much of your free time is spent in improving yourself—engaging in hobbies, taking classes, and spending time by yourself or with your friends? And how much time are you spending with the other person doing relationship activities?

Learn all you can, heal all you can, and stop holding the precious butterfly in your hands so tightly that it can't fly and be free. The energy you spend holding on tightly to the other person and to the relationship keeps you from climbing your own mountain and completing your own healing.

Friendship and Therapeutic Relationships

A growing relationship doesn't have to be with a love partner. In fact, there are tremendous advantages to having a growing relationship with a person who is not a love partner. You can experience the same type of healing with a good friend or a trusted family member. You can still talk about feelings, be vulnerable, share parts of yourself that you have never shared with another. This friendship doesn't have the same thrills, excitement, and passion as a love relationship, but it is safer, seldom brings the emotional pain of the end of a romantic relationship, and can offer healing that is just as deep. It, too, can serve as a laboratory for growth, allowing you to change past patterns.

The participants in our rebuilding seminars easily identify with this type of growing relationship based on friendship. They are open and honest with one another, share important aspects of themselves, feel a closeness and intimacy with others, and realize that these relationships are special and often more healthy and healing than what they have known in the past. Learning to develop friendship-based growing relationships can be one of the most valuable learning experiences from divorce recovery groups.

Therapy can also develop into a growing relationship, depending upon the therapist and the style of therapy. But the same type of growth can take place—and with the safety that comes from clear boundaries, paying for the therapy, and keeping it professional. A therapy relationship that helps you to become fully yourself can be one of the most valuable experiences you will have.

Can a Growing Relationship Last?

Does every growing relationship have to end? Each relationship has a foundation that is unique, both to that relationship and to where you are emotionally when you start the relationship. The foundation for the growing relationship is built for growth and healing; that's its purpose. A long-term committed relationship has a foundation built for longevity. What's the difference?

When you are building a growing relationship, you are in process— unstable, continually growing and changing, healing the wounds of the past. You are different today from what you were yesterday. And you will be different tomorrow. During this period of rapid change, your foundation needs to be flexible, adaptable, changeable—allowing you to be different as you change. That isn't a suitable foundation for a long-term relationship.

The "contract" when you started the growing relationship probably wasn't written, or even spelled out verbally, but it was there, with wording something like this: "I need this relationship so I can find out who I am." The foundation for a long-term relationship is more stable and more permanent (although not rigid). Long-term unions require commitment, purpose, and stability.

If a growing relationship is to become a long-term one, it needs to be jacked up and a new foundation put under it. This can be done in various ways. Some couples have had a "healthy termination" of their relationship so that one or both of them could go be the "young colt"—out running around the pasture investing in themselves rather than investing in the relationship. Then they can get back together and build a relationship with a more permanent foundation.

Changing the relationship can also can be done with good communication. Both partners must become aware of the costs and benefits of making their short-term healing relationship a long-term committed relationship. Both must take ownership of their feelings, contributions, and roles in the new relationship. And communication must be open and honest. If you and your partner talk it out thoroughly, with awareness and accountability, and decide that you want to change the growing relationship into a longer, more committed one, it can be done.

But there is an issue that can arise here. If you are truly changing, you might be a different person than you were when you started the relationship. Maybe your attraction and reason for entering into the relationship was to be with a person who was entirely different than your parents, former lovers, former friends. And the need for a contrasting person is met, maybe you will want relationships with people more like your parents, former lovers, and former friends. So when the need for the different person passes, you may want to end the relationship. Many people in growing relationships outgrow the relationship for a variety of reasons.

Don't move too quickly to try to convert a growing relationship into one of long-term commitment. Both partners must be ready to accept themselves where they are now and to move ahead into a more stable future.

"Why Do I Have to Have So Many?"

Sometimes people ask why they have to have so many growing relationships. A very good question. There are several possible explanations:

- The relationships may only have a fraction of the healing power that is possible because you load them down with the future rather than focusing on the present.

- You don't pay enough attention to your own recovery and healing process because you are so infatuated with how great the other person is.

- You terminate the relationship with a lot of pain because you aren't yet aware of how to have a healthy termination. (This pain increases the need for another relationship to heal the pain of ending that one.)

- You may just simply need a lot of healing from your family of origin and childhood experiences, and it takes several relationships to accomplish that.

- You may have been working through the issues described in previous chapters, but you aren't yet entirely aware of what those issues were. Awareness greatly increases the healing potential in a growing relationship.

- Another possible reason you're having multiple growing relationships is the passion often involved in them. They become so physical that the real teaching of the relationship becomes obscured. You can escape very easily into passionate sex and not ever wake up on the awareness level.

- You and your partner may not be able to connect effectively on an emotional level. If you are not living in the present, if you do not give your complete attention to the relationship, if you avoid intimacy rather than seek it, then you never reach closeness, connectedness, intimacy, healing in the relationship. People can be reluctant to end such relationships because, in essence, they have never been complete on an intimate level.

Each relationship contributes to your growth, and it might be helpful for you to identify and be thankful for each relationship, as well as for each person with whom you have been in relationship. The homework at the end of this chapter will guide you to explore what you have learned and how you have healed in each of the growing relationships you've had.

Please be gentle with yourself. If your inner critic beats yourself up every time you enter into or end a relationship, you will negate the healing. Give yourself a warm fuzzy for each growing relationship you have created, which will maximize the healing that has taken place.

Making Your Primary Love Relationship a Growing Relationship

One of the most exciting ways to have a healing relationship is to make your marriage or primary love relationship into a growing relationship! The same concepts apply; you just bring them to your current union: living in the present, good communication, no future expectations, and taking ownership (both individually, being accountable for your own feelings and attitudes, and jointly, being responsible for shaping this new relationship together).

It won't be easy, but many primary love relationships can be reenergized and reinforced with a stronger foundation under them. If you're interested in carving out a new relationship within your marriage, you may find helpful the discussions on rebellion (chapter 12) and healing separations (appendixes B and C). (Bruce's book with Nina Hart, *Loving Choices*, describes ways to create a growing relationship within a committed love relationship.)

Learning Good Communication Skills

A growing relationship needs good communication, and the quickest way you can improve your skills is to learn to use I-messages instead of you-messages—a communication technique first introduced by Dr. Thomas Gordon and discussed several times earlier in this book, especially in chapter 9, when we were talking about expressing anger.

As a refresher: You-messages are like poisoned darts that you throw at another person, who either becomes defensive or starts thinking what to say (throw) back at you as a result. I-messages let others know that you are accepting responsibility for (owning) your own feelings and attitudes.

I-messages may be difficult for you if you haven't always been in touch with what is going on inside of you. Here's an easy way to start using I-messages: Start each sentence with "I" when you are having important conversations with others. Try using these four kinds of I-messages: "I think _____," "I feel _____," "I want _____," and "I will _____." It is helpful to separate your thoughts from your feelings and to use different kinds of communication for each. Think about what you hope to achieve with your message. If you don't say what you want, you probably won't get what you want. And you need to finish your communication with a commitment about what action you will take. Taking responsible action to help achieve what you want is really putting your money where your mouth is.

Men frequently have difficulty accessing and talking about feelings. Using "I feel" statements may help them overcome this handicap. On the other hand, women can often tell you what others around them want or need, but they can't tell you what they themselves want or need.

Healthy Termination

Another key part of growing relationships is *healthy termination*. Because most of these relationships will end, they will be more growth enhancing for both parties if you learn how to conduct a healthy termination. It's an inherent problem in these relationships: you try to make them last longer than is healthy because you've started attaching expectations for your future to them.

By trying to stretch a short-term relationship into something longer than its "natural life," you make it unduly stressful. When you finish stretching it till it breaks, it snaps back at you like a rubber band—and hurts more than it has to.

If you can back it off into friendship before it gets stretched too far, you are more likely to have a healthy termination to the relationship. If you live in the present, you'll notice when the present becomes less meaningful than it was. The needs that created the relationship have changed, and that's when it's time to start terminating.

Talk about your needs being different. Own what is happening with your feelings, explain how your needs have changed, and share your valuable learning from the relationship. Healthy terminations end with a fraction of the pain that results from trying to stretch the relationship into something it is not.

A healthy termination has its roots in openness and honesty about the needs and desires of both partners when you started the relationship. Pete, an army chaplain, stated it well: "I told her I was a wet little kitty and needed someone to take care of me and lick me dry like the mother cat does. And I also told her I didn't know whether I would want a relationship with her when I finally was dry. We were able to terminate the relationship with a minimum of pain because we had been open and honest from the beginning."

So here are the actions that pave the way for a healthy termination. We encourage you to work them into your growing relationships:

- Communicating openly and honestly.

- Living in the present. Taking one day at a time, rather than making plans for an uncertain "future" together.

- Taking responsibility for your own feelings and expressing them openly. Avoiding games like, "I'm fine. Nothing's wrong."

- Seeing this from the beginning as a short-term relationship. "Commitment" is not part of a growing relationship, unless it becomes a long-term union.

- Talking about your needs. Listening to your partner's needs. Watch for clues that tell you it's time to move on, and let your partner know when they start to show up.

- Planning for the highly probable termination of the relationship. Discuss how you'll handle it when the time comes. (For example: Will alternate living arrangements be needed? Transportation? Are children involved? Will you continue as friends? How about mutual friends?)

The concept of a healthy termination applies to all relationships. Each relationship has its natural cycle of growth. Some are short-term annuals, and others are long-term perennials. It's not easy to recognize just what the life span of a relationship should be. Ownership—acceptance of responsibility for yourselves, your feelings, and what's going on with each of you individually—is a tremendous help in allowing the relationship to find its own natural cycle.

A great deal of the pain in our lives comes from holding on to something too long when we need to let it go. If you believe your happiness is someone else's responsibility, you'll have difficulty letting a relationship have its natural length of life.

Do You Need a Growing Relationship?

There are a number of ways to heal without having a growing relationship. However, it does feel good to have someone's hand to hold while you are waking up. And someone to talk to while you are learning about yourself. They contribute much to the healing experience.

If you can understand that these relationships are a place you can put into practice all the skills that you have read about and learned while reading this book, you'll see the benefits of this relationship even more. We hope that the awareness you've gained from reading this book—and doing the exercises we've suggested—will help you pursue real healing in these kinds of relationships, instead of allowing them to repeat old patterns.

Children and Relatedness

Your children will probably develop growing relationships also. They may suddenly be good friends with other children whose parents are divorcing. They will find they can talk to these friends better than to their "married kids" friends.

You may be surprised to find yourself feeling judgmental toward kids whose parents are divorcing. You may even not want your kids to associate with them. Surprise! You have found some of your own biases and prejudices toward divorce. Remember that your children are going through the divorce process also, and finding friends who are in a similar situation may be helpful. As you have learned, anyone can go through a divorce; it doesn't help to persist in critical attitudes toward people who are ending relationships.

If you are involved in your own growing relationship, where do your children fit in? It depends upon the type of relationship you are creating. If you have a therapy relationship, it may be helpful to share this with your children. They will be more open to talking with others if they realize you are talking to someone.

If your growing relationship is with a friend or family member, you may choose to involve your children in this relationship by sharing with them how good it feels to have a special person to talk to.

If your growing relationship is of the passionate love affair kind, though, then you need to decide carefully how much to include your children in this relationship. Your children have been observing the arguments between you and your ex, so it might be nice to expose them to a more peaceful and loving relationship. However, it's very easy for the excitement of the new relationship to cloud your thinking; you may find yourself wanting to include your children in this relationship more than is appropriate at this stage. Having your new partner spend the night while your kids are there, for example, is usually difficult for children to deal with, and is probably not a good idea.

As we've discussed in this chapter, the chances of a transitional growing relationship lasting and becoming long-term are not high. Your children will very likely have to deal with the rending of another of your relationships. Keep that in mind as you consider how much you want to involve your children in this relationship.

Take responsibility for creating this growing relationship as part of your adjustment process. Awareness of this may help your children to put the relationship in better perspective. You take control of your life by making more aware, loving choices; your children can—and will—follow your example.

Homework for a Growing Relationship

Write responses to the following questions in your journal:

- What is your response to this chapter? Does this discussion square with your experience?

- If you have had one or more growing relationships, describe them. How were they healing? How were they harmful? What did you learn in each one? Were they with a friend, lover, therapist, or family member? How could you make the next one more healing and healthy?

- If you have not had a growing relationship, do you want to? Are you afraid of becoming vulnerable? Are you unable to communicate? Are you afraid of being hurt again?

- If you are in a primary committed love relationship and having a healing separation, do you think it is possible to experience a growing relationship with your partner? Is this a new concept for you?

Bruce observed hundreds of couples create a new and loving relationship from the painful ashes of a dead relationship. If that is your goal, a good way to start is for both partners to read and work your way through this book. Do as much of the homework as you can. Encourage and nurture each other because this process takes commitment, self-discipline, and confidence. And there are no guarantees.

How Are You Doing?

Before you go on to the next chapter, take advantage of this brief self-assessment. It will help you to determine if you're ready to head on up the trail.

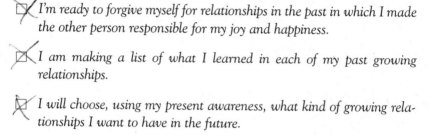

☑ I'm ready to forgive myself for relationships in the past in which I made the other person responsible for my joy and happiness.

☑ I am making a list of what I learned in each of my past growing relationships.

☑ I will choose, using my present awareness, what kind of growing relationships I want to have in the future.

☑ I will take ownership for creating growing relationships as part of my healing process.

☑ I will take ownership of good feelings in my growing relationships; I am becoming the person I choose to be.

☑ I will put into practice all of the relationship skills I am learning in this book; I will use these skills in my future relationships.

☑ I am being open and honest, and using good communication skills, in my current relationships.

☑ I am trying out new healthy behaviors, breaking old patterns, and making my relationships as growing and healing as possible.

CHAPTER 17

Sexuality

"I'm Interested, but I'm Scared"

When you're first separated, it's normal to be extremely fearful of sex. During the adjustment process, you can learn to express your unique sexuality according to your own moral standards. Some singles follow a conventional moral code: no sexual relationships outside of marriage. Others enjoy singles culture and adopt its emphasis on authenticity, responsibility, and individuality. It's time to discover what you believe. (Whatever you decide, remember that if there is to be any sex, it must be safe sex.)

Being Divorced and Middle-Aged Is:

Not taking out the garbage for fear you'll miss that obscene phone call...

Standing out in the middle of the dark parking lot and shouting, "Hey you muggers, the muggee is here!"...

Telling the guy who frisked you and demanded all your money that you have no money, but if he'll frisk you again, you'll write him a check...

Putting a sign on your gate that reads, "All trespassers will be violated"...

Looking under the bed and hoping someone is there.

—Lois

Everyone looks forward to this portion of the climb with great expectations. You may even have jumped ahead to read this chapter first. Maybe you have been anticipating this discussion of sexuality ever since the introduction to the rebuilding blocks in chapter 1. Either way, we urge you to slow down, take a deep breath, and try to put sex in its proper perspective. (At least read chapter 1 first!)

Before We Begin...

We'd like to open this chapter by acknowledging the very wide range of attitudes and beliefs people hold about sex. We know that views span a spectrum, from "no sex outside marriage" to "if it feels good, do it." Sexuality and morality are closely connected in our society, and we respect those who have adopted a strong moral position as well as those who have chosen nonconventional lifestyles.

A very large percentage of those who take part in our divorce seminars do so under the auspices of a faith-based organization, and many faiths maintain that a sexual union belongs only within the committed marriage relationship. Some who agree with that view may find portions of this chapter offensive. We regret that, but we would consider it irresponsible to ignore a subject so central to the concerns of people going through the divorce recovery process.

Because we believe that decisions in the realm of sexual morality are very personal, we have elected not to take a position on the moral issues involved. In short, we do not advocate sexual relationships after divorce, nor do we condemn them. Whatever your own stance, we believe you'll find this chapter a useful examination of the issues involved in developing a sexual relationship—or not. (Still, some readers may prefer to skip this chapter.)

Take It One Stage at a Time

I've had a conflict about having sexual relations while I am single. One part of me says that sex is important to my personal growth, and the other part says that I feel guilty having sex with a woman I'm not married to. What do I do?

—Tom

On this part of the climb up the mountain, you'll want to find your own pathway. Each of us has an individual morality that will largely determine our direction. Because this area requires an effort not only to climb, but also to find your way, you may feel more hesitant and less confident. Take your time and make sure the path you choose really suits you. Of course, you can change paths if one isn't working for you. But some people have paid a tremendous price—emotionally and physically—because they experimented with behavior that was not really compatible with their own values.

There are three typical stages in this rebuilding block: *lack of interest*; the *horny* stage; and the *return to normal*. Each of the stages has powerful effects on the adjustment process. However, not everybody going through the divorce process goes through all three stages of the sexuality process. Some people do not go through the lack of interest stage, and some do not experience the horny stage. However, the stages are very common occurrences that need to be recognized.

You had a sexual relationship—for better or for worse—for all those years you were married, but now your relationship partner is no longer available. You are faced with all of the emotional and social adjustments of ending a love relationship, including what to do with your sexual desires.

"I Wish I Were Single"?

When you were married, did you wonder if all those "free" singles were the sexual athletes they were rumored to be? And did you fantasize about what it would be like to have a date with a different and exciting person each night of the week?

Now you are single. (We trust that, by this point on the trail, you have accepted the reality of your situation.) Look at the people around you. Many are spending evenings alone. Many are out pretending to have fun when in reality they are just plain bored. You may find yourself spending an evening with a person who makes your ex look attractive and desirable—and you never thought anyone could be worse than your ex. And everyone you know seems to be going out with someone and then breaking up—you can't even keep track of who is dating whom. The contrast between your fantasy of the wild single life and what it actually is adds greatly to the trauma of divorce.

"A Date? Well, I Don't Know..."

Take heart: The first part of this sexuality climb is the steepest and most difficult; it gets easier after you become accustomed to being single. You have not been "out on a date" for years, and the first person you ask turns you down. You attend a singles party petrified that no one will ask you to dance—and equally petrified that someone will. At the first contact with the opposite sex, you feel like an awkward junior-high kid on a first date. And wow! If someone should make a pass at you...well, the thought is enough to make you stay home, alone, forever.

Just what is appropriate behavior for an adult who hasn't dated in years? There may have been rules and chaperons at your gatherings when you were a teenager. Your parents probably told you what time to be home. Now you have no one to set the limits but yourself, and your feelings are so confused and uncertain that you can't even rely on them. You envied the freedom of singleness, and now you would give anything to have the security of marriage again. And what about the moral and health issues involved?

Later on in the process, when you've found your individual pathway, things will be more comfortable. After you have overcome your confusion and uncertainty, you'll find that you can express yourself through dating and relationships with the opposite sex. There may be a freedom that you didn't have when you were a teenager doing what was expected of you—or what was not expected.

"I'm Glad You Asked That Question"

Sex can be, for many people, a difficult—even awkward—subject to discuss with others. In the Fisher divorce seminars, sexuality is one of the last of the sessions, to give people time to become comfortable discussing these personal and emotional issues. To help participants become more comfortable, they're asked to *write down* their questions about sexuality—you know, the ones they've always wanted to ask but were afraid to—and the facilitator reads the questions aloud to ensure anonymity. Questions that come up frequently give us insights into the concerns of formerly married people.

A few examples from recently separated people:

- *What do you find attractive and desirable in the opposite sex?*

- *What do you call going out? I hate the word "date"!*

- *How do I tell the person I'm going out with that I don't want anything heavy?*

Those farther along in the recovery process ask other questions:

- *What do you think about a person who will have sex early in the relationship?*

- *How do people feel about having more than one sexual relationship at the same time?*

- *Why don't they call again after we've gone to bed together?*

- *I refuse to consider having sex outside of marriage—would you want to go out with me?*

The adjustments resulting from the changing sex roles cause difficulty for both men and women:

- *What do men think about a woman who asks you out?*

- *Just what do women want? I hold the door open for one woman and she gets irritated. The next woman waits for me to open the door. What am I supposed to do?*

- *I always felt comfortable making complimentary comments to a woman and asking her out. This week, a woman told me she liked my legs and asked me if I would like to go out with her. What do I do?*

- *Who do you think should pay for the date?*

- *Whose responsibility is it for birth control?*

- *Is everybody but me comfortable about using condoms?*

Questions about kids can be difficult too:

- *Who pays for the babysitter?*

- *Who takes the babysitter home?*

- *What do you think about a partner spending the night when children are present?*

- *My children don't want me to date. What do I do?*

- *What do I say to my teenager when she tells me to get home early?*

- *What do I do when the kid answers the doorbell, sees me, and shuts the door in my face?*

Many formerly married people are frightened about AIDS and other sexually transmitted diseases (STDs):

- *I would like to have sex, but I'm deathly afraid of STDs. How can I be sure to avoid getting a disease?*

- *How do I find out if the person may be infected with HIV before we have sex?*

- *What is herpes? Is it really dangerous?*

Formerly married people have many understandable concerns about sexuality. These questions reflect only a few of their anxieties. Dorothy reflected the emotional impact of sexuality, reporting, "I became extremely depressed last week when I realized I was forty years old, divorced, and might never get laid again!"

We don't claim to have answers to all these questions, but we think this chapter will help you clarify your own issues around sexuality.

"Not Tonight, Thanks"

The first stage of the process, while you are in deep grief, is a lack of interest in sex, or maybe a complete inability to perform sexually. Women tend to be completely uninterested in sex; men are often impotent. Just when you are feeling a great deal of emotional pain, the fact that you are uninterested or unable to perform sexually adds to the pain. Many people say, "I was already hurting so much, and now I find that I can't perform sexually. It feels like hitting rock bottom." When they learn that it is perfectly normal and natural to be uninterested in sex while in deep grief, they feel greatly relieved.

Honk If You're...

I became so horny after my separation that I called my friend asking for suggestions of what I could do. Having sex with someone I was not married to was out of the question for me.

—Raquel

Somewhere along the divorce process, perhaps near the end of the anger rebuilding block, you get through the stage of not wanting to or not being able to perform sexually. At that point, you will probably go to the other extreme and reach the *horny* stage. Your sexual desires may be greater than you have ever known in your life. It is almost frightening. Because the needs and desires of this stage are so strong, it is important to understand your feelings and attitudes as much as possible.

Among the many feelings present in the horny stage is a need to prove that you are okay, personally and sexually. It is as though you are trying to solve not only your sexual problems, but all of the other rebuilding blocks as well, using sex as the method. You are trying to overcome loneliness, to feel lovable again, to improve your self-concept, to work through some anger, to develop friendships—and all of these things are concentrated in the sexual drive. It is as though your body is trying to heal itself through sexual expression alone. Some folks find their behavior at the horny stage to be somewhat "compulsive" because of this.

One-night stands are one way people try to deal with the horny stage. We see this approach commonly portrayed in books and movies about divorce. The need to go out and "prove that you are okay" may be so great that some people will do something sexually that they have never done before—without much thought for the moral or health issues.

Another important understanding about the horny stage is that there is a great need for touching during this period. As you go through the divorce process, you will probably experience a heightened need to be physically touched. Touch has remarkable healing qualities. Depending upon the warmth and closeness of your relationship, you likely received much physical touching in your marriage. Now that touching is not there anymore, many people will try to meet their need for physical touch with sex, not realizing that there is a very real difference between physical touching and sexual touching. Although the two are entirely different, you can resolve much of your need for sexual contact by getting the physical touching that you need in nonsexual ways (such as hugs, massages, holding hands, walking arm in arm).

You can resolve the needs of the horny stage by methods other than direct sexual contact. If you understand that a part of the compulsive drive behind the horny stage is to prove that you are okay and to feel good about yourself again, then you can work directly on that. Building your identity and self-confidence and understanding that you are lovable can overcome the loneliness and take away some of the pressures of this stage. And if you can reach your "quota" of hugs, this will also take away some of the pressures. Together, these steps may go a long way toward resolving your needs at this difficult time.

The stereotype about the divorced person being an "easy mark" sexually results from the horny stage. During this period, the divorced person may indeed be an "easy mark," as the sex drive is tremendous. Many people going through the divorce process have sexual relationships somewhat promiscuously—not a recommended practice in the age of widespread herpes, chlamydia, HPV, HIV, and other sexually transmitted diseases.

Getting Back to Normal

> Sex in our marriage was not good. We separated and experienced sexual relationships with other people. Then when we came together again, we were surprised that sex with each other was good. It seemed to free us to be apart and to be with others.
>
> —Mike and Jane

Eventually, you will overcome the horny stage and transition to the third stage of postdivorce sexuality, in which your normal sex drive resumes. (There is, of course, a great deal of variation in sex drive from one person to another, and remember that not everyone experiences all three stages.) Because the horny stage is so compulsive and so controlling, people often find it a relief to return to their normal level of sexual desire.

During the early stages of the sexuality process, you do what you *should* do; then you start doing what you *want* to do. Most people going through divorce experience the evolution of becoming free sexually, in the sense that they are suddenly aware of who they are and what their sexual nature is. This is another growth aspect of the divorce process.

Most people were sexually monogamous in marriage because that is what they believed they should be. Then when they go through the horny stage, they may have many sexual relationships. Finally, they decide to be monogamous again because this is what they want to be.

Consider the impact of this process on future love relationships. The need for sexual experience outside of a committed relationship is much less when one arrives at this third stage. As long as you are in the *should* mode sexually, there is always the temptation to do what you *should not* do. But when you reach this third stage—doing what you want to do and expressing who you really are—the temptation for sex outside a love relationship is greatly diminished.

There's More to Life

> I've agreed with everything you have said until now, but when you state that experiencing sexual relationships while single can be a personal growth experience, I have to strongly disagree. Sex is sacred and should occur only between two people in a sacred marriage.
>
> —Father John

We have blown sex out of proportion in our society, perhaps because we hid it and denied it for so long. The "media view" of sex appears not to have much to do with the real world. Advertising is full of sex in order to sell products. Youth—and the supposed beauty, aliveness, and sexuality of youth—is revered. With such a daily overdose in the media, it's tough to keep a realistic perspective on sexuality when it comes to love relationships and marriage.

Usually missing from popular depictions is the spiritual dimension of human sexuality. Sex is one way of transcending our normal means of expressing ourselves, and it allows us to show our love and concern for another person in a very special and positive way. Sex can be a method of transporting oneself to levels beyond the everyday, to become something greater than what one normally is. But this spiritual dimension that is present in sexuality is also present in overcoming anger, in our ability to communicate, in learning to like another person, and in learning to accept and deal with all of the human emotions. Sexuality, when placed in perspective, may be seen as only one of the many normal healthy elements of our connectedness with our fellow humans.

Our society, with its historical roots in religious belief, has traditionally placed great emphasis on having a sexual relationship only with a marriage partner. Yet the messages we receive are mixed and quite confusing. Many divorced people are amazed to learn that they can have very enjoyable and beautiful sex without being in love with the person. Those who hold more traditional beliefs may feel a great amount of guilt if they have nonmarital sex. And there are a number of people who have adopted a morality concerned only with not catching a disease and not becoming pregnant.

Healthy divorce adjustment requires that you grow beyond an undue emphasis on physical sex and arrive at the point where you can understand the beauty of your sexuality as a special way of sharing and communicating with another person. A personal style of sexuality that is (a) a genuine expression of your individuality, uniqueness, and morality, (b) equally concerned with the needs and well-being of your sexual partner, and (c) not hurtful to anyone else or the larger community is socially responsible, self-fulfilling...and human.

Each person has to develop a personal and individual sexual morality appropriate for her or his own beliefs, values, personality, background, attitudes, experiences, and partner. Many people will choose to have no sexual relationships outside of marriage—a very appropriate choice for them. Others may find sexual experiences an effective way of appeasing postdivorce sexual desire and of healing themselves after ending the love relationship.

Most divorced people are comfortable with only one sexual relationship at a time. In fact, the evidence seems pretty clear that most people need an emotional relationship to support a sexual relationship.

When two people have communication, trust, understanding, and respect for each other, they are comfortable having a sexual relationship, if that is within their moral value system. If you are able to reach this level of self-actualization in your sexual relationship, you will find less need to have relationships outside of marriage if you remarry in the future.

Can We Talk About It?
Open Communication About Sex

Let's now look at some of the other adjustment problems you may experience as you end a love relationship and enter the formerly married culture.

Women often complain that all men are interested in is going to bed with them. Yet we find that very few formerly married people are genuinely able to enjoy cheap and casual sex. There are, unfortunately, many people in our society who have not developed ways of interacting with the opposite sex beyond the sexual arena. It can be and often is the easiest avenue open for contact and, after all, it's one where the potential payoff is great, if temporary. Nevertheless, there are many aspects of relationship other than the sexual component, and your life will be so much richer if you fully develop your range of choices. (In the previous chapter, we looked at developing friendships with the opposite sex that are nonromantic and nonsexual.)

It is interesting to note that, in our seminar questionnaires asking people what they would most like to talk about, the number two choice (after relationships) differs between men and women. In almost all cases for women, the second choice is sexuality, and in almost all cases for men, the second choice is love. Surprised? There's more. Not only are women more interested in talking about sex, they are much more comfortable talking about it than men are. After one session on sexuality, Burt confided that he went home and was unable to go to sleep because he was so shocked by how freely the women in class had talked about sexuality.

We believe that openness is a very healthy style of interaction with others. (You'll recall our discussion in chapter 13 about dropping our masks and being more open in our communication.) Sexuality used to be virtually impossible to talk openly about, so people were prevented from understanding and dealing with their sexual attitudes and feelings. Now, because of greater openness in our society, we are able to understand and develop our sexual feelings just as we understand and develop all of the other human emotions we feel.

Openness in sexual matters leads to another avenue that is very freeing. When you are dating within the society of the formerly married, you can discuss sexual concerns openly and early in your relationships, minimizing all of the little games revolving around "Are we going to bed or not?" Many of the dating relationships that you have will never include sexual intimacy; it will simply not be appropriate. Discussing this and getting it out in the open frees you to allow the relationship to develop more naturally and normally, free of the games that go along with not knowing where you stand sexually with the other person.

If you are early in the rebuilding process and the idea of having a sexual relationship is extremely frightening, you can share this with the other person: "I really need to get out and be with a friend, but anything beyond friendship is more than I can stand emotionally at this point." You'll be surprised at the favorable response from others after you have openly shared like this. Most will understand and accept you because they, too, have gone through painful breakups, if not a divorce, and have experienced some of the same feelings themselves.

Without Using Each Other

There are a considerable number of lonely—even desperate—people who introduce another problem into the culture of divorced people in which they now find themselves. They make the whole problem of sexuality even more difficult because they are basically looking for somebody to use. If you are a kind and caring person, seeing all of the needy people around you may tempt you to help them meet their needs, some of which may be sexual.

The great loneliness and neediness found in the postdivorce culture causes special adjustment problems for those who are caught in the *compassion trap*—the desire to nurture and give to others in response to their apparent needs. If you tend to be that way, you will have to learn to be somewhat selfish. (In this case, "selfish" is also arguably the responsible path.)

There is no way you can meet the needs of all those who are desperate and lonely. You must meet your own needs and take care of yourself first, and you must do so without using other people or allowing others to use you. Do everything you can to feel good about yourself and to grow within yourself so you can become as complete and whole as possible, overcoming your own loneliness and neediness. That will provide you a solid foundation for future relationships, as well as for helping others who are in genuine need.

Roles and Rules: Who Does What to Whom?

Another big problem for many people entering the postdivorce dating pool is the question of rules. You may feel as if you are a bewildered teenager, not exactly understanding and knowing how to behave. Attitudes and social mores around sexuality have changed so rapidly in recent years, hardly anyone can keep up. Set rules of conduct for romantic partners and fixed roles for each gender are a thing of the past. By the time you read this, in fact, things will have likely changed from the time it was written!

The key to these changes is developing the freedom to be yourself. Of course, freedom to be yourself is very difficult to achieve if you don't know who "yourself" is! You'll need to find your way, follow your own values and moral code, become open and honest about who you are, and express your unique individuality as much as possible.

If there ever were "rules" for dating, they are no more! Gender roles are in flux, with both women and men acting as initiators in everything, including sex. In the discussions of sexuality in the Fisher divorce seminars, both genders are asking how the other feels about who makes the first move in sexual contact. Heterosexual men often say they find it very freeing to have the woman be the initiator. They have had to deal with fears of rejection from women all of their lives, and they say it feels good now to have women deal with the risk of being turned down—they feel free from the burden of being the initiator all the time. And women are ready to take the lead.

Despite such comments from men, however, women report that in the real world, some men are still unsure how to respond to assertive women. Although men say they like to be asked out, often they are uncomfortable when the actual situation arises. It appears that, *intellectually*, men like women to initiate; but *emotionally*, men have more difficulty handling sexually assertive women.

Women report confusion also. Women who say they would like to ask men out often get cold feet when the time comes. It's not easy to dismantle old roles and try out new behaviors when you are rebuilding after the loss of a relationship. On the other hand, it is an opportune time to do exactly that. Everything else in your life is changing. Evolving gender roles and sexual mores are resulting in more equality between the sexes and more freedom for individuals to be themselves.

But nothing stays the same; we see the pendulum of social mores swinging back and forth. It's not a smooth road, and periods of rapid social change cause much uncertainty and confusion. Now more than ever, perhaps, it is necessary to know yourself, to adopt values that are both self-fulfilling and respectful of others, and to act in accordance with those values.

Let's Be Careful Out There

If you have decided to be open to new sexual relationships, let us pass along a couple of words of advice: *be safe!*

Safer sex is really important. HIV and other sexually transmitted conditions have had a major impact on sexual behavior around the world. Science and medicine continue to seek ways to deal with these diseases, but each of us has to take responsibility for keeping ourselves and our sexual partners healthy by adopting safer sex practices.

By "safer sex," we mean a conscious decision to minimize the risks of sexually transmitted diseases. The only guarantee against STDs, of course, is either abstinence or an absolutely certain, exclusive monogamous relationship with a love partner who has "tested clean"; but additional measures, including the following, can be taken:

- Regular periodic physical examinations

- Conscientious and unfailing use of condoms (preferably with spermicides) during intercourse

- Awareness and avoidance of common risk factors (such as sex with intravenous drug users)

- Honest and open discussion of sexual history, habits, and preferences with potential partners

- Infrequent changing of partners

Every individual—married or single—of course has the right to freedom of sexual expression, so long as the practice involves consenting adults and purposefully avoids physical or psychological harm to another. No one is obligated to have a sexual relationship with another person (including a marriage partner) unless he or she wishes to do so. Being a sexual person—and all of us are—is a matter of making choices and acting on them. We hope your choices will be informed, safe, fun, relationship-centered—and your own.

Children and Sex

Children of divorce must also deal with the rebuilding block of sexuality. When their parents' relationship ends, where do they find role models for relationships, for sexuality, for becoming mature adults?

It is often confusing for children to see their parents involved in new relationships after the divorce. Even young children somehow sense that this new development may include sex. (In fact, kids know more than you realize about which parents are having sex and which are not!) And if the parents are in the horny stage and sending out all of the sexual vibrations that accompany that stage, what do the children do with that? How do they handle this new behavior in their parents?

Communication may sound like an old answer, but it is critically important at this point. When parents talk with their children frankly and openly about sexuality—at a level appropriate to each child's ability to understand—it is very helpful for the kids and for the parents. Although there is much anxiety and insecurity in the children's lives right now, that very turmoil can be the beginning of learning. Children may well gain a far deeper understanding of sexuality—including their own maturation—as their parents go through this stage of rebuilding.

Children can find role models in their parents, relatives, and grandparents, and their parents' friends. As one teenager stated, "I've got more role models around now than I ever had before!"

How Are You Doing?

We have covered a lot of ground in this chapter, and there is much we have not explored. Sex is often a stumbling block for the divorced person, so be sure you have dealt thoroughly with these issues before you go on. Here are some trail markers for assessing your progress:

- *I am comfortable going out with potential love partners.*

- *I know and can explain my present moral attitudes and values.*

- *I feel capable of having a deep and meaningful sexual relationship when it becomes appropriate.*

- *I would feel comfortable being intimate with another love partner.*

- *My sexual behavior is consistent with my morality.*

- *I am satisfied with my present dating situation.*

- *I am behaving morally, the way I would like to have my children behave.*

- *I feel satisfied with the way I am meeting my sexual needs.*

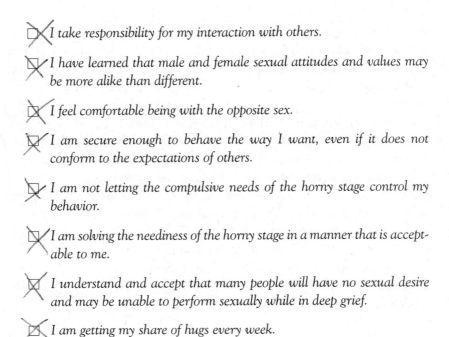

☒ I take responsibility for my interaction with others.

☒ I have learned that male and female sexual attitudes and values may be more alike than different.

☒ I feel comfortable being with the opposite sex.

☒ I am secure enough to behave the way I want, even if it does not conform to the expectations of others.

☒ I am not letting the compulsive needs of the horny stage control my behavior.

☒ I am solving the neediness of the horny stage in a manner that is acceptable to me.

☒ I understand and accept that many people will have no sexual desire and may be unable to perform sexually while in deep grief.

☒ I am getting my share of hugs every week.

CHAPTER 18

Singleness

"You Mean It's Okay?"

Singleness is a time to invest in your own personal growth rather than in other relationships. A period of singleness enables you to build confidence in yourself so you can experience and enjoy being single as an acceptable lifestyle, not as a time to be lonely. It is easy, however, to become stuck in this rebuilding block as a means of avoiding another intimate love relationship.

I've become aware that living as a single person is an affirmation of strength and self, not an embarrassing admission of failure. I'm more relaxed in the company of others—I'm no longer wasting emotional energy being a social chameleon. Postmarital guilt, self-doubts, and questions like "Will I ever love again?" are greatly diminished. I am happy as a single person—something I had not thought possible before.

—Larry

You'll notice a number of people walking by themselves during this part of the climb. They've gained enough confidence in their climbing ability that they're choosing to walk at their own pace rather than following the crowd. Some of these folks have chosen time alone as a way of investing in themselves. Others simply want and need to be by themselves, with their own thoughts, and to enjoy the view alone. This is the stage of *singleness*.

Were You Ever Really Single Before?

Many people never learned to be single before they married. They went from parental homes to marital homes, never even considering that one could be happy living as a single person and never questioning the myth of "happily ever after."

Mona lived with her parents until she married Joe. She went from pleasing one man, her father, to pleasing another man, her husband. When Joe first talked about leaving, she clung to him because the thought of living alone was terrifying. She had never learned to please herself. She had always been a dependent person, and now the thought of being independent, although challenging, was frightening to her. She was embarrassed about how she felt because it really seemed silly to her that a thirty-five-year-old woman did not know her own mind or know what to do with her life.

Only gradually did she adjust to being alone. At first, she searched for other relationships, something or someone to lean on. As she became more and more confident, she began doing more things for herself and enjoying it. She wallpapered a whole bedroom; sawed the boards and pounded the nails for a new patio fence; started going out to movies and concerts by herself while the kids were with Joe. She invited the whole neighborhood over for a party. These activities left her feeling exhilarated, knowing that she did not need anyone. She became a good example of what it means to be an independent person.

Jim represents the male side of this same coin. He had been well cared for by his mother. His clothes were always washed and ironed, meals were on time, and even his room was kept clean. He could devote his time to school, school activities, and his job. When he entered college, he lived in a dorm. Again his meals were provided and he had a minimum of house-keeping chores. When he married Janet, she took over all the things his mother had always done. He felt independent and didn't realize how dependent he actually was. He found out when he left Janet. He was help-less in the kitchen, even in preparing the simplest meal. He had very little understanding of how to wash his clothes and ended up with pink under-wear when he put them in the wash with his red shirt! You can pay for car maintenance, but it is difficult—and very expensive—to hire a full-time cook and housekeeper.

Gradually, Jim's self-prepared meals improved. He finally got brave enough to invite a woman friend to his home to eat, and she was delighted with the meal he prepared. His clothes began to look more cared for. He was very pleased and proud when he learned to iron his own shirts. Learning to care for himself was like growing up—and each accomplish-ment gave him a feeling of success and achievement.

"Me and My Shadow"

The singleness we're talking about is much more than learning to do the tasks that someone else has done for you, of course. It's a whole way of life.

Independence in the realm of dating and love relationships is a good example. A typical comment from a recently separated person might be, "I'll never make it as a single person; I need another love relationship." But during the singleness stage, the same person might say, "Why get remar-ried? I can come and go as I please. I can eat whenever I feel like it. I don't have to adjust my daily living habits to another person. Being single sure feels good!" Before the singleness stage, one may be looking for the "lost half." But during this stage, one reaches the point of comfort in going out alone. No longer is a "date" necessary to avoid embarrassment or a feeling of failure. The quality of relationships improves: now you're choosing the person you go out with, rather than taking whoever seems available, just to be with someone. And the whole evening out may be spent sharing rather than needing. Other people may be encountered and enjoyed for who they are, rather than as potential lifetime companions.

Single and Loving It

One of the homework assignments in the Fisher divorce seminar has to do with developing new interests in the singleness stage. Many people spent their free, recreational time in the past doing what their spouse wanted or what they had learned to do with their parents. Your assignment now is simply to take the time to develop a new interest or to pursue something you may have wanted to do for a long time. It might be to learn to play the guitar, to paint, to drive a car, or to play a new sport. Those who take this homework seriously find many new activities that *they* really enjoy; they no longer settle for what someone else enjoyed.

Singleness is a time for being a responsible adult. The roles each of us plays in our relationships with others are linked to our internal attitudes and feelings. Surprisingly, the link is a two-way street! As you change your actions and your ways of relating to others, you'll find that your attitudes begin to change too. ("Hey, I'm finding out I can get along well as a single person. Look what I'm accomplishing on my own!")

It's easier to make these moves toward independence in the singleness stage than when you were in a long-term love relationship. A neutral environment facilitates both internal and external changes. The singleness stage is a great opportunity to make the internal changes in attitudes and feelings—and the external changes in behavior and relationships—necessary for your growth toward becoming a whole person by yourself.

"I'm Glad to Be Single Again...or Am I?"

Not everything is rosy in the singleness stage, of course. Research shows that single people—particularly women—do not always fare as well economically. Single people are passed over for promotions in some career fields. They're looked upon as fair game romantically and sexually. Despite strengthened laws against sexual harassment, single women in particular may be pressured in the workplace, expected to trade sexual favors for promotions and other opportunities. There are other situations that create discomfort for single people. Alexa complained about her child's Sunday school class. When the teacher asked the children to draw pictures of their families, Alexa's son drew a picture of himself, his sister, and his mother—which was his family. The teacher made him add a man to his drawing because, "We all know that a family consists of both a father and a mother!" Alexa was hurt, disappointed, and angry, and she expressed her negative feelings directly to the minister of the church.

Ursula reported that the Mother's Day sermon at her church was about marital love, ignoring the dozen or more single moms present, who felt completely left out. She let the minister know what a depressing day in church it had been for her. He responded very favorably, meeting with the single mothers and offering a special sermon—with a broader view of motherhood—a couple of weeks later.

Schools are often an irritating problem when you are a single parent. The PTA chairperson calls and asks if Johnny's parents will run the dart booth at the school carnival. The single-parent father explains that he would be happy to take part—but that he'll be alone. The chairperson informs him that it takes two to run the booth and she will ask someone else to handle it. PTA meetings are often couple-oriented and can be pretty uncomfortable for singles who must attend without a partner.

Same thing with parent-teacher conferences. The teacher tells you that "all of the 'problem children' in the room have just one parent," and that's why she wanted to see you. Your child may not be getting "the parenting she needs," and perhaps that's why she is doing so poorly in her schoolwork. What's more, your daughter is "so boy crazy for a fifth-grader!" It is implied that if Mom had a "permanent" relationship with one man, Janie would have a better attitude toward males. You feel angry, vulnerable, and defenseless. What can you say?

You can develop some assertive responses for the most common put-downs and discriminatory acts. You can help to educate others, while maintaining your own integrity, by responding firmly. You'll feel better inside too, rather than going away fuming!

Here's an example: In response to the teacher who insists Janie would be better off in a two-parent household, you might try something like this, "You're right—being a single parent isn't easy. But Janie and I are doing fine these days, and I don't agree that her school performance is suffering because of my divorce. I'll be glad to work with you on special homework or tutoring or other efforts to improve her schoolwork. What suggestions do you have for her study habits? Will you give her extra assignments?"

That way, you're not accepting the teacher's put-down or letting her blame your personal life for Janie's school problems. The responsibility for schoolwork is focused back where it belongs—on teacher-student-parent cooperation—not on your love life.

Successfully Single

It often takes a great deal of inner security to handle the singleness stage successfully. Much of the discussion in this chapter concerns the feelings singles experience in response to society's attitudes. If you have worked your way through the prior rebuilding blocks successfully, it is likely that you will be able to experience a sense of peacefulness and calmness in the singleness stage. You may become slightly upset about the attitudes of others, but you'll be strong enough to handle them. Learn from the external prejudices and use them to become more secure in your own internal feelings.

Singleness can be one of the most productive stages you go through in the climb, in the sense that the old wounds can really be healed. Dealing with the external discrimination may help you to become stronger inside.

One caution: Singleness is an easy stage in which to become stuck. If you have not worked through all of the leftovers concerning marriage and intimacy, you may use the singleness stage as a place to hide. It may sound like it's coming from the singleness stage when you hear someone say, "I'll never marry again." But in many ways, that is the opposite stance of genuine singleness. Fear of intimacy, avoidance of feelings, and opposition to marriage as though it were the worst institution in our society—all indicate that the person is stuck. The goal is to be free to choose singleness or remarriage, not to purposely stay single forever.

Singleness has become an acceptable alternative in our society. A generation or two ago, a single person was looked upon in the community as somewhat weird, one who just did not quite make it to the altar. It was "patriotic" to be married because, after all, the family was the cornerstone of American society. Attitudes are changing; at a talk on love relationships, one woman wanted to know why we had to keep talking about *relationships*. Was it not just as valid to talk about remaining single? Did we have to keep looking toward being in a relationship as the ideal?

The fact that there are an estimated one million divorces in the United States each year makes singleness more acceptable for many. The large number of formerly married people in our society has brought about many changes in attitudes toward singleness. Perhaps we are becoming more accepting of individual differences? Let's hope so!

Children and Singleness

Singleness is an important rebuilding block for children too. They need to learn to be single, individual, independent-from-parents people before they marry for the first time. If children can see and understand the importance of singleness, it will give them a much better chance to develop successful love relationships in their futures.

Parenting is different during the singleness stage. In earlier stages, parents frequently bend themselves out of shape trying to make sure they are lovable, datable, and okay in many other ways. The kids often suffer; their needs are put on the "back burner." In the singleness stage, parents are usually more responsive to the needs of the kids. Susannah had been volunteering in her divorce recovery seminar because she "needed" to feel worthwhile by helping others. When she began to reach the singleness stage, she resigned as a volunteer because she wanted to spend more time with her children. Parents in the singleness stage have begun to rise above their own emotional needs.

How Are You Doing?

At this point in our climb up the mountain, we've gained a big reward: the view from above the timberline. You can see forever! And the singleness stage is definitely above the timberline. You can see the world much more clearly from here. You know yourself much better. You understand others, and your interactions with others, much better. Your view of life is much broader. At the singleness stage, we're almost to the top. Let's hurry and see the view from the peak!

Here are some items to check up on before the final climb:

- ☑ I am comfortable being single.

- ☑ I can be happy as a single person.

- ☑ I am comfortable going to social events as a single person.

- ☑ I see being single as an acceptable lifestyle.

- ☑ I am becoming a whole person rather than a half person looking for my lost other half.

- ☑ I am spending time investing in my own personal growth rather than looking for another love relationship.

- ☑ I can look at my friends as people I want to be with rather than as potential love partners.

- ☑ If I have children and family, I can spend time enjoying being with them rather than begrudging the time they take from my personal life.

- ☑ I have found inner peace and contentment as a single person.

CHAPTER 19

Purpose

"I Have Goals for the Future Now"

Recently separated people tend to live in the past and be very dependent upon others. After they have worked through the divorce process, they begin to live more in the present and be less dependent upon others. Now you can plan for your future as an independent person, with or without a new love relationship.

When I started this divorce seminar, I dreamed I was driving a car that went off a mountain road and I was balancing on the edge of a cliff, too scared to move. When I completed this divorce seminar, I dreamed I was in a big, dark pit with my car, but there was a cement ramp at the end of the pit where I could drive my car out.

—Harry

T ake a look back down the trail. Hasn't this been a rewarding climb? Your highest priority, back in the divorce pits at the bottom of the mountain, was to survive. You weren't thinking about setting any goals for the future. You were getting along from hour to hour, day to day.

Things have changed a lot as we've "gained altitude," haven't they? It was hard work climbing the divorce process trail, but now that you're almost at the top, you have some perspective. You can look back at your past to see how you got to where you are today. You can look at your present situation and recognize how much you have accomplished. You can look at your future and know that you can determine for yourself who you will become.

Looking at Your Past, Present, and Future Life

The trauma of divorce motivates us to take a good hard look at our lives. We tend to go back into the past and dwell a great deal upon the things that we would have done differently if we could live our lives over again. We tend to be so engrossed in the present scene that we are unable to think about the future.

It is time now for you to get out of some of the past thinking and the present pain and to start thinking about goals and decisions for the future.

People in a great deal of emotional pain cannot easily make plans and set goals for the future, and if you are still in a great deal of emotional pain, then you may find it difficult to read this chapter on setting goals. If you've read this book too fast and haven't allowed all of the emotional learning to take place, then you may need to set aside this chapter for now, take some time to go back over the previous material, and do the emotional learning that you need to do.

As we discussed in chapter 11, Bruce's research shows that people who have recently separated have very low scores on the Tennessee Self-Concept Scale. Other research using the Personality Orientation Inventory indicates that recently separated people, and especially dumpees, have a great deal of "living in the past" in their thinking and attitudes. People in the divorce pits have very little hope and goals for the future. They feel they have entered Dante's *Inferno*, where the words above the gate read "All hope abandon, ye who enter here."

But chances are, if you have worked your way carefully through each of the preceding chapters over a period of weeks or months, you are ready to get on with your life. In this chapter, you'll be building on your successful climb up the mountain and doing some goal setting for your future.

Let's get started!

Your Lifeline: An Exercise in Setting Goals

Here's an experiential exercise that will help you to look at your past, your present, and your future life: we want you to draw your own *lifeline*. This lifeline is a graphic timeline, drawn across a sheet of paper from left to right, showing the ups and downs of your life. (See the illustration later in this chapter for an example of how the finished product might look.)

Keep in mind that this project is only for *yourself*—it's not an art project, and you won't be graded! (Although there will be questions on the "test" at the end of the chapter.) Erase or start over as you need to. Make the final product realistic and valuable for *you*. Here's a step-by-step guide to the process:

1. Find as big a piece of clean paper as you can. The bigger it is, the more freedom it gives you to draw your lifeline. A few feet of butcher paper is ideal.

2. Think about your present age and then think about how long you expect to live. Most people, when they think about it, have a sense of how old they are going to be when they die. They may feel they are going to live to be very old, or they may feel they are going to die young. Get in touch with this feeling and see what kind of a life expectancy you have for yourself. Then think about your present age, what percentage of your life you've already lived, and what percentage of your life you've got left to live. For example, if you feel that you may live to be ninety and you are presently forty-five, you have lived 50 percent of your expected life.

3. Draw a vertical line on your sheet of paper such that the amount of space to the left of it signifies how much life you've already lived and the amount of space to the right of it signifies how much you've got left to live. (If you've lived half of your life, the line would be smack in the middle. If you've lived a third of your life, the line would be a third of the way across the paper.) Think about how many years you've probably got left to live compared to how

many years you've already lived. What are you going to do with the remaining years of your life?

4.   Think about whether your life has been basically happy or basically unhappy so far. Draw another line horizontally on the paper reflecting your basic level of happiness. If you have been basically unhappy all your life, draw the line lower down on the page.

Now you're ready to start drawing your lifeline.

Your Lifeline: The Past

Start your lifeline by trying to remember the earliest childhood memory you have. Think about this early childhood memory for a little bit. It may tell you a great deal about yourself and about the rest of your life. Begin your lifeline so it reflects the happiness or unhappiness of this earliest memory. The more unhappy this earliest memory was, the lower you start on the page.

Next, think through the important things you can remember in your early childhood. Identify them in your mind and mark them on your lifeline. If there was an extremely happy event that you remember, mark that on your lifeline, putting it higher on the paper. If there were extremely unhappy things, such as the loss of somebody in your family through death, mark that as something more unhappy.

Keep working through your life as you enter grade school, junior high, and high school, and keep marking the important milestones that stand out in your memory. Think of creating this lifeline as though you were telling a story to a friend—a story about the important things that have happened to you in your life. Include your marriage and any children you may have.

Your Lifeline: The Present

Now think about your divorce and your present emotional situation. Many people who have recently separated will draw their lifelines with the divorce crisis as the lowest point in their lives. This kind of leaves you at a bad place in your lifeline, but remember that you still have the rest of your life left to work on it and to improve yourself to become the kind of person

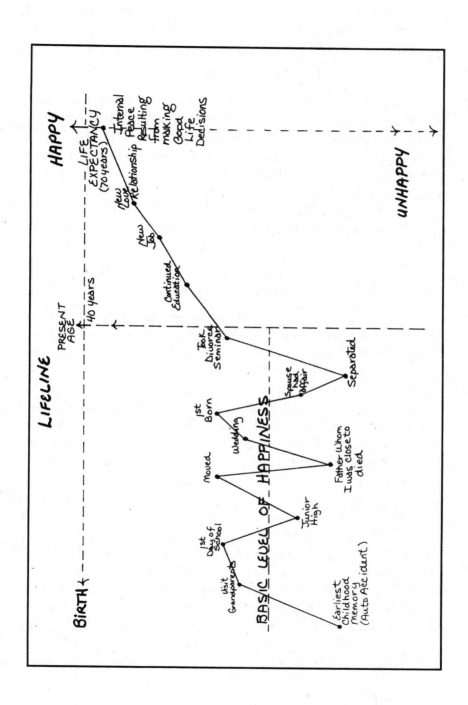

you would like to be. Draw your lifeline to show your level of happiness at the time of your divorce and since then.

Your Lifeline: The Near Future

You've now passed the present, and it's time to start thinking about the future. Set some short-term goals for next month, the next three months, the next six months. Predict what you are going to be doing and how you are going to be feeling in your life. Do you think it is going to be a happier or less happy time than the present? Do you still have some pain to work through, such as the trauma of the final divorce proceedings, a property or custody settlement, or lots of bills to pay with very limited income? Draw the next few months on your lifeline as realistically as possible.

Your Lifeline: The Long-Term Future

Start making longer-term goals by answering these types of question: What do you want to be doing a year from now, five years from now? What are you going to be like in your old age? Will your face reflect the happiness you've known in your life, or will it reflect sadness, bitterness, anger, or negative feelings of some sort? How will retirement affect you? Will you be ready for it—able to handle the adjustment of not working anymore? Have you taken care of your financial needs for your old age? How do you feel about major illnesses possibly occurring in your future life? Have you developed a healthy lifestyle that can help prevent such illnesses? Is your life full of negative feelings that could turn into physical illness as you become older?

You have planted your life into a seedbed, and you're going to grow and mature and harvest the crop. What kind of crop are you going to harvest with your life? Are you going to look back and say, "I've lived the type of life that I wanted to live, and I am ready to die"? Or are you going to look back and say, "Life has somehow passed me by. I'm not ready to die yet"?

What about the person you will be living with? Is it important for you to have another love relationship? To share your life with somebody else as you age? Or would you like to live as a single person and enjoy all of the freedom of being single?

What is important to you in your life? Is it important to make money, to become famous, to have good health, to be successful in your career, to have a happy family? And what does "success" mean to you? What would you do with your life to make it successful? Will you be comfortable with your answers to these two questions: "What contributions will I be remembered for?" and "Will I leave the world a better place?"

Are you becoming the type of person you'd like to be? When are you going to start changing and becoming that person? Today, next week, next month? Or are you never going to get around to being the person you want to be? Today would be a good time to start.

Kids Need Goals Too!

Children feel very confused when their parents are divorcing. While the parents are going through their own pain, the needs of the children are often overlooked. They have no idea where they are going, what's going to happen to them, or how they'll feel tomorrow. They often feel lost, without any goals or direction.

Children face their own stumbling blocks that they can change into rebuilding blocks (see appendix A). If they are given a chance to work through the process themselves, they can begin to develop goals for themselves and for their new family structure. If not, they'll probably feel they are going nowhere.

A structured personal growth program—on either an individual or a group basis—can be very valuable for children at this time. Appendix A presents an outline parents can follow to guide their children through the divorce process, one rebuilding block at a time, just as you've done. Such experiences develop children's skills for dealing with their parents' pain and for meeting their own needs.

The lifeline exercise in this chapter can be adapted for children also, as well as tweens and teens. They don't have the same perspective of time that you have as an adult, but it can be valuable for them to think about their future and to set some goals (typically shorter-term than yours) for themselves.

Divorce is an uncertain and unstable time for kids. It's especially important that we help them to maintain hope for the future, and give them opportunities to develop their own goals.

How Are You Doing?

Now that you've thought about your life and your future as you completed your lifeline chart, take a few moments to assess your progress before you proceed to the mountaintop. It's tempting to sprint to the top when you're this close, but after all your work to get this far, it's worth maintaining a steady pace. Answer these few questions, then go on to the top-of-the-mountain chapter:

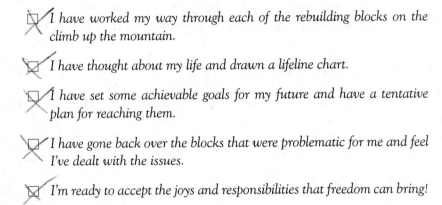

☑ I have worked my way through each of the rebuilding blocks on the climb up the mountain.

☑ I have thought about my life and drawn a lifeline chart.

☑ I have set some achievable goals for my future and have a tentative plan for reaching them.

☑ I have gone back over the blocks that were problematic for me and feel I've dealt with the issues.

☑ I'm ready to accept the joys and responsibilities that freedom can bring!

CHAPTER 20

Freedom
From Chrysalis to Butterfly

Freedom is being able to be fully yourself. By working through the rebuilding blocks, you are building a more fulfilled life and more meaningful relationships in your future. You're becoming free to choose your path to a self-actualized life as a single person or in another love relationship.

I felt many times in my marriage that I was trapped in a prison of love. It was hard to be myself when there were so many demands and expectations placed upon me. When I first separated, I felt even worse. But now I have found that I can fly. I can be me. I feel as if I left the chrysalis and have become a butterfly. I feel so free.

—Alice

Wow! Would you look at that view from here on top of the mountain!

After this page, we want you to stop reading for a moment and take time to go on a fantasy trip. Imagine being on top of a mountain with a view of other peaks and valleys below. Smell the pine trees; let the clear, bright, high-altitude sun warm your skin. Notice the clouds lower than you are, and feel the cool breeze blowing off the snow glaciers. Notice how far away the horizon is out over the plains and how far you can see. Think back about the climb. What was the most enjoyable and interesting portion for you? What was the most difficult part? The most painful? Can you identify the many changes that have taken place within you? Have you really reached the top emotionally, or are you only at the top in your mind? Think about how it feels at the top, having worked so hard in your climb of personal growth.

Take as much time as you want with this fantasy before you go on reading. When you have thought about your fantasy carefully, go ahead and continue reading.

How Far You Have Come!

On the singleness portion of the trail, we hope you found not only that it feels good to be single, but that it may have been the most productive lifestyle for you during the climb. Now you are ready to consider whether you want to begin to develop love relationships again.

How did the process of working your way through these rebuilding blocks affect the way you deal with others? The way you react to loneliness, grief, rejection, guilt, anger, and love significantly determines how you handle your daily life and your interactions with those around you.

If you really work at the rebuilding process, overcoming each stumbling block—including the ones you've had a lot of trouble with—you'll be able to enter into another love relationship (if that's your choice) and make it more productive than the last one. You'll be prepared to meet your own needs, as well as the needs of your loved one, much better than you have in the past. Rebuilding not only helps you to survive the crisis, it also develops your life skills for living alone or in a new love relationship.

A Word to the Widowed

Perhaps you are a widow or widower who was satisfied and happy in your lost relationship. Research indicates that widowed people who elect to marry again have remarriages that are more likely to last. Adjusting to being widowed is a very painful and difficult process, thus most of the blocks in our rebuilding model are applicable and helpful to those going through that crisis. Many widowed people, however, do not have to deal with one of the toughest parts of the adjustment: a previous *unhappy* love relationship.

We've included a special section in the book (appendix D) addressing how the rebuilding model can be applied to the needs of those who are dealing with the pain and challenges of widowhood.

The Air Is Pretty Thin Up Here

For many people, the climb is so difficult that they feel like quitting before reaching the top. Over the years, we've heard countless people say, "I want to stop climbing and take a rest! I'm tired of growing." And many do stop along the way because they are tired or frightened, or feel unable to handle the changes. At such a point, it's time to sit and rest, get your energy back, then keep on climbing. The view at the top is worth it.

Support, hope, and a belief that you can make it are helpful. But it's up to you in the end. Probably the best evidence of the difficulty of the climb is the small percentage of people at the top. Do you have the self-discipline, desire, courage, and stamina to make it?

Now comes the "truth in packaging" disclaimer: We cannot promise that you will be happier, or wealthier, or more fulfilled if you complete the climb. We can assure you that there are fewer turkeys and more eagles at this altitude, but we can't promise that you will find an eagle for yourself (except when you look in the mirror!). The plain hard fact is that you will not necessarily find another "just right" person with whom to create a lasting relationship. What you will find is that you like yourself better, you can enjoy being alone and single, and the people you meet up here will be pretty special—after all, they made this tough climb too!

It is true that there are fewer people here from which to choose. An awful lot of folks just did not make it this far—indeed, many are still at the base camp, playing social games, hiding behind emotional walls, and finding excuses not to undertake the climb. The lack of numbers here may make the process of finding new friends and potential lovers more difficult. But relationships with others at the top are such better quality that quantity is not so important. When you're really at the top, giving off those good vibrations, there are many people attracted to you. (In fact, you may need to be careful—as an eagle now, you look really good!)

Actually, the top of the mountain is not as lonely as parts of the trail were on the way up. And if you are still feeling lonely, maybe you haven't reached the top emotionally. (Have you gone through the book too fast?)

Take a Deep Breath

You may get discouraged at times when you realize that the old patterns have crept back and you really haven't changed as much as you thought. Do you normally put on your right or left shoe first? Try to reverse your routine next week and put on the other shoe first. We'll bet you forget and go back to the old way. It's difficult to make changes in your daily living habits, and even harder to make changes in your personality. Keep up your determination and you will make it. Don't get discouraged—it may come slowly!

You may greatly fear the unknown future. You're not alone! It may be learning to be single; it may be not knowing what to expect or what is expected of you. How do you feel the first time you drive or ride in a city that is unfamiliar to you? Confused, lost, uncertain? How about the way you feel the first time you go to a singles party? There is a certain amount of comfort in the known. (Your old relationship may look good, even if it was like living in hell.)

We doubt you'll want to go back to your old relationship at this point, but if you do, it will be for more positive reasons than fear of the unknown future.

Beyond Singleness

We've talked a great deal during the climb up the mountain about the importance of learning to be single. Let us get in a last word about the importance of relationships. You can become whole by emotionally working hard at it, but we believe there is a part of each of us that needs another person to help us become completely fulfilled. A love relationship is more than icing on the cake, but that analogy seems to fit: the cake is whole without icing, but ever so much sweeter with it! We think each of us needs another person to help us become completely fulfilled and to make life sweeter!

Becoming Free

When you were in the pits of the crisis, you gave no thought to plans and goals for the future. Part of your grief was concerned with loss of your future, since you had to give up the plans and goals you had in that love relationship. But when you came out of the pits, you began looking to the future and making plans again.

Ernie, who worked in a hospital, told his seminar group one evening, "It's like the process in the hospital psych wards. There's a crafts room where the patients spend time. When patients are first admitted, they have no energy to work on crafts. But when they begin to be really interested in crafts, this is a good indication that they're ready to be discharged. I felt ready to be discharged from the divorce pits when I started making plans for the future!"

Research has found that recently separated people, and especially dumpees, are very much "living in the past," thinking mostly about how it "used to be." Farther along in the process, people stop living in the past and start living in the present, enjoying the sunsets. We hope by now you have stopped living in the past and are living in the present and making plans for your own future.

Recently separated people, and again especially dumpees, are very dependent upon others. As people continue to grow in the process, they gain more independence. We hope you have found a good balance between dependence and independence.

The Children of Freedom

As we've made clear, children need to work their way through the rebuilding blocks too, ultimately acquiring the freedom to be themselves, to be free from all the unhealthy needs that control so many people. They need to be free to choose marriage when the time for that comes in the future. Quite frequently, children of divorce say that they will not get married because they saw how devastating divorce was to their parents. Children need freedom of choice in what they will do with their lives, without feeling unduly influenced to either follow or reject their parents' pattern.

All children are not the same, nor do they have the same needs. So even though we generalized a great deal about children in each of the rebuilding blocks chapters, remember that each child is a unique human being and that it is as important for them as it is for adults that they be respected and treated as such. Their differing needs depend upon age, sex, cultural background, number of children in the family, health, availability of extended family and friends and neighbors, physical environment, conditions at school, and the nature of their parents' breakup, as well as the individual personal characteristics of each child.

Kids are stronger than you think and can grow through the rebuilding process right along with you. We encourage you to assist them on the journey, and if you're serious about wanting to do so, you'll find material in appendix A helpful in guiding you.

How Are You Doing?

We thought you might like one last self-assessment to help you see how you are doing in your personal growth. You may wish to check yourself now and occasionally in the future—say, once a month, or at least in two months, six months, a year.

This final checklist includes some important aspects of personal growth that you need to be aware of in order to keep growing. Most of these are areas we've talked about as we climbed the mountain together, and you may want to go back and review them in the book.

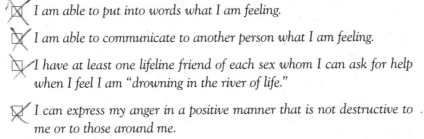

☑ *I am able to put into words what I am feeling.*

☑ *I am able to communicate to another person what I am feeling.*

☑ *I have at least one lifeline friend of each sex whom I can ask for help when I feel I am "drowning in the river of life."*

☑ *I can express my anger in a positive manner that is not destructive to me or to those around me.*

☑ *I am keeping a journal of my feelings and attitudes as I adjust to my divorce crisis.*

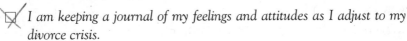

☑ *I have made at least one new friend, or renewed an old friendship, in the past month.*

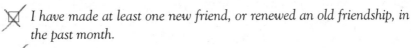

☑ *I have invested quality time with at least one friend this past week.*

☐ I have identified which of the rebuilding blocks I need to work more on and have made a plan to start my further work.

☒ I have invested time in a personal growth experience this past week, such as reading a good book, taking an educational class, attending an interesting exhibit or lecture, improving my diet, watching an educational program on TV, searching online for job opportunities, or beginning an exercise program.

☒ I have seriously considered if I would benefit from a therapy relationship in order to enhance my personal growth or to speed up my adjustment process.

☒ I have received my share of hugs this week to provide me with positive touch.

☒ I have spent time by myself in prayer, meditation, or solitary thought this past week.

☒ I have nurtured myself with a kind deed this past week.

☒ I pay attention to the aches, tensions, and feelings in my body to learn more about myself.

☒ I exercise regularly.

☒ I have made at least one change in my daily living habits that I feel good about this past week.

☒ I nourish my body with a healthy diet (low-sugar and high-fiber foods, fresh fruits and vegetables, whole grains).

☒ I have given emotionally of myself to at least one friend this past week.

☒ I have invested in my spiritual growth this past week.

☒ I like being the person I am.

☒ I am making plans for my future.

☒ I have let the child within me have fun this past week.

☒ I am not carrying around pent-up feelings of anger, grief, loneliness, rejection, or guilt, but have learned to express these feelings in positive ways.

☑ *I am much more in control of my life than I was when my past love relationship ended.*

☑ *I am experiencing the feeling of freedom to be myself.*

☑ *I am actively using the concepts learned from this book to help speed up my adjustment process.*

Well, how are you doing? Are you satisfied with your "report card"? Bring it out again from time to time. It will help you keep track of your progress and remind you of some of the important concepts we've talked about in this climb.

Are You Ready to Fly?

What is this freedom we all seem to be striving for?

Freedom is something you find inside yourself. And you find it by becoming free from unmet needs that control you, such as the need to avoid being alone, the need to feel guilty, the need to please a critical parent, or the need to get free from your own "parent within you."

The butterfly at the top of the mountain stands for the freedom to fly and to land where you choose. You can become free of the bonds that have kept you from being the person you would like to be, the person you were meant to be, the person you are capable of being.

Your worst enemies are those within you, and it is those demons from which you need to free yourself.

Of course, your best friends are inside you as well. Climbing the mountain not only gives you the freedom of choice to seek happiness—either alone or in another love relationship—it also gives you the freedom to be yourself. And that makes the climb of personal growth worthwhile.

It's tough for us to end this book, because we know it represents just a beginning for you. The thousands of people who have gone through the rebuilding process have taught us a great deal about what it means to climb the mountain. We hope you won't put this book away on a shelf, but that you'll use it as often as you need to as a tool to help you rebuild. Share it with a friend, or perhaps give your friend his or her own copy.

Most of all, we wish you success in your continuing personal growth. It's a lifelong challenge!

Kids Are Tougher Than You Think

The Rebuilding Blocks Process for Children
Bruce Fisher, EdD, and Robert Stewart, MA

I thought everything in my life that could go wrong had. But now my kids are acting out. I really don't know what to do.

—Corinne

Sure, single working mothers have problems—real ones. But what about fathers who have custody of their children after a divorce? If you're a man trying to work and raise a child alone, you get no support from anyone. Women are uncomfortable around you—they either think you're on the make or they want to mother you and your child to death. You can't talk to other men: they think you're a little weird if you're worrying about toilet training while they're planning a golf game or a camping trip.

As a single custodial father, I didn't know:

a. What to do when my son woke up screaming with a nightmare
b. How to go about finding a good babysitter
c. How to plan my son's birthday when he turned three
d. How to plan the weekly meals and bake cookies and cakes
e. How to answer questions like, "Why did she go? Where is she? Will I see her again? Does she love me? Will you leave me? Why do I have to go to the babysitter's?"

Harboring all of these insecurities, we both cried a lot.

—Bill

Remember the good old days, Dad—the days before you left home?

—Sheila

Children go through an adjustment process similar to the adult process, but the feelings and attitudes of each rebuilding block may be somewhat different for children. It helps if we realize that our children are also in process, with a mountain of their own to climb.

As family therapists, we believe we are obligated not only to help children adjust to their parents' divorce, but also to help them adjust to the transformation that took place while the parents were going through their own recovery process.

There is a great deal of research about the effects of divorce on children. Some studies say the children are scarred for life; others say the children can actually benefit from their parents' divorce. The most solid research indicates that, while children are likely to experience modestly negative outcomes from their parents' divorce early on, loving parents can help them to prosper in the long run. The people who have done a good job of adjusting are typically better parents. Their children reinforce what much of the research says: children whose parents are adjusting well tend to adjust better also.

Thoughts on Children and Divorce

Many parents try to make up for the guilt they feel about hurting the children with the divorce by playing "superparent." This is usually not helpful to the children.

Kids tend to become stuck on the same building blocks as their parents. The nicest thing you can do for your child is to get your own act together—to work through your own adjustment process—so you can be the warm, supportive parent you are capable of being.

Many times, the children remain strong and supportive to the parents until the parents get their act together. Finally, when the children perceive their parents are strong enough, they take their turn at working through the adjustment process.

In almost every seminar, at least one person is working through his or her parents' divorce of twenty to forty years earlier. We hope your children will not take that long to adjust to the ending of your relationship.

Adults who actively participate in a divorce recovery program often experience tremendous personal growth and change that can affect their children. The children have to adjust not only to their parents' divorce, but also to the personal changes one or both parents have made. We need to do all we can to help our children adjust to what can be major changes in our lives. That's the intention of this appendix.

We hope the material in this section, together with the earlier material on children in the chapters, will help both you and your children transform the divorce crisis into a creative experience.

A Good Divorce Is Better Than a Bad Marriage

Bruce's experience as a juvenile probation officer in the early 1970s is mentioned several times in *Rebuilding*. When he began that work, he at first thought one of the major reasons teenagers got in trouble was because their parents had divorced. This was reinforced by the fact that 48 percent of the children he worked with came from other than a two-parent household. After he went through his own divorce, he recognized that he had been guilty of prejudice against divorced families. It wasn't the divorce itself that was the major cause of kids having difficulties; it was the dysfunctional family that often ended up divorced.

More recent research shows that maybe one-third of children whose parents divorced are doing above average in school and adjustment, another third are doing about average, and the remaining third are doing below average—roughly the same numbers as for intact families. In contrast, children who live within a two-parent dysfunctional family are almost all performing below average. In short, kids are better off with divorced parents than with a high-conflict home life.

Adversarial divorces—and the custody battles that often accompany them—are another source of negative effects on children of divorce. Bruce, in particular, observed that the adversarial process in our courts, which is effective in criminal and civil cases, can feed the anger and vindictiveness of the divorcing parties; in one case he recalled, the judge allowed the noncustodial parent to force five custody hearings for the three children over a two-year period! In that case, the court's handling of the divorce contributed to the children's adjustment difficulties in a way that was almost abusive. Children's pain is already magnified when their parents' divorce is acrimonious rather than amicable; battles in court only extend their period of pain and uncertainty.

Fortunately, parents, and subsequently their children, have a much better opportunity of adjusting to the trauma of divorce today than they did forty, fifty, or sixty years ago. A headline from a *Saturday Evening Post* of 1948 read: children are semi-orphaned by their parents' divorce. Hopefully, we've entered a time when children possibly having four parents instead of two is considered more than acceptable, if not favorable.

Yet we don't want to minimize the difficult adjustment for children when their parents go through a divorce. The consequences of divorce can affect them for many years. Where do the divorced parents sit at their children's weddings? Who brings whom to their graduations? How can the children maintain a close relationship with grandparents when the parents are locked in a divorce battle? How much more likely is it that children of divorce will themselves divorce later in life?

Nevertheless, a good divorce is better for children than living with parents in a destructive marriage. If the parents are able to adjust to their divorce, the chances of the kids adjusting are greatly increased. Many adults are able to be better parents after the divorce, and the children often benefit from this improved parenting. Still, divorce is often the most traumatic event in a child's life, and we need to do what we can to minimize the emotional and psychological hurt and pain.

The Effects of Parental Adjustment on Children

Maybe you've noticed this perplexing phenomenon: when we adults are in the divorce pits, why does everything seem to break down? Does the washing machine know we are going through a divorce? Can the car sense our anxiety? It's completely understandable when people say a little prayer of gratitude or consider it a good day when their computer doesn't crash and their phone doesn't drop a call!

When we are experiencing technological breakdown all around us, our children are often emotionally supporting us more than we would like to admit. They often behave better so they don't upset us. They often do things for us that they wouldn't have thought of doing when we were married. They don't let us know how much pain and anger they are feeling. In essence, they put their own adjustment process on hold as we go through ours.

When we parents begin to sit back and relax because we think we are adjusted, feeling stronger, and over the divorce, look out! That's often when our children sense at some level that they can start working through the rebuilding blocks—that they don't have to walk around on tiptoe anymore. Corinne, quoted at the beginning of this appendix, complained to her seminar group about her kids acting out. But maybe her kids were actually giving her a compliment! Finally feeling free enough to act up, what the children really might be saying with their behavior is, "You've adjusted and are strong enough that I can now work through my process. I need to cry, to be angry, and to act out my hurt. I think you're finally ready to handle me while I work through my pain." Parents' faces light up with relief when they consider this possibility.

We've said it before and we'll say it again: kids are tougher than you think.

Stumbling Blocks for Children

As your children make the climb up the divorce recovery mountain, there are eight stumbling blocks they may encounter, expressed as follows:

1. **"I don't know what divorce is."** Your children may not know what the word "divorce" means or how it will work in your lives together. It's not uncommon for children to hold myths about divorce or to drift toward believing their worst fears when left to discover things on their own.

2. **"I don't like all the changes happening around me."** Divorce has brought a complete overhaul to your children's life as they knew it. There are many logistical changes they may have needed to adjust to (residence, neighborhood, school, friends, personal space, and so forth), perhaps in a short period of time.

3. **"I have all these different feelings stuck inside me."** Your children are most likely experiencing a wide range of emotional responses related to the divorce. They may be feeling sad, angry, worried, confused, relieved, and many other emotions without any knowledge of what to do with their feelings.

4. **"I wonder if I am responsible for my parents' divorce."** Children feel responsible in a variety of ways. Some believe they actually did something bad to cause their parents to get divorced. Other children feel responsible for helping their parents feel better about what has happened. Finally, some children believe that the reason

they don't get to see the noncustodial parent more often is that there's something wrong with them.

5. **"I don't know if we are a family anymore."** Your children may be wondering how to relate to you and your former partner now that the two of you are no longer in relationship. Some children wonder if it is okay to love both parents or if they need to pick a side. Children also wonder what it means to be a family now that everyone no longer lives together.

6. **"I wish my parents would get back together."** This is a fantasy children keep alive because they are unhappy with what the divorce has meant for their lives. Uncertainty, instability, and disruption are not their friends. Many children kindle hope as a way of moderating the stress of watching their parents separate. Other children who are having difficulty with the other stumbling blocks may want to change what they are experiencing by wishing for something different.

7. **"I think it will be all good, or all bad, if my mom or dad finds a new partner."** This block concerns your children's view of the future. Some children think if you find a new partner, everything will be okay; somehow the family is incomplete until they have a new mommy or daddy. Other children resist their parents' interest in someone new because it is a concrete sign that their parents will not get back together. Children who view your finding a new partner through either the "all good" or "all bad" lens may be stuck at this block.

8. **"I feel like the only kid in the world whose parents are divorcing."** During the divorce process, children often believe they are alone and have no friends. They are lonely, usually have feelings of low self-worth (as they wonder what they did wrong to cause the divorce), and keep looking for new friends.

Rebuilding Blocks for Children

Stumbling blocks trip children up, but rebuilding blocks are the tools they use to get back on their feet. With the rebuilding blocks for children—which differ from those in the recovery model for adults—the experience of divorce is accepted and the foundation for recovery is built. The crisis becomes an experience that may actually encourage your children's growth and maturity. As children change each of the stumbling blocks into the following rebuilding blocks, they become stronger:

1. **"I know what divorce is and what it means for me."** At this block, your children gain a clear understanding and definition of "divorce." They also learn what it will and won't mean for their individual lives.

2. **"I'm finding out how to handle the changes I am experiencing."** Here, your children discover some healthy ways to cope with the various events taking place around them. They may not like the changes, but they are finding nondestructive ways to work with them.

3. **"I'm letting my feelings out without hurting myself or others."** At this point, your children become more aware of their feelings and discover appropriate ways of expressing them. To reach this block, children usually need to feel safe sharing their feelings with at least one parent.

4. **"I know divorce is a grown-up problem."** Your children are letting go of their need to take responsibility for what has happened between you and your former partner. Your children develop good boundaries, learning the difference between what they can and cannot control.

5. **"I can still love my mom and my dad."** Your children realize they do not have to choose sides between their parents. They have a new definition of their family that includes both Mom and Dad, separately.

6. **"I'm accepting that my parents will not get back together."** Your children grow toward accepting that you and your former partner will not be back together. They learn to feel safe even as they acknowledge that their wish won't come true.

7. **"I can see things I will like, and things I won't like, if my mom or dad finds a new partner."** Your children are moving away from viewing your dating as either all good or all bad. They find a balanced perspective on both the positive aspects and the challenges that will arise if you find a new partner.

8. **"I'm learning to be a friend to myself through my parents' divorce."** A child who reaches this point has neared the end of the climb. The sense of self-worth evident in this statement makes the climb worthwhile. At this stage, children have grown from loneliness into a feeling of emotional closeness with themselves and others.

9. The last rebuilding block doesn't have a corresponding stumbling block: **"I have the freedom to be myself."** When you and your children reach the top of the mountain, the view of yourself, others, and life itself is spectacular. The personal freedom and intimacy both children and parents feel is great. Together, you and your children have transformed the crisis into a creative experience.

Each of the rebuilding blocks represents an adjustment for children as they experience the stages of divorce recovery. It is likely that your children will gain in wisdom, strength, and maturity as they climb to the top of the mountain.

Rebuilding Together

One symbolic activity you can do with your children is to take them on a hike. This is especially good if you live close to mountains or foothills, so you can pick a trail and climb to the top. Shared outdoor activities can really bring children and parents together. You and your children already know that adjusting to divorce is a lot like climbing a mountain. All of you can gain powerful insights by physically hiking even partway up. In urban areas, you could plan a challenging course in a safe neighborhood and include some stair-climbing along the way.

If you decide to do this activity, it will help if each of you pays attention to the feelings you notice on your journey. Which aspects of your hike were exciting? Which were frustrating? What challenges did you encounter? How did you feel at the end of your hike? How about when you reached your goal? What was it like for you and your children to accomplish this goal together? What are you learning about adjusting to the ending of your love relationship? What are you learning about your children? What are your children learning about you?

The Healing Separation

An Alternative to Divorce

Bruce Fisher, EdD

I have a vision of a relationship more beautiful and loving than both of us can imagine or know. It is truly a relationship that is a laboratory for growth, where we are able to grow and completely be ourselves, while still in relationship with each other. I am not a whole enough person to be able to have such a healthy relationship with you without building a better relationship with myself first. I think I will need to separate and live apart from you for a while. I love you.

—Nina

For many years, a popular women's magazine ran a monthly column called "Can This Marriage Be Saved?" which gave advice to couples who were really in trouble. For those who want to try to save their marriages, there's a very powerful tool that has helped a number of relationships called the "healing separation." Please give it thoughtful consideration if you've not yet actually divorced.

A healing separation is a structured time apart that can help a couple heal a relationship that isn't working. It can also help revitalize and renew a relationship that is working. The healing separation is designed to transform the basis of a love relationship—moving it from neediness to health. A successful healing separation requires that both partners be committed to personal growth and to creating healthier relationships with themselves and each other. Such a framework will allow them to carve out a new and more fulfilling relationship than they've known in the past.

When a relationship is in trouble, the couple has essentially three choices: (1) continue as is; (2) end the relationship; or (3) carve out a new relationship. If the relationship is already crumbling, not many couples want to continue it as is. That leaves choices 2 and 3. Chances are they haven't thought much about the third choice—it probably seems impossible. What's more, they don't know how to go about it. So their choice, almost by default, is to end the relationship. And up goes the divorce rate.

There is another alternative: partners can work out a new relationship with themselves and with each other. The healing separation offers a process within which to do just that.

What Is a Healing Separation?

The healing separation, like the old-style trial separation, involves living apart for a while, with the decision as to whether or not to end the relationship put off until some future time. Unlike unplanned and unstructured separations, however, the healing separation is a working separation in which you and your partner dedicate yourselves to investing in your own personal growth. If you can create a better relationship with yourself, that can allow you to have different and healthier relationships with others. Sometimes your work during a healing separation may be on "the old relationship," and sometimes it may be on "the old you." The healing separation is a creative way to strengthen both partners and build a new relationship without dissolving the partnership.

As we talked about at the beginning of this book, a relationship between two people is analogous to a bridge. Each partner forms one end and provides half the support for the bridge. The connection between the two—the bridge—is the relationship itself. A healing separation gives the partners time to concentrate on themselves, on their own supportive end structures, rather than on the relationship. It's a scary process because neither person is tending the relationship bridge for a while—it could collapse. Nevertheless, it may be worth the risk. When the two ends are eventually rebuilt, the possibility exists for a new healthy relationship bridge to be built, supported by bridge ends that are now stronger.

What Are the Purposes of a Healing Separation?

The goals of a healing separation are more profound than simply decisions about whether you'll continue your love relationship. There appears to be a high correlation between the amount of personal growth each person does and the success of the healing separation. If both parties are committed and motivated to work on their self-relationship, the chance of their new relationship lasting is good.

Here's a list of purposes for a healing separation:

- To take the pressure off a troubled relationship. A love relationship is a changing pattern of interaction between two people who themselves are changing as they develop emotionally, socially, physically, and spiritually. This evolution of the relationship may result in strains and pressures upon the relationship, and a crisis may develop. During this crisis, it is difficult for the partners to make rational and objective decisions concerning their future. A time apart pending a final decision may be an advantageous alternative for the couple to consider.

- To enhance your personal growth so that you can work through the stumbling blocks mentioned in this book. Changing stumbling blocks into rebuilding blocks can be the end result of a successful healing separation.

- To transform your relationship into something more beautiful and loving than you ever thought possible. You could find yourself in a relationship that not only allows you to be yourself, but enhances your individual identity and offers more love and joy than you ever imagined. You could deepen your concept of what love is, creating a relationship that has no boundaries or limits, one that has evolved and transformed to a level of love usually associated with spiritual love.

- To end your love relationship on a positive note and have the ending be a creative and constructive experience. To reach this goal might mean the ending has a minimum of stress, anxiety, and court battles, with everyone feeling good about the way it worked out. Remaining friends and being able to co-parent peacefully could be important by-products of this healthy ending.

Who Should Consider a Healing Separation?

Here are some key characteristics of partners who might want to try a healing separation:

- You are experiencing sad and unhappy feelings, or feeling suffocated, or experiencing tremendous pressures, or feeling depressed, possibly even suicidal. You need to separate in order to survive and continue living.

- Your partner has refused to take any responsibility for the relationship difficulties and has refused to become involved in counseling or other growth activities. The separation is one way to "hit your partner over the head with a two-by-four" in order to get his or her attention.

- You are going through the rebellion process identified in chapter 12. You feel the need for emotional space and decide to separate to relieve the internal pressures.

- You are in the process of healing your childhood abuse and neglect and need to be alone in order to complete the process.

- You have begun an important personal transformation, perhaps psychological or spiritual in nature, and you want to invest as much time and effort as possible in your own process. You find that the time and effort spent in the relationship competes with and limits the amount of time you can spend with yourself.

- You have not been able to gain enough emotional space in the love relationship and need more space in which to survive, grow, evolve, or transform.

- You're caught in conflict: wanting to continue the love relationship, but unable to break the old patterns. Living together encourages continuing the old patterns of interaction. You want to "divorce the old relationship" so you can carve out a new one that is more healthy and less needy. A time apart may allow you to create new ways of interacting by developing a new and different relationship with yourself.

- You need an understanding of how it feels to be single. Perhaps you went directly from your parental home to a marriage home without experiencing the single life. You missed experiencing one of the developmental stages of growth and development: that of being an independent adult. Many people wrongly believe the single life to be one of freedom with no responsibilities—an escape from the stress of living with a love partner. Having some time apart from the love partner may provide a more realistic view of the difficulties of living as a single person.

- You may need to express your independence from your family patterns for the first time. You may have built a love relationship bridge much like your parents' bridge. Now you're attempting to get free from your parents' influence, and you need to have distance from your love partner because your patterns with your partner are too similar to those you experienced with one or both parents.

- You and your partner are projecting your unhappiness onto each other, making the other "responsible" for your unhappiness. You have not learned to take individual ownership of your own feelings. Time apart—with a plan for personal growth—could help both of you learn to accept adult responsibility for your lives.

Dumpers and Dumpees Again: The 80/20 Rule

A separation is seldom started as a mutual decision. In the Fisher divorce seminar, some 84 percent of couples ended their relationships when the dumper decided to leave. A similar division is estimated for a healing separation; that is, one partner is likely to be the initiator and the other is likely to be reluctant perhaps 80 percent of the time. Sounds like quite an obstacle to the success of the healing separation, doesn't it? How can a couple overcome the differences in attitude, goals, and motivation of the initiator and the reluctant one?

First of all, couples must rethink the question "Who's to blame?" When a relationship is not working as well as it should, both parties are equally responsible for the malfunctions. That statement is not easy to understand and really believe at first—even for therapists. But the longer we work with couples, the more we find that when you peel off the layers of pain and get to the core issues, the responsibility for the problems is equal. Thus the problems are mutual even though one person was the initiator in the separation. When you begin to understand and accept the notion of mutual responsibility for the problems, you have begun to build a foundation for a successful healing separation—and a successful new relationship.

Research with the Fisher Divorce Adjustment Scale indicates that the dumpee experiences much more anger and painful feelings than the dumper. Probably the reluctant one in a healing separation will experience more emotional pain. Whatever strong feelings are experienced by either party will need to be worked through before the separation truly becomes healing.

The parties in a healing separation have more alone time to work on themselves, on their careers, on projects and hobbies. This can be a positive aspect and helpful to both parties. The reluctant one may learn to appreciate having extra time to work on personal growth and eventually appreciate the initiator's decision to have a healing separation.

When the reluctant one finally understands that the initiator was experiencing so much internal pain and emotional pressure that separation was a matter of survival, it helps the reluctant one to understand and accept the initiator's decision.

Experience has shown that it is more likely for the initiator of a healing separation to be the female partner. Here are a few of the reasons:

- Research indicates married females are more unhappy than married males.

- Females are more likely to be open to new ways of improving relationships.

- The person who is experiencing personal change and transformation—perhaps one who is healing past abuse, usually female—will seek time and space to do that work.

- The person who is going through a spiritual transformation is usually female.

- The female partner, most often the submissive one in our male-dominated society, is more likely than the dominant one to seek equality.

- When a relationship is not working, the male will often leave the relationship, not knowing or believing that there is a possibility of changing it. If the female partner initiates the separation, the traditional "macho male" will often seek the ending of the relationship rather than agree to a healing separation. It takes a male who is sensitive, patient, caring, flexible, and open to change to participate in a healing separation.

Interestingly, after a few weeks, men who agree to work on the relationship often admit, "I didn't think I needed this program. I was just doing it for her because I thought she needed it, but the learning over these past weeks has helped me discover that I need this more than she does."

Guidelines for a Successful Healing Separation

Following the guidelines below will improve the chances of success of your healing separation. They're not all absolute rules, but if you ignore more than one or two, your prospects will be hurt.

1. Probably the most important requirement for both of you is a strong commitment to make the healing separation work. Feelings of love and commitment are tremendously helpful to motivate you both.

2. Make a list that describes what your ideal love relationship would be like. Think of what aspects would be important to you. Allow yourself to develop a fantasy of what your relationship might be like after the healing separation. Share and discuss your lists with each other.

   Commit yourselves to communicating with each other in an open and honest manner. Learn to use I-messages rather than you-messages. Communicate by stating, "I think _____," "I feel _____," "I want _____," "I need _____," and "I will _____." Learn to be as honest as you can be with yourself and with your partner. Learn to say what is true for you. Complete honesty may include owning that portion of the relationship problems for which you have been responsible. Are you part of the problem or part of the solution?

3. Do not file for divorce or start any court proceedings during the healing separation. You must agree to not take any legal action without first conferring with the other person. The adversarial legal system is antithetical to the goals of a healing separation. Even the threat or the thought of the other person filing is enough to release the brakes of the train headed for dissolution, so you need to make it clear in the healing separation agreement (see appendix C) that neither of you will consider undertaking any court action. The exception to this is when one or both of you needs to let the old relationship die by having a final decree stating you are divorced. You need to work toward obtaining the final decree together and avoid the adversarial court process. Anything you can do to help end the old relationship is helpful in the healing separation. This may be the step that really gets your partner's attention and lets the other person know you are serious in your need for emotional space.

4. Quality time together might nourish this new relationship (see the next section). It is helpful to think of the new relationship as a tender young plant just emerging from the seedbed. It needs frequent, gentle, and loving care to grow and not be squashed by the storms of the healing separation.

5. Continuing a sexual relationship may help nurture the relationship, but it could also hurt. Review the material in chapter 17 for cautions.

6. Sometimes you will need to talk out issues with a person other than your partner. You will need a good support system or a therapy relationship, or both, to resolve these issues without them being added to the storms that will most likely occur during a healing separation.

7. It is a great time to keep a personal journal. You will need a place to express and dissipate the strong feelings that are bound to emerge during this difficult time and a place to sort out the many thoughts and feelings you are experiencing.

8. Read, take classes, attend lectures and seminars. Awareness can really help to put the brakes on your runaway relationship train. Reading and learning all you can will help make the process healing rather than destructive.

9. You will need to do some self-care so you don't become emotionally and physically drained. The whole process can be very draining emotionally, and sometimes you feel like giving up because you don't have enough energy to continue. What can you do to restore yourself and keep from becoming emotionally drained?

10. Use the "Contract for a Healing Separation" in appendix C—with modifications to suit your relationship needs—as a firm commitment to each other. A formal agreement such as this will give your healing separation the best chance of success.

11. Seriously consider an ongoing therapy relationship (preferably joint counseling) with an experienced licensed marriage and family therapist or psychologist.

Other Considerations

Quality time together. You may find it beneficial to set times to be together on a regular basis during the separation, as often as feels right and okay. It should be agreeable to both of you to spend "quality time" together. This quality time might include one or more of the following activities: (a) important sharing and active listening, using good communication skills; (b) verbal intimacy and/or sexual intimacy, if appropriate; (c) time to nurture each other; (d) trying out new patterns of interaction leading to carving out a new relationship; (e) doing fun activities together; (f) sharing your personal growth with the other person.

When your old dysfunctional patterns of interaction start happening, you need to be apart rather than continuing the old unproductive patterns of behavior together. Remember to stay honest with each other!

Length of separation. You may be asking, "How long are we going to be separated?" Part of the goal for this process is to encourage and support you to be as fearful and insecure as possible! It would be easy for you to make a commitment for three months and then use that deadline as a way of not dealing emotionally with the problems. "I can put up with anything for three months" might be your attitude. It is suggested that you agree on a time limit for your healing separation, but realize it needs to be flexible and may be renegotiated. This insecurity of not knowing how long you will be separated may help to keep you on your toes, and you may be able to use the insecurity of no time limit as motivation to keep growing.

Insecurity about the future of your relationship can be frightening. You don't know how much to work on yourself and how much to work on the relationship. (If you've been trying to change your partner, that may be one of the reasons you're having a healing separation!) Sometimes it feels as if you are walking on ice. One false step and down you go, into the icy water of loneliness, rejection, guilt, anger, and the other feelings of the divorce pits.

The healing separation will probably consume a year or so of your life.

Timing of when to move back in together. The question of when to end the separation by moving back in together is crucial. Usually, the couple is uncomfortable living apart, and the pain motivates them to move back in together too quickly. One party is usually pushing to live together more quickly than the other. Males usually want to resume cohabitation sooner than females. The reluctant partner usually wants to move back in together before the initiator does. Time itself is a factor: early in the process, one or both are eager to move back in together; the longer the separation lasts, the more hesitant both partners are to return to their previous living arrangement.

It is very destructive to move back in together too quickly and have the patterns of the old relationship come back. This increases the possibility of separating again, and each separation increases the chances of the relationship ending.

Take your time about moving back in together. Beware of the "honeymoon phase." You may start to feel emotionally close, intimate; sexual satisfaction may improve (maybe because you have let go of sexual expectations); you want to live together again—but maybe for the wrong reasons. Wait until you both agree that you sincerely choose to be in relationship with each other and to share the rest of your lives with each other. Paradoxically, when you both believe you can live alone the rest of your lives and be happy, it may be a good indicator you are ready to live together again.

Outside love relationships. As a general rule, having an extra love relationship during a healing separation will diminish your chances of improving your relationship with yourself. Time and energy invested in the outside relationship diminishes the time and energy available to invest in your own growth as a person.

Partners who initiate the separation seeking personal growth, healing, or transformation are so involved in their personal growth process that an extra relationship is often not of interest. They have a strong commitment to the healing separation and are willing to risk everything in their relationship with their reluctant partners just so they can work toward becoming whole people.

Reluctant partners have many opportunities for outside relationships, but they usually find out they are more "married" than they thought. Often they discover that a potential new partner carries the potential for a multitude of new problems. Dating may leave them much more committed to the healing separation.

The person, male or female, who initiates a separation while in the rebellion process is much more likely to have an outside relationship that looks like an affair and may include sexual intimacy. He or she usually thinks of it as part of the process—the primary purpose is to have someone to talk intimately with—and does not think of it as an affair. This extra relationship may become a long-term union, but the chances of it becoming a healthy relationship are small.

Outside relationships usually have an adverse effect upon a healing separation because the people involved make the extra relationship more important than it is. A partner who is in rebellion finds it exciting and believes it has much promise for the future. (This excitement rarely lasts beyond the early or "honeymoon" stage.) The other partner will feel hurt, rejected, and angry about the extra relationship and may decide to end the healing separation and let go of the relationship altogether.

Lack of support. Another area of difficulty in a healing separation is your support system. Both partners need an emotional support system to help them deal with the pressures of the difficult situation. The problem is that very few people have seen a healing separation in action—they might not even believe the concept—and the view of many friends and relatives will be that the relationship is going to end. Thus when you need emotional support the most, your friends are going to be urging you to end the relationship, saying things like, "You're still in denial. Can't you see that the relationship is over? ... Are you codependent? You don't seem to be able to disentangle.... You are just opening yourself up to be taken to court by some shark attorney. You'd better strike first.... Why are you staying in limbo? You need to get on with your life.... Why don't you get rid of that bum?"

The idea of a healing separation is contrary to the values of many people. A commitment "till death do us part" is a strong belief in our society, and a healing separation is somehow seen as undesirable, not spiritually okay, a form of radical behavior. That's one of the reasons many people are unable to support and accept the couple attempting this alternative to divorce.

You need the support of your friends, but it can make you more insecure if they tell you the relationship is going to end. So continue to reach out and build your support system, but understand that some people may not always be there to help you make the healing separation succeed. (Maybe having them read this material will help them be more supportive of you?)

Paradoxes of a healing separation. There are many paradoxes (perhaps even contradictions) in healing separations. Here are some of the more important ones:

1. The person who initiates a separation often does it out of a need for emotional space. But the reluctant one often uses and benefits from the emotional space as much as or more than the initiator.

2. Initiators appear to be selfishly seeking ways of meeting their own needs, but often they are providing an opportunity for their reluctant partners to meet their needs.

3. The initiator appears to be leaving the relationship but may actually be more committed to the relationship than is the reluctant one.

4. As soon as initiators feel they have the emotional space they need, they reach out and ask for more closeness with the reluctant one.

5. The initiator wants the separation but is not looking for another relationship. The reluctant one wants the relationship to continue but is more likely to enter into another love relationship.

6. When the partners separate, they are often more "married" than they were when they were living together.

7. Most love partners project some of their hang-ups onto the other person. The healing separation makes these projections more obvious and identifiable. It's harder to blame another person for what happens when he or she doesn't live there anymore!

8. One of the reasons initiators give for wanting a separation is the opportunity to enhance their personal growth. But reluctant partners may experience as much or more personal growth during a separation.

9. The initiator may actually elect to have the marriage legally ended by a final court dissolution so the partners can begin again to build and create a new and different relationship.

10. The healing separation makes it look to others as if the relationship is not working, when in reality, it may be the healthiest it has ever been.

11. In the process of seeking a clearer personal identity, the initiator may find a stronger sense of "relationship identity"—personal identity as part of a relationship.

12. Initiators often give reluctant partners what they need rather than what they want.

Is This a Healing Separation or Denial?

It is a time for action, not promises. If both parties are not actively engaged in working on themselves and rebuilding their ends of the relationship bridge, it is probably not a healing separation but a step toward the ending of the relationship.

Here are some important questions to consider when determining if you are working on a new beginning or working toward the end:

- Are you both working at this healing separation, or is only one of you investing in your own personal growth?

- Are both parties involved in counseling?

- Are both parties reading self-help books?

- Are both parties spending time alone, or are they continually with people in situations that are not growth-producing?

- Are both parties avoiding excessive drug and alcohol use?

- Are both parties investing in themselves, or are they investing in another relationship outside of this one?

- Are the two people having any quality time together that includes good communication?

- Are both parties attempting to become more aware of their individual contribution to the difficulties in the relationship?

- Are both parties looking at how they can grow, instead of expecting the other person to make all the changes?

- Do both believe the partner is the problem and there is nothing one can do to change or grow until the other changes?

How does your healing separation rate on these questions? Are both of you working at the relationship? If only one of you is, then you are most likely in denial and your relationship is going to end.

Afterword

The structure of the healing separation is designed specifically for couples in a primary love relationship; the lessons are most relevant to their needs. Nevertheless, the lessons presented in this appendix will work for many kinds of relationships, including friendships, family relationships, coworkers in a business setting, therapy. A "time-out" is often helpful to allow the people involved to gain breathing space and perspective—a chance to take a fresh look at what's actually happening in the relationship and to build a foundation for a stronger partnership in the future.

Checklist for a Healing Separation

Both partners should read this material about the healing separation and complete the following checklist:

☐ *I recognize the reasons I entered into this relationship that contributed to my need for a healing separation.*

☐ *I have identified and own some of my contributions to our need for a healing separation.*

☐ *I am committed to working on my own personal growth and development during this healing separation.*

☐ *I am aware of my own personal process that has resulted in my need for more emotional space at this time of my life; or*

☐ *I am aware of my own contributions to my partner's need for more emotional space.*

☐ *I am working on my own personal growth so I will have a healthier relationship with myself.*

- ☐ I am committed to making this healing separation a creative experience.

- ☐ I am committed to learning as much as possible from my relationship partner during this healing separation.

- ☐ I am avoiding the behaviors that may lead this healing separation toward the rocks of divorce.

- ☐ I am working on relieving the internal pressures that contributed to my need for more emotional space.

- ☐ I have completed my part of the healing separation agreement form (in the next section).

- ☐ When the time is appropriate, I will communicate with my partner about ending the healing separation, either by ending the relationship or by moving back in and living together again.

- ☐ I am avoiding blaming and projecting upon my partner.

- ☐ I am avoiding the "helpless victim" role; I don't believe there is "nothing I can do" about my situation.

Contract for a Healing Separation

A healing separation is a very challenging experience, which may result in increased stress and anxiety for both partners. Some structure and awareness can help improve the chances of success of the healing separation. Unplanned and unstructured separations will most likely contribute to the ending of the relationship. This healing separation agreement attempts to provide structure and guidelines to help make the separation a more constructive and creative experience and to greatly enhance the growth of the relationship rather than contributing to its demise.

A. Commitment to a Healing Separation

With the awareness that our love relationship is at a point of crisis, we choose to try a working and creative healing separation in order to obtain a better individual perspective on the future of our relationship. In choosing this healing separation, it is acknowledged that there are aspects of our relationship that are destructive to us as a couple and as individuals. Likewise, we acknowledge that there are positive and constructive elements in our relationship that could be deemed assets and upon which we may be able to build a new and different relationship. With this in mind, we are committed to do the personal, social, psychological, and spiritual work necessary to make this separation a healing one.

At some future time, when we have experienced the personal growth and self-actualization possible in a healing separation, we will make a more enlightened decision about the future of our love relationship.

B. Goals of Our Healing Separation

Each partner agrees to the following goals for this separation:

1. To provide time and emotional space outside of the love relationship so I can enhance my personal, social, spiritual, and emotional growth

2. To better identify my needs, wants, and expectations of the love relationship

3. To help me explore what my basic relationship needs are and to help me determine if these needs can be met in this love relationship

4. To experience the social, sexual, economic, and parental stresses that can occur when I have separated from my partner

5. To allow me to determine if I can work through my process better alone than I can in the relationship

6. To experience enough emotional distance so I can separate out my issues that have become convoluted and mixed up together with my partner's issues in our relationship

7. To provide an environment in which to help our relationship heal, transform, and evolve into a more loving and healthy relationship

C. Specific Decisions Regarding This Healing Separation

1. Length of Separation

We agree our separation will begin on _____ and will end on _____ .

(Most couples have a sense of how long a separation they will need or want. It may vary from a few weeks to six months or longer. The length of time agreed upon may be renegotiated at any time at the initiation of either partner. Since it was explained in appendix B, "The Healing Separation," that it's preferable to keep the end date fluid and negotiable, this contract term would be a good topic of conversation for a communication exercise.)

2. Time to Be Spent Together

We agree to spend time together when it is agreeable to both parties. This time might be spent having fun, talking, parenting together, or sharing each other's personal growth process. We agree to meet for _____ hours _____ times the first week, then to negotiate the time together for each succeeding week. We agree to discuss and reach an agreement if this time together is to include a continuing sexual involvement with each other.

(A healing separation ideally should include some quality time together on a regular basis. Some people will enjoy their newfound freedom and desire very little such time. Conversely, when the person needing more emotional space separates, he or she may want even more time together. This may be confusing to the person who didn't want a separation. Partners who feel suffocated emotionally desperately want out. But when they get out of what felt like a tight place, the need for emotional space is decreased tremendously.

It is important that the time together be quality time and be spent creating a new relationship. When the old patterns start occurring, in whatever form that may take, one solution is to end the quality time together and be apart. There are arguments for and against a continued sexual involvement with each other. Ideally, sexual contact can enhance intimacy and make the separation less stressful and hurtful. Sex may, however, result in problems of the sort discussed in chapter 17, creating confusion for the potential dumpee if the dumper is just trying to "let him/her down easy.")

3. Personal Growth Experiences

Partner A agrees to participate in such personal growth experiences as:

_____ Individual counseling

_____ Marriage counseling

_____ Involvement in relationship-building educational or support programs

_____ Reading self-help books

_____ Keeping a journal

_____ Starting or maintaining an exercise program

_____ Starting or maintaining a diet program

_____ Involvement in a personal-growth group, such as an anger management group

Partner B agrees to participate in such personal growth experiences as:

_____ Individual counseling

_____ Marriage counseling

_____ Involvement in relationship-building educational or support programs

_____ Reading self-help books

_____ Keeping a journal

_____ Starting or maintaining an exercise program

_____ Starting or maintaining a diet program

_____ Involvement in a personal-growth group, such as an anger management group

(Ideally, a healing separation would include as many personal growth experiences as are feasible, practical, and helpful. Note that professional counseling is strongly encouraged, because if you haven't been able to make your relationship work before this healing separation, you'll likely have difficulty making it work without some form of outside help, guidance, information, and support.)

4. Relationships and Involvements Outside of the Relationship

Partner A agrees:

_____ To develop a support system of important friends

_____ To become more involved socially with others

_____ To not date potential love partners

_____ To remain emotionally monogamous

_____ To remain sexually monogamous

_____ To become involved in clubs, church groups, and other social group activities

Partner B agrees:

_____ To develop a support system of important friends

_____ To become more involved socially with others

_____ To not date potential love partners

_____ To remain emotionally monogamous

_____ To remain sexually monogamous

_____ To become involved in clubs, church groups, and other social group activities

(Ideally, a joint decision and compromise should be made concerning social involvement and romantic or sexual relationships outside of this relationship.)

5. Living Arrangements

Partner A agrees to:

_____ Remain in the family home, *or*

_____ Move out and find an alternative living arrangement, *or*

_____ Alternate living in the family home with partner B so the children can remain in the family home

Partner B agrees to:

_____ Remain in the family home, *or*

_____ Move out and find an alternative living arrangement, *or*

_____ Alternate living in the family home with partner A so the children can remain in the family home

(Experience has shown that an in-house separation, with both parties continuing to live in the family home, results in a less creative experience. It seems to dilute the separation experience and keeps both parties from experiencing as much personal growth as is possible with separate living arrangements. It also may not provide enough emotional space to the person who needs it.)

6. Financial Decisions

Partner A agrees to:

_____ Maintain joint checking account jointly

_____ Maintain joint checking account separately

_____ Open new checking account

_____ Pay auto expenses

_____ Pay household living expenses

_____ Pay child support of $_____ monthly

_____ Pay home mortgage and utilities

_____ Pay medical and dental bills

Partner B agrees to:

_____ Maintain joint checking account jointly

_____ Maintain joint checking account separately

_____ Open new checking account

_____ Pay auto expenses

_____ Pay household living expenses

_____ Pay child support of $_____ monthly

_____ Pay home mortgage and utilities

_____ Pay medical and dental bills

(Some couples will decide to continue joint checking accounts, savings accounts, and payment of bills. Other couples will completely separate financial aspects of the relationship. Experience with divorcing couples indicates that one person will often completely close out checking and savings accounts without the other person's knowledge or consent. If there is any chance for potential disagreement, each person could take out half of the assets and open a separate account.)

7. Motor Vehicles

Partner A agrees to operate _____ vehicle, and Partner B agrees to operate _____ vehicle.

(It is suggested that ownership and titles not be changed until a decision has been made about the future of the love relationship.)

8. Children Involved in This Relationship

1. We agree to:

    _____ Joint custody

    _____ Sole or physical custody temporarily granted to _____

2. We agree to the following visitation schedule:

    _____

    _____

3. The medical and dental expenses and health insurance will be the responsibility of:

    _____ Partner A

    _____ Partner B

4. We agree to the following suggestions, designed to help the healing separation be a positive experience for our children:

    a. Both parents will remain committed to maintaining a good-quality relationship with each child involved. Each child should continue to feel loved by both parents.

    b. The parents will be as open and honest with the children about the healing separation as is appropriate.

    c. The parents will help the children see and understand that the physical separation is an adult problem for which they are in no way responsible.

d.   Neither parent will express anger or negative feelings toward the other parent through the children. It is very destructive to children to become caught in their parents' emotional crossfire.

e.   The parents will avoid forcing the children to take sides in the parental arguments concerning differing attitudes and viewpoints.

f.   Neither parent will put the children in a position of spying and reporting on the behavior of the other parent.

g.   Both parents will remain committed to working with each other on parenting the children and to effectively co-parent with as much cooperation as possible.

(It is important when a couple does a healing separation to minimize the emotional trauma for the children involved.)

9. Signing the Agreement

We have read and discussed the above healing separation contract and agree to the above terms. Furthermore, each of us agrees to inform the other partner of any desire to modify or change any terms in this agreement or to terminate this agreement.

_____

Partner A   Date

_____

Partner B   .   Date

Rebuilding Blocks for Widows and Widowers

Authors' Note: This section for the widowed was compiled and written by Nelse Grundvig of Bismarck, North Dakota, and Robert Stewart of Denver, Colorado. We're grateful to Nelse and Robert for this important contribution that allows widowed people to participate in and benefit from the rebuilding model.

The purpose of this appendix is to shed some light on the unique issues affecting the widowed. The rebuilding concepts are thus translated into a language that better fits widowed people.

Dumper and Dumpee for the Widowed

You may be asking, "What does 'dumper' or 'dumpee' have to do with me? I am widowed." At first glance, these terms do not seem to apply to your case. The person you loved did not leave the relationship to continue with his or her life. Your love partner left the relationship in one of two ways: through sudden death or through lingering illness. Remember, though, that dumpers are those who begin to grieve before the end of the relationship. Dumpees begin the grieving when the relationship ends. Using these definitions, it is possible to apply the terms to yourself.

A widow or widower whose spouse died quickly is forced to begin the grieving process abruptly and can feel emotionally numb at first. The full impact of what has happened is often not felt until after the funeral. In one sense, the widowed have been dumped on—they did not choose to end the relationship. Therefore, the surviving spouse is similar to the dumpee in a divorce, experiencing many of the same thoughts and feelings, because the death occurred suddenly.

However, when the death is slow, over a long period of time, the surviving spouse may experience thoughts and feelings more parallel to the dumper's. Widows whose spouses die after a prolonged illness will be more likely to start the grieving process before the death of their loved one. They may react to the death of their spouse with relief. They will often appear to be coping well, but they have had more time to react to the situation because they started grieving at a different point in the relationship.

It is also possible for the widowed to have some combination of dumper and dumpee thoughts and feelings. You may not precisely fit into one of the categories. What is important is that you become aware of, and acknowledge, how you are experiencing your spouse's death. You may have conflicting feelings regarding how being widowed will impact your life. You may have some underlying judgments regarding those feelings that hinder you from fully embracing what you are experiencing.

The following is an attempt to translate the rebuilding blocks into a more meaningful exploration of the issues directly impacting your life.

Denial

Denial is an emotional safety valve. When faced with something physically painful, the body will try to compensate; when in severe pain, it can even cause unconsciousness. Emotions can respond to pain in a similar way.

For dumpees, denial is reflected in statements like, "This can't be happening to me" and "This is a sick joke. It can't be true." In extreme cases, denial may include clinging to the delusion that the spouse will return. You may have said to yourself, "When I go home today, my wife will be in the kitchen cooking dinner, like she always is" or "If I just wait long enough, he'll be back."

Dumpers also experience denial, but usually before the actual death. Denial for you occurs when you first hear the news that your spouse is dying. "He isn't really dying" or "Medicine will find a cure" are statements that may indicate denial. It may be difficult to distinguish between denial and hope. However, an unwillingness to even acknowledge the possibility of death is a strong sign you may be struggling with denial.

The important thing to remember about this stage is that it occurs very strongly at first and does not fade entirely until the grieving process is well under way.

Fear

Fear may be your predominant emotion. It is one of the reasons for denial—facing the fear seems like too much to bear. There are two primary categories of fear you may experience: (1) fear of dying and (2) fear of living. When your spouse died, you came closer than ever to your own mortality. Many people avoid facing the fact that death is inevitable. When your spouse died, your own underlying fear that you, too, will die may have surfaced. This is especially true if your spouse died suddenly. You may also fear dying because your spouse is no longer available to meet your needs or take care of you. Many widows or widowers were totally dependent in some way upon their spouses. A common fear thus becomes "What's going to happen to me now?"

The fear of living may take on any number of faces. You may fear all the lifestyle adjustments and new choices ahead. You may fear your own feelings and thoughts related to your spouse's death, especially if you experienced some relief, which is likely to be true when death occurred over a period of time.

Adaptation

We live in a couple's world. When we pledged "till death do us part," none of us planned to actually see the end of our marriage. Oh, we knew that we would not live forever, but we never consciously thought that our spouse would die. Well, yours did, and here you are, still alive, left to make a thousand adjustments—the first one being dealing with the fact that you are now single.

You may resist accepting this fact. What if someone asks you out on a date? That would be absolutely terrifying. All the dynamics of potentially starting a new relationship may seem so complicated. Stepping into the unknown of meeting another person is one of the major adjustments of being widowed. The longer the marriage, the more difficult this prospect may be. You may cling to an image of your love partner and may have an even more idealized image now that your partner is dead.

It may sound cruel, but the death of your spouse is an opportunity for self-examination. How do you view yourself, life, and others? In which areas have you fallen into a rut or become stagnant? The death of your spouse is a way for you to examine any ways in which you have taken life for granted.

This time is also an opportunity to consider why you got married in the first place. Did you experience a successful, full, interactive relationship? Were you satisfied with the nature and dynamics of the relationship? As you adjust to singleness, introspection is an option for increasing your present awareness and future freedom.

Loneliness

You may be feeling the loneliest you've ever felt. It's painful to live with the knowledge that your spouse is not going to laugh at your jokes or be there for you when you cry. You may have had a time apart before, such as a vacation, business trip, or hospitalization, but you have not experienced this depth of loneliness. Now that the relationship has permanently ended, the other person is no longer there, and you feel totally alone.

That loneliness is magnified by the question "Am I going to be lonely like this forever?" You begin to wonder if you'll ever have the companionship of a love relationship again. Even with the comfort and encouragement of children and friends, this feeling can be overwhelming.

You may have felt lonely while in the relationship, especially if your spouse was in the hospital or diagnosed with a terminal illness. That form of loneliness is a special kind of pain, and the death of your spouse may actually ease some of that burden.

Socially, you might isolate yourself. You feel like the third wheel on a bicycle—not really fitting in, not needed. You imagine that everyone is talking about you, while privately, you wonder who really cares about your pain. When someone asks you about your dead spouse, you don't know whether to be offended, cry, or just walk away.

You may try to escape the feelings of loneliness by being in a crowd or constantly having people around you. You may seek relief by becoming super busy, doing anything to avoid being home alone. You may find people to go out with just to keep from being alone, even if you don't enjoy their company. Sometimes anything is better than being home alone with all those feelings and memories.

As time goes on, you will move beyond loneliness into accepting your *aloneness*. Aloneness is the process of becoming comfortable with yourself. It involves a willingness to stop running from the pain and accepting all aspects of who you are during this time. It also means realizing there is a uniqueness to your experience that others may not be able to share in or fully understand.

To reach this point, we have to realize that the fear of being alone is much worse than actually being alone. When we experience being alone, we discover resources we never knew we had. We also learn to gather the resources we need but don't have. We are then able to accept that aloneness is part of the human condition.

Being alone can become a way of healing ourselves. You need time to be introspective and reflective, to reconnect with disowned thoughts and feelings. Through reclaiming feelings and thoughts, you come to realize that you are not empty, but rather full, when alone. This inner fullness comes when you allow yourself to grow and develop, reaching a point of comfort when not in the company of others. Eventually, you will reach the point of understanding that being with another person to escape loneliness is destructive and painful. Learning what you need for healing—so that you can choose to enter into a relationship rather than needing one to escape loneliness—will be one of your greatest challenges.

Friendship

When we experience pain, especially emotional pain, it is often helpful to share that pain with friends. It is not that they can remedy our pain, but the act of sharing seems to lessen the burden. Unfortunately, many of the friends we had while married will no longer be with us now that we are single.

There are several reasons why you may experience the loss of friends. The first is, as a single, you may be seen as a threat to your married friends, as you are now an eligible love object. If a relationship is not secure, you may pose a threat. It is also threatening to others to acknowledge that one's partner is mortal. Since your partner has died, you are a reminder of this fact.

Another reason you may lose friends is that since you are now single, you have become, regardless of your willingness to accept it, a member of a different subculture: that of single adults. It may be more difficult for you to relate to your married friends. If you want to keep your friends, you must remember that the similarities of your past are now differences; other similarities will have to be strengthened. Also, you may want to reach out to others who are in a similar situation, that of being single again, as they have circumstances you can relate to.

Rejection and Guilt

It may not sound rational, but you can feel rejection because you are still alive. We may feel that our spouse chose death rather than living with us. This is a normal thought and part of the grieving process. However, rejection implies there is something wrong with you. You may begin searching for some imagined defect in your personality. What is so terrible about you that your partner would choose death over life with you? Perhaps you feel guilty because you did not express your feelings of love often enough. Another cause for guilt is surviving or moving on with your life. You can feel guilty because you did not want to be left alone, even if it meant your spouse suffered. If your spouse was experiencing pain, you may feel guilty because of your relief from the stress of watching a loved one suffer.

This is not all negative. If, when looking at your own behavior, you find that it causes difficulty in your interactions with others, you can change that. The goal of working through this process is to be able to see yourself as a loving and beautiful person and to come to appreciate yourself as if you are your own best friend.

Guilt is not entirely useless. It helps us realize we have not lived up to our own standards. However, excessive guilt is destructive. When we live our lives with "ought tos," "should haves," and "could have beens," we are not able to live life fully. We end up becoming inhibited and controlled. If you have not lived up to realistic expectations, you may need to make amends (if possible) and change behaviors in the future. If the guilt you feel is based on unrealistic expectations, you need to remind yourself that you did the best with what you had at the time.

The goal here is to be able to look rationally at your guilt and see if it is appropriate. To feel guilty because we want to go on with our lives, or because we prayed for the suffering of our loved one to end, is normal. However, to feel guilty because you didn't prevent your spouse's death is being unfair to yourself.

Grief

People experience the stages of grieving in many different ways. But some patterns do emerge, regardless of whether one is in the dumper or dumpee role. You will most likely experience denial, bargaining, anger, depression, and eventually acceptance.

Grief is an important part of the healing process once your partner has died. The death of your spouse included a funeral, a burial, and the surrounding of friends and relatives. However, the grief process is not something that has a time limit. Well-intentioned people will say, "Isn't it time for you to move on with your life? It has been X number of months." What they don't realize is that we need to grieve in order to say good-bye to the relationship and that we have to say good-bye not only to our spouse, but also to our way of life. We often limit ourselves by not allowing ourselves to cry and feel the pain. Unfortunately, this only forestalls the grieving process; it doesn't put it aside. We need to acknowledge the pain and the loss of control in our lives. Only then are we able to move on with our lives.

There are two different faces to the bargaining phase of the grief process. For dumpers, it often takes the form of, "I'd do anything to prevent this from happening to my love partner." For dumpees, it may mean attending church to guarantee safe passage for your loved one or a willingness to give anything to ensure that the pain will be less. Bargaining can be helpful. Many people come to support groups in an effort to bargain away their grief. In these cases, the person grieving will try to get into another relationship to shortcut the pain and insecurity of being alone. It should be stressed that if you are hurting from a past relationship, you will not be able to dedicate the needed time and energy to create an authentic intimate relationship.

The depression stage usually lasts one day longer than we thought we could stand. We spend so much of our energy being concerned with our love partner that when we do not have access to that partner, it hurts. You may have the feeling that everything you touch dies. This is not the case, but the feelings of depression still need to be examined and dealt with. Some people argue that depression is anger that has no external outlet. Whatever the cause, it is important to realize that others have, or are experiencing, the same emotion.

When you finally stop asking, "Why did my spouse have to die?" the process of acceptance is well under way. The emotional pain of separation does lessen over time. Hopefully, the pain you are experiencing will enable you to learn who you are and to reach out toward a full and enriching experience. Acceptance is funny because we don't know we have reached it until we are confronted by either our past or someone else's pain. Acceptance can be achieved partially and can slip away when we have uncovered some painful feelings from our past. When acceptance does slip from us, it is often an indicator that we need more self-discovery and personal growth.

Anger

Anger is a natural part of the grieving, and therefore the healing, process. You may have many targets for your anger. God is often a good target, because God took your love partner away. You might feel angry with your dead spouse for leaving you, or friends and clergy for not realizing your emotional pain. Even those who understand and are willing to help may become targets of your anger. You may also feel angry at yourself because your emotional upheaval makes it difficult to go on with life.

Anger is a feeling, and feelings are a part of life. You may be tempted to deny or suppress your anger. However, anger can be very constructive as a positive energy force because it leads you to acknowledge your humanness and the humanness of others. As you work through your anger, you begin to experience feelings of peace and of letting go what you could not, and cannot, control.

Letting Go

This difficult and painful process is about releasing our emotional ties to our former spouse. At some point, your heart releases all the rights and privileges of being married to your spouse. Your mind declares that it is time to go on with what you still do have, as your focus moves away from what was toward what can be.

An example of someone who has not disentangled from the past is a widow who still wears her wedding band or still refers to herself as "Mrs. John Doe" (where John Doe is the name of her dead spouse, of course). A part of you may resist the disentanglement process. You may experience anger or guilt as you attempt to let go.

This final stage of the grieving process can be much easier if you have, or develop, other interests, such as a job or hobby, and if you maintain a good support system. To help you disentangle, we suggest you move the bedroom furniture, put away personal belongings of your dead spouse, and experiment with some small changes in your life. Later, when you have fewer emotional ties to your past, you can revisit those items you have put away. However, you may want to have a friend nearby when you journey back into those memories.

Self-Worth

Your self-concept may be at an all-time low when your love relationship ends. So much of your personality was invested into the relationship that it is devastating to face the empty place in your identity. All too often, you thought of yourself only in terms of the relationship. When you used to introduce yourself to others, you often referred to yourself as "the husband of" or "the wife of." When you weren't with your mate, others would jokingly ask, "Where's your better half?"

Dr. Fisher found that it's common for people to have a poor self-image immediately following the loss of a love relationship. He argues that our self-image is a learned attitude. The way we refer to ourselves as "the spouse of," "children of," or "parents of" gives us a sense of identity. When you are widowed, you lose that identification. If your self-esteem has dropped and remains low, the grieving process can become even more difficult.

Transition

You are in the midst of perhaps the greatest transition of your life. What makes it even more difficult is that it wasn't one that you chose. In all aspects of your life, you are moving from a lifestyle of marriage toward becoming single.

Beneath this transition may be an even larger one: a transition from unconscious influences over your life into a new freedom. With your spouse no longer a part of your life, you may begin to evaluate many of the choices you made in your marriage, including the motivations behind those choices. You may experience a new awareness of how leftovers from your past may still be influencing your life.

Openness

Openness refers to your willingness to drop your guard, a willingness to pursue intimacy with another person. The thought of becoming vulnerable to another may stir up feelings of fear and guilt. You may have created masks to keep people from knowing your pain during the grieving process. Perhaps you have hid behind masks your entire life. Taking the chance to "let someone in" may seem too risky.

There are many masks you might take on to protect yourself during this time. One common one is that of the "merry widow." Everything is seen in a positive light; all pain is covered up. Another mask is that of the "busy beaver," which refers to the widowed who preoccupy themselves with only logistical details and keep conversations on the surface. There are many different masks. Have you adopted a mask to help cope with the pain and uncertainty of this time?

Masks are not always bad. They are often necessary for surviving difficult circumstances, such as losing a spouse to death. There comes a time, though, when the energy required to maintain the mask hinders personal growth and the potential for intimacy. At that point, the mask is a burden. You will need to decide when the time is right to begin letting others see beyond your mask.

Try writing down the masks you wear to protect yourself. Which, if any, developed as a result of your spouse's death? What feelings does each mask hide or protect? Which would you like to let go of?

Love

Typically, "love" is defined only in terms of some external object, usually a person. However, the beginning point of true love is yourself. You may discover some parts of yourself you consider unacceptable; grieving has a way of exposing deeper parts of our being. Learning to embrace those parts is the beginning point of loving others. How can you love others if you don't love yourself?

You have lost the one person toward whom you directed your love. Now you may feel lost trying to direct that same love inward. Perhaps you have not experienced the beauty of that type of acceptance from another person, making it even more difficult to give it to yourself. Yet this time can become an opportunity to appreciate the unique person you are. In the midst of caring for yourself, you may begin to discover the desire to experience love again with another. You may find it difficult to avoid comparing potential future partners to your former spouse. You may wish to find someone to replace your spouse. While the desire is understandable, it is not possible. However, experiencing intimacy is.

Trust

You may be thinking, *Don't love others; they can die on you.* When you get past this thought, though, those who are available just don't seem to measure up. What's happening is that you might be making yourself unavailable so you won't get hurt again. Being with others requires that we share ourselves. When we trust, we expose ourselves to pain. If we don't trust, however, we merely exist and fail to live life.

You lived, your spouse died, and yet if you fail to get involved in life, you are the one who is acting emotionally dead. Lack of trust is not necessarily a bad thing, but failure to trust anyone, including yourself, causes pain, doubt, and fear that only you can feel.

Relatedness

As you continue along the "climb," as it is referred to in the rebuilding process, you may find others to connect with along the way. It is not uncommon for the widowed to seek out others from whom they can receive comfort, support, and encouragement. These "growing" relationships are not necessarily romantic and often are short-lived.

Sexuality

When you were married, you knew what to expect sexually from your spouse. You may not have always had your needs met or felt satisfied in this area of the relationship, but what you did have was familiar. For some, the thought of entering a new sexual relationship may be exciting. For many, however, the unknown variables make this stressful.

You are also faced with a new set of choices. What are your values around sex? Losing our love partner creates the need for sexual fulfillment and exposes the fears we have about becoming intimate with another person. You may even feel guilty for being sexually attracted to someone new.

Singleness

Earlier in the grieving process, you may have felt like you could not live without another love relationship. When you get to the point of saying, "I am content being single," then you reach a stage of personal satisfaction. This doesn't mean you will be single for the rest of your life, but it does mean you have accepted your aloneness.

If most of your identity revolved around being related to your former spouse, singleness may at first feel like failure. Something inside you may say, "I'm only okay if I'm married." Although this is a difficult belief to change, it is possible for you to renew your view of yourself. This renewal is an awakening—an understanding that your value as a human being does not come from being related to another person. You are valuable even if you are alone. In your marriage or family of origin, you may have either not felt valued or, somewhere along the way of bonding, given up your value. Now you have an opportunity to reclaim what is rightfully yours.

Purpose

This exciting time signals that you are nearing the end of the grieving process. You begin to feel alive as if for the first time. You may be opening up to experiences that before you had taken for granted or simply neglected, because you were immersed in the pain of losing your spouse.

During this period, you stop defining your life in the context of your former marriage. You begin to develop purpose based upon your needs, perceptions, and goals. This may be a time to evaluate the direction your life has been going and decide if it's the path you really want. You also begin living more in the present, letting go of the past, while planning ahead for the future.

Freedom

Freedom is about fully being yourself. It is accepting, and acting upon, an integration of your various personality parts. You are free to feel, to think, and to relate. Assuming you are successful in resolving the former rebuilding blocks, you are now free to become the person you want to be. You realize that relationships can be your teachers and that connecting to others means reconnecting with yourself. You have climbed the mountain and are now ready to move on with your life. You have grieved the loss of your former love partner and are now open to experiencing intimacy with others.

Congratulations!

Resources

Books You May Find Helpful

(Keyed to rebuilding topics)

Ahrons, C. 1998. *The Good Divorce*. New York: HarperCollins. *(Divorce and Divorce Recovery)*

Alberti, R., and M. Emmons. 2008. *Your Perfect Right: Assertiveness and Equality in Your Life and Relationships*. 9th ed. Atascadero, CA: Impact Publishers. *(Self-Worth)*

Ansari, A., and E. Klinenberg. 2015. *Modern Romance*. New York: Penguin Press. *(Relatedness)*

Beck, A. 1989. *Love Is Never Enough*. New York: Harper Perennial. *(Relatedness)*

Beckfield, D. 2004. *Master Your Panic and Take Back Your Life: Twelve Treatment Sessions to Conquer Panic, Anxiety, and Agoraphobia*. 3rd ed. Atascadero, CA: Impact Publishers. *(Fear)*

Blinder, M. 1989. *Choosing Lovers: Patterns of Romance: How You Select Partners in Intimacy, the Ways You Connect, and Why You Break Apart*. Centennial, CO: Glenbridge Publishing Ltd. *(Relationships, Love, Sexuality)*

Bloomfield, H. 2011. *Making Peace with Yourself: Turning Your Weaknesses into Strengths*. Kindle ed. New York: Ballantine Books. *(Self-Worth)*

Borysenko, J. 2009. *It's Not the End of the World: Developing Resilience in Times of Change*. Carlsbad, CA: Hay House. *(Guilt/Rejection)*

Bourne, E. J. 2015. *The Anxiety and Phobia Workbook*. 6th ed. Oakland CA: New Harbinger. *(Fear)*

Bray, J. H., and J. Kelly. 1999. *Stepfamilies: Love, Marriage, and Parenting in the First Decade*. New York: Broadway Books. *(Stepfamilies)*

Bridges, W. 2004. *Transitions: Making Sense of Life's Changes.* Rev. ed. New York: Da Capo Press. *(Transition)*

Deits, B. 2009. *Life After Loss.* New York: Da Capo Press. *(Grief)*

Einstein, E., and L. Albert. 2006. *Strengthening Your Stepfamily.* Atascadero, CA: Impact Publishers. *(Stepfamilies)*

Ellis, A. 2001. *Feeling Better, Getting Better, Staying Better: Profound Self-Help Therapy for Your Emotions.* Atascadero, CA: Impact Publishers. *(Guilt/Rejection)*

Ellis, A., and R. Tafrate. 1997. *How to Control Your Anger Before It Controls You.* New York: Carol Publishing Group. *(Anger)*

Fisher, B., and N. Hart. 2000. *Loving Choices: An Experience in Growing Relationships.* Atascadero, CA: Impact Publishers. *(Relatedness)*

Gibran, K. 1923. *The Prophet.* New York: Alfred A. Knopf. *(Inspirational)*

Hendricks, G., and K. Hendricks. 2015. *Conscious Loving Ever After: How to Create Thriving Relationships at Midlife and Beyond.* Carlsbad, CA: Hay House. *(Relatedness)*

Jampolsky, G. 2010. *Love Is Letting Go of Fear.* 3rd ed. Berkeley, CA: Celestial Arts. *(Fear)*

Keen, S. 1992. *Fire in the Belly: On Being a Man.* New York: Bantam Books. *(Women and Men)*

Kingma, D. A. 2012. *Coming Apart: Why Relationships End and How to Live Through the Ending of Yours.* Rev. ed. San Francisco: Conari Press. *(Letting Go)*

Klinenberg, E. 2012. *Going Solo: The Extraordinary Rise and Surprising Appeal of Living Alone.* Cambridge, MA: MIT Press.

Kübler-Ross, E., and D. Kessler. 2005. *On Grief and Grieving.* New York: Scribner. *(Grief)*

MacGregor, C. 2001. *The Divorce Helpbook for Kids.* Atascadero, CA: Impact Publishers. *(Children of Divorce)*

MacGregor, C. 2004. *The Divorce Helpbook for Teens.* Atascadero, CA: Impact Publishers. *(Children of Divorce)*

MacGregor, C. 2005. *Jigsaw-Puzzle Family: The Stepkids' Guide to Fitting It Together.* Atascadero, CA: Impact Publishers. *(Children of Divorce)*

MacGregor, C., and R. Alberti. 2006. *After Your Divorce: Creating the Good Life on Your Own*. Atascadero, CA: Impact Publishers. (*Divorce and Divorce Recovery*)

McKay, G., and S. Maybell. 2004. *Calming the Family Storm: Anger Management for Moms, Dads, and All the Kids*. Atascadero, CA: Impact Publishers. (*Anger*)

McKay, M., P. D. Rogers, and J. McKay. 2003. *When Anger Hurts: Quieting the Storm Within*. 2nd ed. Oakland, CA: New Harbinger. (*Anger*)

Palmer, P. 2000. *I Wish I Could Hold Your Hand: A Child's Guide to Grief and Loss*. Atascadero, CA: Impact Publishers. (*Grief*)

Palmer, P., and M. Froehner. 2010. *Teen Esteem: A Self-Direction Manual for Young Adults*. 3rd ed. Atascadero, CA: Impact Publishers. (*Self-Worth*)

Paul, J., and M. Paul. 2002. *Do I Have to Give Up Me to Be Loved by You?* 2nd ed. Center City, MN: Hazelden. (*Love*)

Peck, S. 2003. *The Road Less Traveled: A New Psychology of Love, Traditional Values, and Spiritual Growth*. New ed. New York: Simon & Schuster/Touchstone. (*Inspirational*)

Perry, L. D. 2007. *Drunk, Divorced, and Covered in Cat Hair: The True Life Adventures of a 30-Something Who Learned to Knit After He Split*. Deerfield Beach, FL: HCI Books. (*Singleness*)

Phelps, S., and N. Austin. 2002. *The Assertive Woman*. 4th ed. Atascadero, CA: Impact Publishers. (*Women and Men*)

Rathus, S. A., and J. S. Nevid. 2013. *Human Sexuality in a World of Diversity*. 9th ed. New York: Pearson Education. (*Sexuality*)

Rofes, E., ed. 1981. *The Kids' Book of Divorce: By, for, and About Kids*. New York: Vintage Books. (*Children of Divorce*)

Rye, M. S., and C. D. Moore. 2015. *The Divorce Recovery Workbook: How to Heal from Anger, Hurt, and Resentment and Build the Life You Want*. Oakland, CA: New Harbinger. (*Divorce and Divorce Recovery*)

Satir, V. 1988. *The New Peoplemaking*. Mountain View, CA: Science and Behavior Books. (*Relationships, Families, Trust*)

Schwartz, P. 2014. *Dating After 50 for Dummies*. Hoboken, NJ: Wiley. (*Singleness*)

Sills, J. 2009. *Getting Naked Again: Dating, Romance, Sex, and Love When You've Been Divorced, Widowed, Dumped, or Distracted.* New York: Hachette/Springboard. *(Sexuality)*

Solin, K. 2015. *The Boomer Guide to Finding True Love Online.* Pompano Beach, FL: 21st Century Lion Books. *(Singleness)*

Stahl, P. 2000. *Parenting After Divorce.* Atascadero, CA: Impact Publishers. *(Children of Divorce)*

Temlock, M. 2006. *Your Child's Divorce: What to Expect—What You Can Do.* Atascadero, CA: Impact Publishers. *(Parenting, Families)*

Turkle, S. 2012. *Alone Together: Why We Expect More from Technology and Less from Each Other.* New York: Basic Books. *(Relationships)*

Walton, B. 2000. *101 Little Instructions for Surviving Your Divorce: A No-Nonsense Guide to the Challenges at Hand.* Atascadero, CA: Impact Publishers. *(Divorce and Divorce Recovery)*

Webb, D. 2000. *50 Ways to Love Your Leaver.* Atascadero, CA: Impact Publishers. *(Letting Go)*

Wenning, K. 1998. *Men Are from Earth, Women Are from Earth.* New York: Jason Aronson. *(Women and Men)*

Williams, R., and V. Williams. 1998. *Anger Kills: Seventeen Strategies for Controlling the Hostility That Can Harm Your Health.* New York: Harper Paperbacks. *(Anger)*

Wilson, C. A., and E. Schilling. 1992. *Survival Manual for Men in Divorce: Straightforward Answers About Your Rights.* Boulder, CO: Quantum Press. *(Divorce and Divorce Recovery)*

Wilson, C. A., and E. Schilling. 2000. *Survival Manual for Women in Divorce: 185 Questions and Answers.* 3rd ed. Boulder, CO: Quantum Press. *(Divorce and Divorce Recovery)*

Wilson, K. K. 2003. *Transformational Divorce: Discover Yourself, Reclaim Your Dreams, and Embrace Life's Unlimited Possibilities.* Oakland, CA: New Harbinger. *(Divorce and Divorce Recovery)*

Wisdom, S., and J. Green. 2002. *Stepcoupling: Creating and Sustaining a Strong Marriage in Today's Blended Family.* New York: Random House/Three Rivers Press. *(Stepfamilies)*

Zimmerman, J., and E. S. Thayer. 2003. *Adult Children of Divorce: How to Overcome the Legacy of Your Parents' Breakup and Enjoy Love, Trust, and Intimacy.* Oakland, CA: New Harbinger. *(Adaptation)*

Online Resources You May Find Helpful

http://www.rebuilding.org
This site provides more information on Bruce Fisher's work, on his ten-week divorce recovery seminar, and on locations around the world where the seminar is offered.

http://www.psychologytoday.com/basics/relationships
Most posts to the *Psychology Today* website (affiliated with the magazine) are by psychologists and other professionals in human services. While divorce recovery is not a specific topic of emphasis, the site has a "Relationships" section with lots of helpful ideas. There is also a "Find a Therapist" section.

http://www.parentswithoutpartners.org
Parents Without Partners (PWP), the largest international nonprofit membership organization devoted to the welfare and interests of single parents and their children, is generally acknowledged to be the granddaddy of support groups. Mainly catering to divorced men and women since it first began in the late 1950s, PWP now offers a resource center open to all, as well as a directory of local chapters and a listing of local and international PWP events.

http://www.divorcemag.com
Divorce Magazine's online site is packed with divorce-related information and support.

http://www.facebook.com/DivorceMagazine
Divorce Magazine's Facebook page presents the usual social media info, what's happening currently and where, and connections with other resources.

http://www.divorcesource.com and http://www.divorcesupport.com
These paired sites—with emphasis on legal issues—provide links for fathers' and mothers' rights, domestic violence, publications for more information, bulletin boards, and chats.

http://www.divorcenet.com
Produced by the highly regarded self-help legal publisher Nolo Press, this site has a number of chat support groups, an attorney resource center, and a state-by-state listing of legal provisions, as well as bulletin board discussions on a number of topics.

http://www.singlemoms.org
Featuring a network of local groups, this site is dedicated to providing resources, support, and information for all single parents (not just mothers).

http://www.divorcecare.org
A faith-oriented, highly organized program of divorce recovery support groups, most sponsored by churches. Emphasizes Bible-based "expert" information rather than personal growth.

http://www.stepfamilies.info/stepfamilyprogram
The National Stepfamily Resource Center's site offers access to a free, video-format, research-based interactive program featuring ten common challenges in stepfamilies. Also offers a library of useful information on topics related to parenting, stepparenting, co-parenting, and managing a healthy couples relationship.

Bruce Fisher, EdD, (1931–1998) developed the 'rebuilding' model of divorce recovery nearly forty years ago. As founder and director of the Family Relations Learning Center in Boulder, CO, he personally trained thousands of individuals and therapists in this approach, enriching the lives of hundreds of thousands worldwide. He was a popular divorce therapist, author, teacher, and clinical member of the American Association for Marriage and Family Therapy. *Rebuilding*, Fisher's best-selling guide to surviving divorce, has over a million copies in print in the United States, and editions in ten languages. His other books include *Loving Choices*, with Nina Hart, and the *Rebuilding Facilitator's Manual*, with Jere Bierhaus.

Robert Alberti, PhD, has received international recognition for his writing and editing, often praised as the "gold standard" for psychological self-help. Recently retired from a long career as a psychologist, marriage and family therapist, book author, editor, and publisher, Alberti's now-inactive professional affiliations include Life Membership and Fellowship in the American Psychological Association, Clinical Membership in the American Association for Marriage and Family Therapy, and more than fifty years of professional membership in the American Counseling Association. His publishing achievements include eight books, newsletters for a number of organizations, dozens of articles, and the editing of more than 100 popular and professional psychology books by other authors. Alberti's "formal" publications career began in 1970, with the first edition of *Your Perfect Right*, coauthored with Michael Emmons. Now in its tenth revised edition, *Your Perfect Right* has over 1.3 million copies in print in the United States, and has been published in translation in more than twenty languages around the world. Alberti collaborated with the late divorce therapist Bruce Fisher on the third edition of *Rebuilding*, and recently completed the revised fourth edition.

Foreword writer **Virginia M. Satir** (1916-1988) was one of the most well-loved and highly respected contributors to the field of marriage and family therapy. She is recognized as a founder of family systems theory. Her many books, including her best-seller *Peoplemaking*, were influential in establishing the framework for family therapy, and comprise a major component of the foundation of the profession as it is currently practiced. Satir wrote this foreword for the first edition of *Rebuilding*.